D0189724

THE JOHN HARVARD LIBRARY

# CANNIBALS ALL!

*or Slaves Without Masters*

*By*

GEORGE FITZHUGH

Edited by C. Vann Woodward

THE BELKNAP PRESS OF
HARVARD UNIVERSITY PRESS
*Cambridge, Massachusetts*
*London, England*

*Fifth Printing, 1980*

*Library of Congress Catalog Card Number 60–5400*

ISBN 0–674–09451–4



*Printed in the United States of America*

# CONTENTS

# GEORGE FITZHUGH, *SUI GENERIS*

If social theories regularly shared the fate of the social systems in which they were born, the history of thought would be a thin and impoverished thing of purely contemporary dimensions. The theories of George Fitzhugh came very near suffering the fate that befell the social order and institutions he defended. It was not merely that he was the spokesman of a cause that was overwhelmed in military disaster and an order that was leveled by revolutionary action. Nor was it simply that he was the outspoken champion of the discredited, despised, and abolished institution of Negro slavery. More important than the fall of the old order in explaining the eclipse of Fitzhugh was the sensational, if temporary, triumph of the system he opposed, a triumph that followed hard upon the collapse of the order he championed.

The fact was that the very aspects of "free society" that Fitzhugh most fiercely attacked, the aspects he repeatedly prophesied would spell the doom and downfall of that system, were the features that flourished most exuberantly in the decades following Appomattox. These features were an economy of laissez faire capitalism, an ethic of social Darwinism, and a rationalistic individualism of a highly competitive and atomized sort. Even part of his beloved South joined in the pursuit of these heresies.

It is little wonder that one writer could ask, "But who in America would be reading Fitzhugh in twenty years?" The question was intended to be rhetorical and the answer was, of course, "Nobody." In the America of the post-Civil War period, admittedly, it is impossible to imagine a more completely irrelevant and thoroughly neglected thinker than George Fitzhugh.

The lapse of a century, however, has altered the perspective from which earlier generations assessed the significance of Fitzhugh's thought. The triumph of a highly individualistic society no longer seems as permanent in this country as it once did; nor does the disappearance of all forms of slavery before the advance of progress seem inevitable in the rest of the world. The current of history has changed again. Millions of the world's population are seeking security, abandoning freedom, and finding masters. It is not the sort of socialism that Fitzhugh advocated, nor the slavery he defended, but another type of system that he feared which is fulfilling his prophesies. Even in those societies where socialism is abhorred, mass production, mass organization, and mass culture render his insights more meaningful than they ever were in the old order of individualism.

It was Fitzhugh's constant complaint that his contemporary opponents rejected his theory out of hand without evaluation or understanding. He would have been more crushed by the total neglect of posterity, even in the South, until quite recently. For an intellectual tradition that stands in desperate need of contrast and suffers from uniformity – albeit virtuous liberal uniformity – this oversight is unfortunate. Granting his wicked excesses and sly European importations, Fitzhugh could at least furnish *contrast*. The distance between Fitzhugh and Jefferson renders the conventional polarities between Jefferson and Hamilton, Jackson and Clay, or Hoover and Roosevelt – all liberals under the skin – insignificant indeed. When compared with Fitzhugh, even John Taylor of Caroline, John Randolph of Roanoke, and John C. Calhoun blend inconspicuously into the great American consensus, since they were all apostles in some degree of John Locke.

With such a wealth of sterling and illustrious examples of the Lockean liberal consensus, from Benjamin Franklin to Abraham Lincoln and on down, surely a small niche could be found in our national Pantheon for one minor worthy who deviated all down the line. For Fitzhugh frankly preferred

Sir Robert Filmer and most of his works to John Locke and all his. He saw retrogression in what others hailed as progress, embraced moral pessimism in place of optimism, trusted intuition in preference to reason, always preferred inequality to equality, aristocracy to democracy, and almost anything — including slavery and socialism — to laissez faire capitalism. Whatever his shortcomings, George Fitzhugh could never, never be accused of advocating the middle way. Granting all his doctrine to be quite un-American, one might still ask that Fitzhugh's thought be re-examined, if only for the sharp relief in which it throws the habitual lineaments of the American mind.

Louis Hartz, who applauds America's rejection of Fitzhugh, has deplored the prevailing indifference to what he calls "The Reactionary Enlightenment" of the Southern conservatives. "For this was the great imaginative moment in American political thought," he writes, "the moment when America almost got out of itself, as it were, and looked with some objectivity on the liberal formula it has known since birth." While in his opinion the movement ran to fantasy, extravagance, and false identifications, he calls it "one of the great and creative episodes in the history of American thought," and its protagonists "the only Western conservatives America has ever had." [1]

Hartz is quite justified in placing Fitzhugh near the center and in the forefront of the Reactionary Enlightenment. He goes further to pronounce him "a ruthless and iconoclastic reasoner," "the most logical reactionary in the South," and to attribute to him "a touch of the Hobbesian lucidity of mind." He is on more doubtful ground when he pronounces the Virginian a "more impressive thinker" than the great Carolinian, John C. Calhoun, but he qualifies his praise with numerous charges of inconsistency, irresponsibility, and even insincerity. In commenting upon the South's shift from the

[1] Louis Hartz, *The Liberal Tradition in America* (New York, 1955), pp. 147, 176.

liberal doctrine of the Revolution to ante bellum conservatism, Hartz writes: "Fitzhugh substituted for the social blindness of Jefferson a hopeless exaggeration of the truth. The South exchanged a superficial thinker for a mad genius." [2] I would not agree fully with either the praise or the indictment implied, but would cordially endorse the demand for serious attention to a neglected and provocative thinker.

It would be misleading, however, to leave the impression that George Fitzhugh was typical of the Southern thinkers of his period or representative of the pro-slavery thought or of agrarian thought. Fitzhugh was not typical of anything. Fitzhugh was an individual — *sui generis.* There is scarcely a tag or a generalization or a cliché normally associated with the Old South that would fit him without qualification. Fitzhugh's dissent usually arose out of his devotion to logic rather than out of sheer love of the perverse, but evidence warrants a suspicion that he took a mischievous delight in his perversity and his ability to shock. He once wrote teasingly to his friend George Frederick Holmes, referring to his *Sociology for the South,* "It sells the better because it is odd, eccentric, extravagant, and disorderly." [3] He was always a great one for kicking over the traces, denying the obvious, and taking a stand on his own.

For one thing, Fitzhugh was decidedly *not* an agrarian, for in his opinion "the wit of man can devise no means so effectual to impoverish a country as exclusive agriculture." Manufacturing and commerce were the road to wealth. "Farming is the recreation of great men, the proper pursuit of dull men." [4] As for that sacred Southern dogma of free trade, it was a snare and a delusion, another fraud perpetrated by the Manchester heresy, to be avoided at all costs.[5] Those

[2] *Ibid.*, pp., 159, 182, 184.

[3] Fitzhugh to Holmes, April 11, 1855, quoted in Harvey Wish, *George Fitzhugh, Propagandist of the Old South* (Baton Rouge, 1943), pp. 126–127.

[4] George Fitzhugh, *Sociology for the South, or The Failure of Free Society* (Richmond, 1854), pp. 15, 156.

[5] *Ibid.*, pp. 7–33.

who dismiss Fitzhugh and his friends as bemused romantics enamored of feudalism will have to reckon with the Virginian's praise of Cervantes, who "ridded the world of the useless rubbish of the Middle Ages, by the ridicule so successfully attached to it."[6] And those who identify the pro-slavery argument with a poisonous racism will have to take into account Fitzhugh's rejection of it. He deplored "the hatred of race" and anything that "cuts off the negro from human brotherhood," "because it is at war with scripture, which teaches that the whole human race descended from a common parentage; and, secondly, because it encourages and encites brutal masters to treat negroes, not as weak, ignorant and dependent brethren, but as wicked beasts, without the pale of humanity."[7]

Apart from his ideas, Fitzhugh had traits of personality and character that discourage classifying him with any type. In many ways he was the antithesis of the fierce-eyed, grim-faced polemicist who stares out from the picture galleries of the 1850's, whether in the wing for Southern fire-eaters or the wing for abolitionists. Fanaticism is not compatible with a temperament that selects Falstaff and Sancho Panza as favorite characters of fiction. He made much of his remote family connection with the prominent abolitionist leaders Gerrit Smith and James G. Birney, and his acquaintance with other abolitionists. He sought them out, cultivated them. "We have an inveterate and perverse penchant of finding out good qualities in bad fellows," he wrote. "Robespierre and Milton's Satan are our particular friends."[8] There was none of the suspicious recluse in him. "We admire them all, and have had kindly intercourse and correspondence with some of them," he said of the abolitionists. He referred often

[6] George Fitzhugh, *Cannibals All! or, Slaves Without Masters* (Richmond 1857), p. 132 [all page references to *Cannibals All!* are to the John Harvard Library edition].

[7] Fitzhugh, *Sociology*, p. 95, also p. 147. In 1861, however, Fitzhugh became a convert to the theory of the innate inferiority of the Negro race. Wish, *Fitzhugh*, pp 298–299.

[8] Fitzhugh, *Cannibals All!*, p. 97.

to his debate with Wendell Phillips and to the "generous reception and treatment we received, especially from leading abolitionists, when we went north to personate Satan by defending Slavery." [9] Even after the war, when his world was in ruins, his home part of a battlefield, and his enemies were plotting more mischief, he could write in the old vein: "Love is a pleasanter passion than hate, and we have been hating so intensely for the last six years, that we are now looking about for something to love. . . . We are resolved to hate no one, and to quarrel with no one. No, not even with Thad. Stevens and his men." [10] If candor and magnanimity could disarm hostile critics, Fitzhugh was well endowed.

George Fitzhugh was born in Prince William County, Virginia, on the Northern Neck between the Potomac and the Rappahannock Rivers on November 4, 1806. He sprang from a numerous family that included men of large landed property and prominence in the history of Virginia. He was descended from William Fitzhugh, "a fair classical scholar, a learned, able, and industrious lawyer, a high tory, high Churchman," who came to the colony in 1671 as land agent for Lord Fairfax. George Fitzhugh's father, a doctor and small planter, did not prosper, and the paternal estate passed out of family hands shortly after his death in 1829. That year, however, the son improved his lot somewhat by marrying Mary Brockenbrough of Port Royal, Caroline County, and promptly moving into his wife's home. This was described later by an unsympathetic neighbor as a "rickety old mansion, situated on the fag-end of a once noble estate." [11]

Like the mansion, the village of Port Royal had seen better days, but it was prettily seated on the banks of the Rappahannock, and Fitzhugh became devoted to the village and its few citizens. Its most distinguished citizen, the great

[9] *Ibid.*, p. 86.

[10] George Fitzhugh, "Thad. Stevens's Conscience — The Rump Parliament," *De Bow's Review*, After the War Series, II (1866), 469–470.

[11] Wish, *Fitzhugh*, pp. 1–13.

Jeffersonian intellectual, John Taylor of Caroline, had died five years before young Fitzhugh moved to Port Royal. It is not known whether Fitzhugh ever met Taylor, but he did have several of the famous agrarian's books in his library and their influence may be detected in his own works. He acquired several slaves through his marriage, practiced law in a desultory way, and fathered a family of nine children.[12] He was a confirmed homebody. "Love and veneration for the family is with us not only a principle, but probably a prejudice and a weakness. We were never two weeks at a time from under the family roof, until we had passed middle life, and now that our years almost number half a century, we have never been from home for an interval of two months."[13] His one visit in the North came in 1855, when he visited Gerrit Smith in Peterboro, New York, and debated Wendell Phillips in New Haven.

In formal education, Fitzhugh never progressed beyond the old field school. His learning in the law he picked up on his own. His real education came of his independent, undirected, unsystematic, but wide reading. "We are no regular built scholar – have pursued no 'royal road to mathematics,' nor to anything else," he confessed. "We have by observation and desultory reading, picked up our information by the wayside, and endeavored to arrange, generalize, and digest it for ourselves."[14] Unlike many defenders of the South, he took pains to read the opposition. "We have whole files of infidel and abolition papers, like the *Tribune*, the *Liberator* and *Investigator*," he reported. "Fanny Wright, the Devil's Pulpit and the Devil's Parson, Tom Paine, Owen, Voltaire, et *id genus omne*, are our daily companions."[15] He also read some of the British economists, as well as a few of the English and Continental socialists. In the main, however, he relied upon conservative British journals to keep him abreast of

[12] *Ibid.*, pp. 14–18.
[13] Fitzhugh, *Cannibals All!*, p. 192.
[14] *Ibid.*, p. 67.
[15] *Ibid.*, p. 192.

current thought and literature, periodicals such as the *Edinburgh Review*, the *Westminster Review*, *Blackwood's Magazine*, and the *North British Review*. More in keeping with his station and his time were his love of the Latin classics and his habit of quoting from them.

Of all his contemporaries, Thomas Carlyle seems to have made the most profound impression upon Fitzhugh. The Scot was then at the height of his popularity, and his Virginia admirer quoted him often and with relish, especially his diatribes against the cant of philanthropists and his Olympian thunder against the "Dismal Science," its professors, and their miserable "laws of the shop-till." Carlyle's essay, "The Present Age," furnished the text and suggested both title and subtitle of *Cannibals All!* [16] Carlyle's attack upon the British abolitionists and West Indian emancipation was naturally grist for the pro-slavery propaganda mill, but Fitzhugh was interested in the broader implication of Carlylean doctrine, particularly his diatribes against the "Mammonism" of the industrialists and the wickedness of Manchester economics. The Virginian identified himself willingly with Young England, Disraeli, and Tory socialism.

Fitzhugh's activity in politics was only local, and he never stood for elective office. He was acquainted with a number of Virginia politicians, however, and managed to ingratiate himself with President Buchanan, who appointed him law clerk in the office of the Attorney-General. His literary apprenticeship, late in starting, was served first as a writer for the *Federalsburg Democratic Record*, 1849–1851, and later as editorial writer for the *Richmond Examiner* in 1854–1856 and for the *Richmond Enquirer* in 1855–1857. His most significant journalistic writing was for *De Bow's Review*, edited by the fiery champion of the South, James D. B. De Bow of New Orleans. According to the reckoning of Harvey Wish, Fitzhugh published "well over a hundred articles" in that

[16] Printed in Thomas Carlyle, *Latter-Day Pamphlets* (London, 1850). See pp. 52–53, 56.

journal between 1855 and 1867. He also placed occasional essays in the *Southern Literary Messenger* of Richmond, and after the war in *Lippincott's Magazine* of Philadelphia and the *Southern Magazine* of Baltimore.[17]

The political crises of Europe and America in 1848 and 1849 appear to have stimulated Fitzhugh's first independent publications, two pamphlets that appeared in Richmond in 1850 and 1851 and were later reprinted as an appendix to *Sociology for the South.* In the first and more important of them, *Slavery Justified*, he announced several themes that he was to repeat and elaborate in later works. "Liberty and equality," he declared in his opening sentence, "are new things under the sun." France and the Northern states of the union, the only parts of the world that had given the combination an extensive trial, had proved the experiment was "self-destructive and impracticable" and had "already failed." The evidence of failure was the social distress, economic suffering, and political revolt in both countries. "How can it be otherwise," he asked, "when all society is combined to oppress the poor and weak minded?" Since " 'Every man for himself, and devil take the hindmost' is the moral which liberty and free competition inculcate," and since "half of mankind are but grown-up children" it was apparent that "liberty is as fatal to them as it would be to children." What the weak needed was protection, that is, masters, and so they turned to socialism and communism. Plantation slavery of the South was "the beau ideal of Communism; it is a joint concern, in which the slave consumes more than the master, . . . is far happier . . . is always sure of a support . . . and is as happy as a human being can be." To call free labor "wage slavery" as the socialists did was "a gross libel on slavery," for the condition of free labor was "worse than slavery." The wage system was a contradiction of human needs. "Wages are given in time of vigorous health and strength, and denied when most needed, when sickness or old age has

[17] Wish, *Fitzhugh*, pp. 343–344.

overtaken us. The slave is never without a master to maintain him." The consequence was that "At the slaveholding South all is peace, quiet, plenty and contentment. We have no mobs, no trades unions, no strikes for higher wages, no armed resistance to the law, but little jealousy of the rich by the poor. We have but few in our jails, and fewer in our poor houses."[18]

The one cloud in this otherwise idyllic picture of Southern felicity was the free Negro, the few hundred thousand of their race who were deprived of the protection and security of slavery. Their miserable condition was proof of the curse that freedom would prove to their race: another experiment in liberty that ended in failure. The free Negroes of the North were "an intolerable nuisance," and resentment against them there had provoked stringent discriminatory laws and proscription. The answer to the question that formed the title of his second pamphlet, *What Shall be Done with the Free Negroes?*, was, return them to slavery. The Negro was fitted only for that status. "We have fully and fairly tried the experiment of freeing him . . . and it is now our right and our duty, to listen to the voice of wisdom and experience, and re-consign him to the only condition for which he is suited."[19]

For all his professed love of learning and devotion to logic, Fitzhugh was a propagandist and not infrequently displayed the tactics of that craft, as well as an occasional sample of its disingenuousness. He excused the irregularity of his warfare on the ground that it was necessitated by the nature of his adversaries. "They are divided into hundreds of little guerrilla bands of Isms," he said, "each having its peculiar partisan tactics, and we are compelled to vary our mode of attack from regular cannonade to bushfighting, to suit the occasion." And so he did, shifting his ground, masking his

[18] Fitzhugh, *Slavery Justified — Liberty and Equality — Socialism — Young England — Domestic Slavery,* reprinted in Appendix of *Sociology for the South,* pp. 226–258.

[19] Reprinted, *ibid.,* pp. 259–306.

batteries, and resorting to a variety of tricks to confuse his opponents. He deliberately adopted a style, he said, "in which facts, and argument, and rhetoric, and wit, and sarcasm, succeed each other with rapid iteration." [20] More serious was the damaging admission he made in a personal letter to his friend Professor Holmes in 1855. "I assure you, Sir," he wrote, "I see great evils in slavery, but in a controversial work I ought not to admit them." [21]

Fitzhugh's first book, published in 1854, was also the first published in America bearing the new word "sociology" in its title.[22] *Sociology for the South, or the Failure of Free Society* opened with an aggressive assault upon Adam Smith, laissez faire, and all the political economists who advanced the proposition that social well-being was "best prompted by each man's eagerly pursuing his own selfish welfare unfettered and unrestricted by legal regulations, or governmental prohibitions. . . ." He pronounced that philosophy "false and rotten to the core." Such a system not only opened the way for the rich and strong to exploit the poor and weak individuals, but under the guise of "free trade" it paved the way to empire by enabling the industrial and commercial economies to exploit countries with agricultural economies. "Thus is Ireland robbed of her very life's blood, and thus do our Northern states rob the Southern." [23]

The remedy for these ills was not less government but more government. "Government may do too much for the people, or it may do too little," he thought. "We have committed the latter error." [24] Like his contemporary, Henry C. Carey of Philadelphia, Fitzhugh advocated a system of vigorous government participation in economic development, but he urged it upon Virginia and the Southern states as a solu-

[20] Fitzhugh, *Cannibals All!*, p. 239.

[21] Fitzhugh to Holmes, April 11, 1855, quoted in Wish, *Fitzhugh*, p. 111.

[22] Henry Hughes of Mississippi published *A Treatise on Sociology* (Philadelphia, 1854) the same year.

[23] Fitzhugh, *Sociology*, pp. 11–14; see also p. 133.

[24] *Ibid.*, p. 145.

tion to *their* problems. Both his economic and social aims and his means of attaining them were departures from the Jeffersonian tradition. He stressed the social values of manufacturing and commerce and the need for the growth of cities in the South to foster these arts. Government should be employed vigorously for planning and promoting schemes of internal improvements, developing financial and marketing facilities, and fostering transportation, particularly the building of railroads. "Our system of improvements, manufactures, the mechanic arts, the building up of our cities, commerce, and education should go hand in hand." Above all it was important to provide public education. "Poor [white] people can see things as well as rich people. We can't hide the facts from them. . . . The path of safety is the path of duty! Educate the people, no matter what it may cost! "[25]

After disposing of the classical economists to his satisfaction, Fitzhugh turned to the socialists. He was concerned here mainly with English and French socialists, and he treated them with a great deal more respect than he had Adam Smith and the classical economists. Few realized, he wrote "how much of truth, justice and good sense, there is in the notions of the Communists, as to the community of property." They fully acknowledged the obligations of society to the weak and the propertyless and exhibited a sense of responsibility and morality that was foreign to the capitalistic economists. Socialism was, after all, only "the new fashionable name for slavery." If classical economics was "the science of free society," he would pronounce socialism "the science of slavery." Slavery's only quarrel with socialism was the refusal of the latter to acknowledge fully the failure of free society and its futile attempt to build upon institutions and ideas of a discredited order. "We slaveholders say you must recur to domestic slavery," he insisted, "the best and most common form of Socialism. The new schools of Socialism promise something better, but admit, to obtain that some-

[25] *Ibid.*, pp. 144–148; see also p. 153.

thing, they must first destroy and eradicate man's human nature."[26] In that the socialists shared the fallacies of the philosophers who founded free society.

The trouble started with John Locke and the Enlightenment of the eighteenth century. "The human mind became extremely presumptuous" in that era, he wrote, "and undertook to form governments on exact philosophical principles, just as men make clocks, watches or mills. They confounded the moral with the physical world, and this was not strange, because they had begun to doubt whether there was any other than a physical world." Under their spell, Jefferson and a few misguided patriots embellished an otherwise healthy colonial rebellion with the abstractions of the Declaration of Independence and the Virginia Bill of Rights. These principles were "wholly at war with slavery" and, "equally at war with all government, all subordination, all order," in fact. "Men's minds were heated and blinded when they were written, as well by patriotic zeal, as by a false philosophy, which, beginning with Locke, in a refined materialism, had ripened on the Continent into open infidelity." For a long time these abstractions were a dead letter, had little effect, and did little harm, since inherited English institutions continued with little change. "Those institutions were the growth and accretions of many ages," he pointed out, "not the work of legislating philosophers." But now that the abolitionists were inflamed with these notions, Locke and Jefferson should be firmly refuted and repudiated.[27]

Fitzhugh opened up on the "self-evident truths" and "inalienable rights" with the zeal of an iconoclast. What was really self-evident was that "men are not born physically, morally, or intellectually equal," and that "their natural inequalities beget inequalities of rights." "It would be far nearer the truth to say, 'that some were born with saddles on their backs, and others booted and spurred to ride them,' – and

[26] *Ibid.*, pp. 42, 47, 61, 72.
[27] *Ibid.*, pp. 175–177.

the riding does them good." The ideal of equality was not only false but immoral. "If all men had been created equal, all would have been competitors, rivals, and enemies." Nature had a better plan. "Subordination, difference of caste and classes, difference of sex, age, and slavery beget peace and good will." Life and liberty were obviously not "inalienable" since "they have been sold in all countries, and in all ages, and must be sold so long as human nature lasts." [28] His distant kinsman, George Mason, author of the Virginia Bill of Rights, had carried self-deception to the point of solemnly forbidding "such harmless baubles as titles of nobility and coats of arms," and this in the face of "the right secured by law to hold five hundred subjects, or negro slaves, and ten thousand acres of land, to the exclusion of everybody else . . . an exclusive hereditary privilege far transcending any held by the nobility of Europe. . . ." This was arrant hypocrisy. "We have the *things*, exclusive hereditary privileges and aristocracy, amongst us, in utmost intensity; let us not be frightened at the *names* . . ." [29]

Fitzhugh did not place his faith in paper institutions—declarations, bills of rights, or even written constitutions—but in organic, flesh-and-blood institutions:

> State governments, and senators, and representatives, and militia, and cities, and churches, and colleges, and universities, and landed property, are institutions. Things of flesh and blood, that know their rights, 'and knowing dare maintain them.' We should cherish them. They will give permanence to government, and security to State Rights. But the abstract doctrines of nullification and secession, the general principles laid down in the Declaration of Independence, the Bill of Rights, and Constitution of the United States, afford no protection of rights, no valid limitations of power, no security to State Rights. The power to construe them, is the power to nullify them.[30]

"Institutions are what men can see, feel, venerate and understand," such institutions as were associated with Moses, Al-

[28] *Ibid.*, pp. 177–183.
[29] *Ibid.*, pp. 184, 190–191.
[30] *Ibid.*, pp. 188–189.

fred, Numa, and Lycurgus. "These sages laid down no abstract propositions, founded their institutions on no general principles, had no written *constitutions.* They were wise from experience, adopted what history and experience had tested, and never trusted to *a priori* speculations, like a More, a Locke, a Jefferson, or an Abbé Sieyès." The teaching of history was "that it is much better, to look to the past, to trust to experience, to follow nature, than to be guided by the *ignis fatuus* of *a priori* speculations of closet philosophers." [31]

Encouraged by the reception of his *Sociology* in "the confidence that we address a public predisposed to approve our doctrine, however bold or novel," [32] Fitzhugh plunged into the most productive period of his life. Between 1854 and 1857 he was not only writing editorials for the *Richmond Examiner* and *Richmond Enquirer* and articles for *De Bow's Review*, but he was also at work on his major book, *Cannibals All! or, Slaves Without Masters*, published in Richmond in 1857.

If he considered the *Sociology* "bold" and "novel," he undoubtedly thought of its successor as still bolder and even more novel. The very title, *Cannibals All!* proclaimed the moral relativism with which he proposed to affront conventional American values. He realized at the outset, he said, that "our analysis of human nature and human pursuits is too dark and sombre to meet with ready acceptance." [33] Nothing daunted, he set out to perform a sort of Nietzschean transvaluation of American values, a subversion of the national faith in progress and the goodness of human nature, as well as the characteristic addiction to liberalism, optimism, and respectability. "But if you would cherish self-conceit, self-esteem, or self-appreciation," he warned, "throw down our book; for we will dispel illusions which have promoted your happiness, and show you that what you have considered and practiced as virtue is little better than moral Cannibalism." In

[31] *Ibid.*, pp. 183, 187.
[32] Fitzhugh, *Cannibals All!*, p. 7.
[33] *Ibid.*, p. 35.

the Virginian's inverted hierarchy of values, freedom was slavery and slavery freedom, respectability was criminal and crime respectable. His premise was that "all good and respectable people are 'Cannibals all,' who do not labor, or who are successfully trying to live without labor, on the unrequited labor of other people: – Whilst low, bad, and disreputable people, are those who labor to support themselves, and to support said respectable people besides." [34]

Fitzhugh was saying what Thorstein Veblen unconsciously paraphrased nearly half a century later: "Those employments which are to be classed as exploit are worthy, honorable, noble; other employments, which do not contain this element of exploit, and especially those which imply subservience or submission, are unworthy, debasing, ignoble." [35] Like Veblen, the Virginia sociologist accounted reputability proportional to guile: "The more scalps we can show, the more honored we are." But unlike him, Fitzhugh made no pretense of detachment and moral neutrality. "You are a Cannibal!" he charged, "and if a successful one, pride yourself on the number of your victims, quite as much as any Fiji chieftain, who breakfasts, dines and sups on human flesh." [36]

Fundamental to his critique of free society and his defense of slavery was an extreme form of the labor theory of value, which he had absorbed, he said, from the socialists. "My chief aim," he wrote in his Preface, "has been to show, that *Labor makes values, and Wit exploitates and accumulates them;* and hence to deduce the conclusion that the unrestricted exploitation of so-called free society, is more oppressive to the laborer than domestic slavery." [37] His attack was directed at the moral complacency and assumption of superiority in the North. "We are, all, North and South, engaged in the White Slave Trade," he insisted, "and he who succeeds

[34] *Ibid.*, p. 16.

[35] Thorstein Veblen, *The Theory of the Leisure Class, An Economic Study in the Evolution of Institutions* (New York, 1899), p. 15.

[36] Fitzhugh, *Cannibals All!*, pp. 39, 17.

[37] *Ibid.*, p. 5.

best, is esteemed most respectable. It is far more cruel than the Black Slave Trade, because it exacts more of its slaves, and neither protects nor governs them." Proof of it lay in the admittedly greater profitability of free labor, which to Fitzhugh only meant that the employer of free labor retained more and gave labor less of the value created than did the owner of slave labor. "You, with the command over labor which your capital gives you, are a slave owner — a master, without the obligations of a master. They who work for you, who create your income, are slaves, without the rights of slaves. Slaves without a master!" In his opinion the masters of free labor "live in ten times the luxury and show that Southern masters do," while "Free laborers have not a thousandth part of the rights and liberties of negro slaves." On the other hand, "The negro slaves of the South are the happiest, and, in some sense, the freest people in the world." [38]

In Fitzhugh's philosophy the idea of progress was a modern delusion. Modern history, in fact, was a record not of progress but of retrogression. He advanced the theory in his *Sociology* that "the world has not improved in the last two thousand, probably four thousand years, in the science or practice of medicine, or agriculture," and that it had actually been "retrograding in all else save the physical sciences and the mechanic arts. . . . It is idle to talk of progress, when we look two thousand years back for models of perfection." [39] Bourgeois criteria were "purely utilitarian and material," typified by the sentiments and philosophy of Benjamin Franklin, which were "low, selfish, atheistic and material." Acceptance of these criteria tended "to make man a mere 'featherless biped;' well-fed, well-clothed and comfortable, but regardless of his soul as 'the beasts that perish.' " [40]

In *Cannibals All!* he repeated his attack on the idea of progress and elaborated his theory of retrogression in the arts,

[38] *Ibid.*, pp. 15, 17–19.
[39] Fitzhugh, *Sociology*, pp. 157–159.
[40] *Ibid.*, p. 90.

but to this he added a rejection of the Whiggish interpretation of history. He grounded his critique on something rather similar to the Marxian dialectic of class struggle. His writing by this time reveals acquaintance with Marx's *Communist Manifesto*, and he interpreted each political upheaval in terms of material advantages or disadvantages accruing to conflicting social classes. The theory advanced in William Blackstone's *Commentaries* that the appearance of the House of Commons near the reign of Henry III "was the dawn of approaching liberty," he rejected out of hand. "We contend that it was the origin of the capitalist and moneyed interest government, destined finally to swallow up all other powers in the State, and to bring about the most selfish, exacting and unfeeling class despotism." The emancipation of the serfs was not "another advance towards equality of rights and conditions," as Blackstone claimed, because "it aggravated inequality of conditions, and divested the liberated class of every valuable, social, and political right." Blackstone was also wrong in holding that the Reformation "increased the liberties of the subject," for "in destroying the noblest charity fund in the world, the church lands, and abolishing a priesthood, the efficient and zealous friends of the poor, the Reformation tended to diminish the liberty of the mass of the people, and to impair their moral, social and physical well-being." [41]

In leveling his sights on the Glorious Revolution of 1688, Fitzhugh was striking close to the philosophical underpinnings of the American Revolution. His interpretation of the events of 1688 was similar to that later advanced by Marx. Far from "the consummation or perfection of British liberty" usually pictured, the Glorious Revolution in Fitzhugh's view was "a marked epoch in the steady decay of British liberty." What really happened was that the powers of the house of Commons were increased at the cost of prerogatives of the Crown, the Church, and the nobility, "the natural friends, allies, and

[41] Fitzhugh, *Cannibals All!*, p. 107.

guardians of the laboring class." The settlement and the subsequent chartering of the Bank of England "united the landed and moneyed interests, placed all the powers of government in their hands, and deprived the great laboring class of every valuable right and liberty. The nobility, the church, the king were now powerless; and the mass of people, wholly unrepresented in the government, found themselves exposed to the grinding and pitiless despotism of their natural and hereditary enemies." The subsequent history of Britain was another story of "Slaves without Masters," the degradation of the masses. He quoted Charles Dickens as saying, "Beneath all this, is a *heaving* mass of poverty, ignorance and crime." Those who persisted in describing this sad decline as "progress" were afflicted with a wilful blindness.[42]

It is of possible significance that upon the title pages of his two books, the subtitles, *Failure of Free Society* and *Slaves Without Masters*, are printed in larger type than the main titles. At any rate the disparity suggests the predominance of attack over defense in the author's polemics. In both works the great bulk of space is given over to the shortcomings and failing of free society. The ferocity of Fitzhugh's indictment of the capitalist economy surpasses that of John Taylor at the beginning of the century and the Southern Populists toward its close, and is equaled only by the severity of the socialist attack. He could snarl at "this vampire capitalist class" as bitterly as any socialist. In fact Fitzhugh exploited and quoted extensively from many of the sources that Karl Marx used ten years later in the first volume of *Capital* to marshal evidence of the inhumanity of British industrial capitalism. Prominent among these sources were the reports of Parliamentary Commissions appointed to investigate conditions among coal, iron, and textile workers in the 1840's. He also relied upon Tory reformers and British journals, particularly the *Edinburgh Review*, which he called "a grand repository of the ignorance,

[42] *Ibid.*, p. 108. Cf. Karl Marx, *Capital* (Chicago, 1919), I, 795–796.

the crime, and sufferings of the workers in mines and factories . . . in fine, of the whole laboring class of England." [43]

It was perhaps the abundance of material at hand that caused Fitzhugh to concentrate mainly upon British rather than American conditions. He made no more allowance than did Marx for the occasional exaggerations of reformers and spared his readers none of the horrors of the evidence. One is treated to the full measure of misery in the Scottish coal pits with their sub-human child laborers from five to thirteen years of age, who did not see the light of day for weeks on end; their naked men and "almost naked" women workers harnessed to coal carts and toiling twelve to fourteen hours a day. There were the child calico-printers of Lancashire who were kept at their tasks for fourteen or sixteen consecutive hours and grew up with pipe-stemmed legs, pinched faces, and brutalized minds. There were the metal workers of Wolverhampton "cruelly beaten with a horsewhip, strap, stick, hammer handle, file, or whatever tool is nearest at hand." [44] Was it any wonder, asked Fitzhugh, that an American abolitionist after intensive study of British labor conditions declared that "he would sooner subject his child to Southern slavery, than have him to be a free laborer of England." [45] If the degraded workers of England were to be enslaved, in fact, they would "by becoming property, become valuable and valued" and would be elevated from their present plight at least to the status of domestic animals.[46]

In his attack upon free society in America, Fitzhugh borrowed freely from the tactics northern abolitionists employed in their propaganda against Southern slavery. The criminology of the subject was employed as fair description of conditions, and the occasional instance of sadism and depravity presented as the prevailing practice. Just as the abolitionists made effective use of quotations from Southerners and slave-

[43] Fitzhugh, *Cannibals All!*, p. 158.
[44] *Ibid.*, pp. 167–176.
[45] *Ibid.*, p. 109.
[46] *Ibid.*, p. 155.

holders upon the evils of the slave society, so Fitzhugh employed to the fullest the testimony of abolitionist reformers upon the failing of free society. He described the testimony of "the actual leaders and faithful exponents of abolition" whom he quoted as "our trump card." Out of their own mouths he would prove "the inadequacy and injustice of the whole social and governmental organization of the North." Since many of the abolitionists were passionate critics of free society and entertained schemes for reform of the North as well as the South, each with his own panacea, Fitzhugh did not lack for live ammunition from their publications.[47]

It was good propaganda to catalogue the desperate remedies and wild panaceas to which the breakdown of free society had driven the reformers, and Fitzhugh did so regularly: "Mr. Greeley's Phalansteries, Mr. Andrews' Free Love, Mr. Goodell's Millennium and Mr. [Gerrit] Smith's Agrarianism," to say nothing of the multitudinous nostrums of Mr. Garrison, "King of the Abolitionists, Great Anarch of the North." [48] Why all the remedies if there were no diseases in free society?

> Why have you Bloomer's and Women's Right's men, and strong-minded women, and Mormons, and anti-renters, and "vote myself a farm" men, Millerites, and Spiritual Rappers, and Shakers, and Widow Wakemanites, and Agrarians, and Grahamites, and a thousand other superstitious and infidel Isms at the North? Why is there faith in nothing, speculation about everything? Why is this unsettled, half demented state of the human mind co-extensive in time and space, with free society? Why is Western Europe now starving? and why has it been fighting and starving for seventy years? Why all this, except that free society is a failure? Slave society needs no defence till some other permanently practicable form of society has been discovered. Nobody at the North who reads my book will attempt to reply to it; for all the learned abolitionists had unconsciously discovered and proclaimed the failure of free society long before I did.[49]

It was not the slaveholders but the abolitionists who "have

[47] *Ibid.*, pp. 85, 93–95.
[48] *Ibid.*, p. 211.
[49] Fitzhugh to A. Hogeboom, January 14, 1856, *ibid.*, p. 103.

for years been roaring . . . to the Oi Polloi rats, that the old crazy edifice of society, in which they live, is no longer fit for human dwelling, and is imminently dangerous." [50] Yet the same philosophers were inviting the South to abandon its stable society, demolish its tested and benevolent institutions, and move into the rickety edifice of free society which the abolitionists had already condemned as uninhabitable.

Fitzhugh's books appeared at the height of the sectional controversy over slavery and the literary war it induced. It is all the more difficult for that reason to assess their relative importance and distinguish their influence from that of the many other pro-slavery books of the period. His *Sociology* profited much from the wholehearted endorsement and several notices it received from George Frederick Holmes, foremost reviewer in the South. De Bow and other Southern editors gave it space and frequent notice, and the first printing of the book was almost sold out in a few months. Fitzhugh complained of "the affectation of silent contempt" by the Northern press, and such attention as he got in that quarter was in the main hostile. Among Southern writers who revealed the influence of the *Sociology*, whether admitted or not, Professor Wish mentions Edmund Ruffin (who did acknowledge the impact of Fitzhugh's "novel and profound views"), Albert Taylor Bledsoe, William J. Grayson, James D. B. De Bow, George D. Armstrong, and Thornton Stringfellow.[51]

The response to *Cannibals All!* was also flattering in the South, though some of its critics in that quarter were troubled by its concession to socialism and by its carelessness and inconsistencies. Even De Bow thought the author "a little fond of paradoxes, a little inclined to run a theory into extremes, and a little impractical." But on the whole the Southern reception was enthusiastic. The book, after all, marked an advance to "higher ground" in the Southern position at the

[50] *Ibid.*, p. 96.

[51] Wish, *Fitzhugh*, p. 126; and for summary of critical reception of the *Sociology* see pp. 113–125.

climax of the sectional controversy. It virtually ignored defensive tactics and concentrated upon aggressive strategy along radical anti-capitalist lines.[52]

The legend of the satanic champion of evil from Port Royal had grown in anti-slavery circles since the appearance of his first book, and *Cannibals All!* was received as the last word in diabolism. William Lloyd Garrison, according to Professor Wish, gave it "considerably more attention than perhaps any other book in the history of the *Liberator.*" Garrison quoted long passages from the book as horrible examples of the extremes to which "this cool audacious defender of the soul-crushing, blood-reeking system of slavery" could go as the spokesman of "the cradle-plunderers and slave-drivers at the South." Surely *Cannibals All!* could be written down as the "gospel according to Beelzebub that is preached at the South." In another mood he called Fitzhugh "the Don Quixote of Slavedom – only still more demented" than the Knight of La Mancha. "If he is not playing the part of a dissembler, he is certainly crack-brained, and deserves pity rather than ridicule or censure." But Garrison spared him neither censure nor ridicule: the Virginian was "demoniacal," his writings "idiocy." Granted that Fitzhugh showed a certain ingenuity and cleverness in pointing out the failings of free society, these were as nothing compared to the abominations of slave society. Granted the South might be free of "Isms" – so was despotic Russia.[53]

Many of Fitzhugh's more startling phrases and paradoxes, taken out of context, lent themselves admirably to quotation by Republicans or antislavery people for the purpose of discrediting the South or the Democrats. The more extreme pronouncements of the Virginian were thereby represented erroneously not only as typical of *his* views, but also those of his party and his region. Abraham Lincoln was a faithful

[52] *Ibid.*, p. 198. The criticism of *Cannibals All!* is summarized in pp. 195–199.

[53] *Boston Liberator*, March 6, 13, April 19, 1857, quoted in Wish, *Fitzhugh*, pp. 200–203.

reader of Fitzhugh's articles and editorials in the *Richmond Enquirer* and cited them in his speeches during the years 1856 to 1859 as representative of the wicked purposes of Democrats and slaveholders. He even went so far as to connive in planting one of the *Enquirer* articles in a pro-slavery paper of Springfield, which could then be quoted to the embarrassment of local Democrats.[54] William Herndon, his law partner, bought a copy of *Sociology for the South* and reported that, "This book aroused the ire of Lincoln more than most pro-slavery books." If he read as far as page 94 in that work, Lincoln found this passage: "One set of ideas will govern and control after awhile the civilized world. Slavery will every where be abolished, or every where be re-instituted." He could have found the same idea in different words in *Cannibals All!* [page 106]. Actually, in replying to charges of Senator Stephen A. Douglas regarding the famous House Divided speech of 1858, Lincoln said in a speech at Cincinnati, September 17, 1859: 'But neither I, nor Seward, nor [Congressman John] Hickman is entitled to the enviable or unenviable distinction of having first expressed that idea. The same idea was expressed by the Richmond 'Enquirer' in Virginia, in 1856, quite two years before it was expressed by the first of us." Lincoln mistakenly attributed the irrepressible conflict idea to Roger A. Pryor, editor of the paper, but the author of the unsigned editorial of May 6, 1856, to which he referred was really Fitzhugh.[55]

The strain of irresponsibility in his writings involves Fitzhugh in the guilt of his generation. It is somewhat ironical, however, that the Virginian should have been associated in such a personal way with the origins of the irrepressible conflict and House Divided ideas, or that he should have sometimes been made a symbol of Southern intransigence and militant disunionism. He actually deplored nullification,

[54] Albert J. Beveridge, *Abraham Lincoln, 1809–1858* (Boston, 1928), II, 30–31.

[55] See Wish, *Fitzhugh*, pp. 150–159, 288, on the whole House Divided speech matter.

opposed secession till the last moment, and dreaded disunion. In all probability, he no more desired a bloody showdown than did Lincoln. The final words of *Cannibals All!* were a friendly appeal to the abolitionists:

> Extremes meet — and we and the leading Abolitionists differ but a hairbreadth. . . Add a Virginia overseer to Mr. Greeley's Phalansteries, and Mr. Greeley and we would have little to quarrel about. . . . We want to be friends with them and with all the world; and, as the curtain is falling, we conclude with the valedictory and invocation of the Roman actor — "Vos valete! et plaudite!"

Like many Americans of his day, George Fitzhugh was absorbed in the great sectional crisis, and his mind was molded by the titanic surge and flow of the struggle. Unlike all but a very few, however, he managed to achieve a modicum of timelessness and universality in his theories that places them just beyond the destructive reach of historical relativism and should spare them dismissal as the cynical rationalization of outmoded institutions. In the opinion of Charles A. Beard, Fitzhugh's thought was "unlimited in its sweep," a "universal view" that "exceeded the planting view and the agrarian view in its scope of details, in its diversity of content, and in its reach of time." [56] He would seem to deserve some attention outside the context of slavery and the Civil War.

In so far as the phrase is permissible at all, Fitzhugh was an American original. For many reasons he rejected the political principles of the Enlightenment upon which Jefferson based his thought. He found the economic determinism of Madison inadequate for his purposes, as well as the narrow capitalist-versus-agrarian dialectic of the other sage of Port Royal, John Taylor. The parochialism of Calhoun appealed to him, but not the Carolinian's legalistic constitutionalism, and most certainly not his heretical adaptation of Lockean theory. Unlike his Southern predecessors and contemporaries, Fitzhugh's approach was not political, or economic, or le-

[56] Charles A. Beard, *The American Spirit* (New York, 1942), p. 288.

galistic, but sociological and psychological – both with an antique flavor, and yet more attuned to the modern than to the eighteenth- or nineteenth-century mind. His belated discovery of his intellectual obligations to the ancients is revealing of both his naïveté and his originality. He wrote Professor Holmes in 1855:

> I received from Mr. Appleton's, a week ago, Aristotle's Politics and Economics. I find I have not only adopted his theories, his arguments, and his illustrations, but his very words. Society is a work of nature and grows. Men are social like bees; an isolated man is like a bird of prey. Men and society are coeval. . . . Now, I find that, although Locke, Rousseau, Adam Smith, Jefferson, Macaulay, and Calhoun are against me, Aristotle, Carlyle, you, and all the leading minds of the day are with me. . . . I used to think I was a little paradoxical. I now fear I am a mere retailer of truisms and common places.[57]

If man were a social and political animal from the word go, and if society were an organism – as organic as an elaborated and diversified beehive – then all the talk about compacts, and social contracts, and man-in-a-state-of nature, and natural rights, and consent of the governed, and equality was arrant nonsense. Hobbes was as wrong as Locke, and Jefferson as wrong as Calhoun, and Adam Smith was out of his mind. Society was an organic continuum, inegalitarian and hierarchical. The inequalities explained and necessitated the hierarchy. They also required that government recognize the facts of life, refuse to be blinded by laissez faire dogmas, and intervene to protect the weak from the strong. An ethic of devil-take-the-hindmost led straight to tyranny and anarchy. Inequality was both necessary and desirable, and stability was important above all. This did not exclude change. Growth meant change, and society was a growing organism. But it had to grow according to the laws of growth, slowly, with uninterrupted continuity of institutions and moral values – not in fits and starts and revolutions according to the

[57] Fitzhugh to Holmes, April 11, 1855, quoted in Wish, *Fitzhugh,* pp. 118–119. See also *Cannibals All!,* pp. 12–13.

specifications and theories of philosophers and utopian dreamers. "Such is the theory of Aristotle," he wrote, "promulgated more than two thousand years ago, generally considered true for two thousand years, and destined, we hope, soon again to be accepted as the only true theory of government and society." [58]

There came a point, however, where Fitzhugh departed from the Aristotelian way. While man was social, he was not rational. He was, in fact, fundamentally irrational, guided not by reason but by instinct, custom, habit, and requiring tradition and religion and stable institutions to keep him in line. Fitzhugh held and often expressed a profound skepticism of all atomistic and rationalistic theories of human nature and a strong aversion to rationalistic philosophers. "Modern philosophy treats of men only as separate monads or individuals," he complained.[59] His attitude was not that of anti-intellectualism, but he distrusted intellect that departed from experience and history and tradition and arrogantly spun lofty abstractions. Especially did he distrust intellect fired by moral passion and conviction of self-righteousness. "In fine, all of the greatest and darkest crimes of recorded history have been perpetrated by men 'terribly in earnest' blindly attempting to fulfill, what they considered, some moral, political or religious duty." There had been too much of that type of intellect loosed upon mankind, he wrote after the war, too much in the South as well as the North.[60]

In renouncing Locke and rationalism and the Enlightenment, Fitzhugh had no notion of renouncing the heritage of the America Revolution – the true heritage, that is. Not at all, he declared. "All the bombastic absurdity in the Declaration of Independence about the inalienable rights of man, had

[58] Fitzhugh, *Cannibals All!*, p. 71. See also Arnaud B. Leavelle and Thomas I. Cook, "George Fitzhugh and the Theory of American Conservatism," *Journal of Politics*, VII (1945), 145–168.

[59] Fitzhugh, *Cannibals All!*, p. 54.

[60] Fitzhugh, "Terribly in Earnest," *De Bow's Review*, After the War Series, II (1866), 172–177.

about as much to do with the occasion as would a sermon or oration on the teething of a child or the kittening of a cat . . . Our institutions, State and Federal, imported from England where they had grown up naturally and imperceptibly . . . would have lasted for many ages, had not thoughtless, half-informed, speculative men, like Jefferson, succeeded in basing them on such inflammable materials. . . . The Revolution of '76 was, in its action, an exceedingly natural and conservative affair; it was only the false and unnecessary theories invoked to justify it that were radical, agrarian and anarchical." These were the theories of John Locke, "a presumptuous charlatan, who was as ignorant of the science or practice of government as any shoemaker or horse jockey." These theories had not inspired the Revolution of '76, but by slow fuse had eventually touched off "the grandest explosion the world ever witnessed," the Revolution of '61. "The French Revolutions of '89, 1830, and 1848, were mere popguns compared to it; as we all see and feel, for its stunning sound is still ringing in our ears." He wrote that in 1863 when, indeed, the stunning sound of revolution was deafening.[61]

While Fitzhugh expressed distrust for any book on moral science less than four hundred years old, he made one significant exception, Sir Robert Filmer's *Patriarcha.* This was the work of the forgotten Kentish monarchist and conservative whom Locke had felt it necessary to belabor extensively in his *Treatise.* Filmer's stress upon the patriarchal family, rather than his defense of the divine right of monarchs, was what struck the deep responsive chord in Fitzhugh. For the Virginian the family was everything, and society, government were but the family writ large – the authoritarian, patriarchal family. Aristotle had taught him "that the family, including husband, wife, children, and slaves, is the first and most natural development of that social nature." It was the

[61] Fitzhugh, "Revolutions of '76 and '61 Contrasted," *ibid.*, IV (1867), 36–42. This was originally published in the *Southern Literary Messenger,* XXXVII (1863), 718–726.

model of all institutions: "this family association, this patriarchal government . . . gradually merges into larger associations of men under a common government or ruler." It was the disproof of Locke, for "Fathers do not derive their authority, as heads of families, from the consent of wife and children." It was the justification of domestic slavery, for "besides wife and children, brothers and sisters, dogs, horses, birds and flowers — slaves also belong to the family circle," and there they, like other weaker members, received the care, protection, and control they needed.[62]

There is a possible clue in Fitzhugh's thought to the provocative questions and indictments advanced by Louis Hartz in his treatment of the Reactionary Enlightenment. Because Hartz finds "beneath the feudal and reactionary surface of Southern thought" nothing but slavery, he concludes that the massive structure of reaction was "a simple fraud" and that, "Fraud, alas, was the inevitable fate of Southern social thought." He goes on to say, "They exchanged a fraudulent liberalism for an even more fraudulent feudalism: they stopped being imperfect Lockes and became grossly imperfect Maistres. This was the meaning of Fitzhugh's 'great conservative reaction'. . . ." Not only did their system not fit the American liberal formula, "the real trouble with it was that it did not fit any formula, any basic categories of Western social theory." [63]

Fitzhugh did find a formula, and he did not go back to feudalism nor forward to Maistre for it — only back to the seventeenth century, to John Locke's chosen antagonist, Sir Robert Filmer. And in seventeenth-century Kent, as well as in Virginia of that and the two following centuries, as Peter Laslett has pointed out, the patriarchal family was a pretty "basic category." That was why Locke took Filmer seriously. "Filmerism," says this historian, "was above all things the exaltation of the family: it made the rules of domestic society

[62] Fitzhugh, *Cannibals All!*, in order of quotation, pp. 193, 72, 243, 205.
[63] Hartz, *The Liberal Tradition*, pp. 146–148.

into principles of political science."[64] The gentry of Kent were a close-knit community. "The genealogical interrelationships between its members were extensive, complicated and meticulously observed by all of them: it is astonishing how distant a connexion qualified for the title 'cozen.' The reason for this excessive consciousness of kinship was patriarchalism."[65]

This Kentish cousinage and its "excessive consciousness of kinship" extended across the Atlantic. "By 1660," writes Laslett, "this group of interrelationships existed in two places in the world: in middle eastern Kent and in Virginia in the area of the James River. This process, by which an English county society reproduced its names, its attitudes, its literary interests, even its field sports, in the swamps of the Virginia creeks, had begun with the foundation of the Virginia Company of London in 1606. . . . The story of the early Virginian planters' families illustrates the most important feature of the English gentry of the time – the immense strength of the family bond and the extraordinary cohesion of the grouping of families by locality. There could be no more vivid illustration of patriarchalism at work."[66] As for the Kentish gentry, "The most characteristic thing they produced was the political thinking of Sir Robert Filmer and the most surprising was the society of the Old South in the United States."[67] In fact, the transplanted patriarchal offshoot outlasted the original: "the descendents of the Virginian planters, who became the slaveholders of the Southern States, were the heads of a classic type of patriarchal household, so that it survived until the middle of the nineteenth century even in such a rationalistic and egalitarian society as the

[64] Peter Laslett, "Sir Robert Filmer, The Man and the Whig Myth," *William and Mary Quarterly*, Ser. 3, V (1948), 544.

[65] Peter Laslett, "The Gentry of Kent in 1640," *Cambridge Historical Journal*, IX (1948), 150.

[66] *Ibid.*, pp. 161–162.

[67] *Ibid.*, pp. 162–163.

U.S.A." [68] The English historian even suggests that the Southern branch had "lineaments even more strongly marked than in England, perhaps because there were then no towns of any consequence." [69]

But what of the Revolutionary generation of the Virginia Enlightenment — the Masons, the Randolphs, the Jeffersons, the Madisons, the Washingtons — and their apparently firm commitment to the antithesis of Filmerism, to the Lockean principles of rationalistic individualism and its picture of an atomistic society? Whatever principles these gentry subscribed to in the 1770's and later, they were one and all patriarchs on their own — Thomas Jefferson included. The anthropological, sociological, and political realities of Virginia society were those of the patriarchal family. Those realities might better be understood in Filmerian than in Lockean terms. And curiously enough, many of these Revolutionary Lockeans were blood relatives — remote "cozens" of Sir Robert himself. "In Virginia the Filmers and the Filmer conections," writes Laslett, "were associated with all the great families which finally gave to the thirteen colonies their Revolutionary leadership in the 1770's — the Washingtons, the Byrds, the Berkeleys, and the Randolphs and so the Jeffersons. Whatever the subsequent literary and philosophical reputation of Sir Robert Filmer, he had been a great genealogical success." [70] Sir Robert was a family man in more ways than ideological.

It was not "simple fraud" that led George Fitzhugh to seize upon Filmer in his search for some ideological basis on which to construct his defense and his understanding of Virginia society, even in mid-nineteenth century. As a sociologist he had got hold of some firm anthropological data. It is rather more a wonder that the patriarchs of Revolutionary Virginia

[68] Peter Laslett (ed.), "Introduction" to Sir Robert Filmer, *Patriarcha and Other Political Works* (Oxford, 1949), p. 26.

[69] Laslett, "The Gentry of Kent," p. 150n.

[70] Laslett (ed.), "Introduction" to Filmer, *Patriarcha,* p. 10.

should have temporarily embraced Locke than that their sons should have returned to Filmer.

In an elaborate comparison, Fitzhugh identified the South and its heritage and tradition with Filmer, and the North and its tradition and heritage with Locke. The English Tories, with whom he identified the South, "are conservative, for the most part, agreeing with Sir Robert Filmer"; while the English Whigs "are progressive, rationalistic, radical, and agree with Locke in his absurd doctrines of human equality and the social contract." These were "the antinomes or opposing forces" in the mother country: Filmer *versus* Locke. "The North and the South would pretty well supply the places, or act the part, of these forces in America." [71]

Fitzhugh's home at Port Royal was shelled by Union troops during the war, while he and his family were refugees in Richmond. After the war and for more than a year during the Johnsonian Reconstruction, he was employed, oddly enough, as an agent of the Freedmen's Bureau and served with a Negro freedman as an associate judge of the Freedmen's Court. From this vantage point he viewed the Reconstruction drama and wrote about it philosophically, sometimes humorously, but rarely with any bitterness. After the death of his wife in 1877 he moved to Kentucky to live with a son, and finally to Texas with an impoverished daughter. There he died, nearly blind, in 1881 at the age of seventy-four.

In the many articles he published in *De Bow's Review* after the war, Fitzhugh counseled the South to accept the new order, but he showed little disposition to retract any of his ante-bellum theories. In 1867 he had the hardihood to reprint an article he had written in 1863 at the crest of the Confederate tide: ". . . we begin a great conservative reaction," he had announced. "We attempt to roll back the

[71] Fitzhugh, "The Impending Fate of the Country," *De Bow's Review*, II (1866), 569.

reformation in its political phases, for we saw every where in Europe and the North reformation running to excess, a universal spirit of destructiveness, a profane attempt to pull down what God and nature had built up and to erect ephemeral Utopia in its place." [72]

In 1857 he had defiantly addressed to the abolitionists a boast of the security and confidence of the Old Regime: "Is our house tumbling about our heads, and we sitting in conscious security amidst the impending ruin?" he asked. "No! No! Our edifice is one that never did fall, and never will fall; for Nature's plastic hand reared it, supports it, and will forever sustain it." [73] So far as the record reveals, he never had the hardihood to reprint that, but as a philosopher he may have reflected upon it from time to time.

*Baltimore, 1959* C. VANN WOODWARD

## EDITOR'S NOTE

In the interest of the modern reader, inconsistent spellings that appeared in the original edition have been regularized. In particular, proper names have been changed to correspond to current spelling, and typographical errors have been silently corrected. In cases where the rhetorical intent of the author would not be affected and readability would be increased, modern usage in punctuation has been adopted.

I have received valuable suggestions from several friends who have kindly read the manuscript of the introductory essay on Fitzhugh. In particular I wish to acknowledge the help of Professors Thomas I. Cook and Charles A. Barker of Johns Hopkins, Bernard Bailyn of Harvard, Eric McKitrick of Rutgers, and Stanley Elkins of Chicago. Professor Henry T. Rowell of Johns Hopkins kindly helped me with the identification of the Latin quotations. For translations of the latter I relied upon the Loeb Library versions. For biographical data I have leaned heavily upon the work of Harvey Wish, *George Fitzhugh, Propagandist of the Old South.*

[72] Fitzhugh, "Revolutions of '76 and '61 Contrasted," *ibid.*, IV (1867), 43.
[73] Fitzhugh, *Cannibals All!*, p. 97.

# CANNIBALS ALL!

## OR,

## SLAVES WITHOUT MASTERS

BY

GEORGE FITZHUGH

OF PORT ROYAL, CAROLINE, VA.

"His hand will be against every man, and every man's hand against him." — GEN. XVI. 12.

"Physician, heal thyself." — LUKE IV. 23.

# DEDICATION

TO THE HONORABLE HENRY A. WISE.[1]

Dear Sir:

I dedicate this work to you, because I am acquainted with no one who has so zealously, laboriously, and successfully endeavored to Virginianise Virginia, by encouraging, through State legislation, her intellectual and physical growth and development; no one who has seen so clearly the evils of centralization from without, and worked so earnestly to cure or avert those evils, by building up centralization within.

Virginia should have her centers of Thought at her Colleges and her University, centers of Trade and Manufactures at her Seaboard and Western towns, and centers of Fashion at her Mineral Springs.

I agree with you, too, that State strength and State independence are the best guarantees of State rights; and that policy the wisest which most promotes the growth of State strength and independence.

Weakness invites aggression; strength commands respect; hence, the Union is safest when its separate members are best able to repel injury, or to live independently.

Your attachment to Virginia has not lessened your love for the Union. In urging forward to completion such works as the Covington and Ohio Road, you are trying to add to the wealth, the glory, and the strength of our own State, whilst you would add equally to the wealth, the strength, and perpetuity of the Union.

I cannot commit you to all the doctrines of my book, for you will not see it until it is published.

With very great respect,

Your obedient servant,

GEO. FITZHUGH.

*Port Royal, Aug. 22, 1856.*

[1] Henry Alexander Wise (1806–1876), Governor of Virginia, 1856–1860.

# PREFACE

I have endeavored, in this work, to treat the subjects of Liberty and Slavery in a more rigidly analytical manner than in *Sociology for the South*[1]; and, at the same time, to furnish the reader with abundance of facts, authorities, and admissions, whereby to test the truth of my views.

My chief aim has been to show that *Labor makes values, and Wit exploitates and accumulates them*, and hence to deduce the conclusion that the unrestricted exploitation of so-called free society is more oppressive to the laborer than domestic slavery.

In making a distinct onslaught on the popular doctrines of Modern Ethics, I must share the credit or censure with my corresponding acquaintance and friend, Professor H. of Virginia.[2]

Our acquaintance commenced by his congratulating me, by letter, on the announcement that I was occupied with a treatise vindicating the institution of Slavery in the abstract, and by his suggestion that he foresaw, from what he had read of my communications to the papers, that I should be compelled to make a general assault on the prevalent political and moral philosophy. This letter, and others subsequent to it, together with the reception of my Book by the Southern Public, have induced me in the present work to avow the full breadth and scope of my purpose. I am sure it will be easier to convince the world that the customary theories of our Modern Ethical Philosophy, whether utilitarian or sentimental, are so fallacious or so false in their premises and

[1] *Sociology for the South, or the Failure of Free Society* (Richmond, 1854).

[2] George Frederick Holmes (1820–1897), professor of various subjects at the University of Virginia, 1857–1897.

their deductions as to deserve rejection, than to persuade it that the social forms under which it lives and attempts to justify and approve are equally erroneous, and should be replaced by others founded on a broader philosophical system and more Christian principles.

Yet, I believe that, under the banners of Socialism and, more dangerous because more delusive, Semi-Socialism, society is insensibly and often unconsciously marching to the utter abandonment of the most essential institutions – religion, family ties, property, and the restraints of justice. The present profession is, indeed, to stop at the half-way house of No-Government and Free Love; but we are sure that it cannot halt and encamp in such quarters. Society will work out erroneous doctrines to their logical consequences, and detect error only by the experience of mischief. The world will only fall back on domestic slavery when all other social forms have failed and been exhausted. That hour may not be far off.

Mr. H[olmes] will not see this work before its publication, and would dissent from many of its details, from the unrestricted latitude of its positions, and from its want of precise definition. The time has not yet arrived, in my opinion, for such precision, nor will it arrive until the present philosophy is seen to be untenable, and we begin to look about us for a loftier and more enlightened substitute.

# INTRODUCTION

In our little work, *Sociology for the South,* we said, "We may again appear in the character of writer before the public; but we shall not intrude, and would prefer that others should finish the work which we have begun." That little work has met, everywhere, we believe, at the South, with a favorable reception. No one has denied its theory of Free Society, nor disputed the facts on which that theory rests. Very many able co-laborers have arisen, and many books and essays are daily appearing, taking higher ground in defence of Slavery, justifying it as a normal and natural institution, instead of excusing or apologizing for it as an exceptional one. It is now treated as a positive good, not a necessary evil. The success, not the ability of our essay, may have had some influence in eliciting this new mode of defence. We have, for many years, been gradually and cautiously testing public opinion at the South, and have ascertained that it is ready to approve, and much prefers, the highest ground of defence. We have no peculiar fitness for the work we are engaged in, except the confidence that we address a public predisposed to approve our doctrines, however bold or novel. Heretofore the great difficulty in defending Slavery has arisen from the fear that the public would take offence at assaults on its long-cherished political axioms, which, nevertheless, stood in the way of that defence. It is now evident that those axioms have outlived their day – for no one, either North or South, has complained of our rather ferocious assault on them – much less attempted to reply to or refute our arguments and objections. All men begin very clearly to perceive that the state of revolution is politically and socially abnormal and exceptional, and that the principles that would justify it are true in the particular, false in the general. "A recurrence to fundamental principles" by an oppressed people is treason if it fails, the noblest of heroism if it eventuates in successful revolution. But a "frequent recurrence to fundamental principles" is at war with the continued existence of all government, and is a doctrine fit to be sported only by the Isms of the North and the Red Republicans of Europe. With them no principles are considered established and sacred, nor will ever be. When, in time of revolution, society is partially disbanded, disintegrated, and dissolved, the doctrine of Human Equality may have a hearing, and may be useful in stimulating rebellion; but it is practically impossible, and directly conflicts with all government, all separate property, and all social existence. We cite these two examples, as instances, to show how the wisest and best of men are sure to deduce, as general principles, what is only true as to themselves and their peculiar circumstances. Never were people blessed with such wise and noble Institutions as we; for they combine most that was good in those of Rome and Greece, of Judea, and of Mediæval England. But the mischievous absurdity of our political axioms and principles quite equals the wisdom and conservatism of our political practices. The ready appreciation by the public of such doctrines as these encourages us to persevere in writing. The silence of the North is far more encouraging, however, than the approbation of the South. Piqued and taunted for two years, by many Southern Presses of high standing, to deny the proposition that Free Society in Western Europe is a failure, and that it betrays premonitory symptoms of failure, even in America, the North is silent, and thus tacitly admits the charge. Challenged to compare and weigh the advantages and disadvantages of our domestic slavery with their slavery of the masses to capital and skill, it is mute, and neither accepts nor declines our challenge. The comparative evils of Slave Society and of Free Society, of slavery to human Masters, and of slavery to Capital are the issues which the South now presents, and which the North avoids. And she avoids them because the Abolitionists, the only assailants of Southern Slavery, have, we believe, to a man, asserted the entire failure of their own social system, proposed its subversion, and suggested an approximating millennium, or some system of Free Love, Communism, or Socialism, as a substitute.

The alarming extent of this state of public opinion, or, to speak more accurately, the absence of any public opinion, or common faith and conviction about anything, is not dreamed of at the South, nor fully and properly realized, even at the North. *We* cannot believe what is so entirely different from all our experience and observation, and *they* have become familiarized and inattentive to the infected social atmosphere they continually inhale. Besides, living in the midst of the Isms, their situation is not favorable for comprehensive observation or calm generalization. More than a year since, we made a short trip to the North, and whilst there only associated with distinguished Abolitionists.[1] We have corresponded much with them, before and since, and read many of their books, lectures, essays, and speeches. We have neither seen nor heard any denial by them of the failure of their own social system; but, on the contrary, found that they all concurred in the necessity of radical social changes. 'Tis true, in conversation, they will say, "Our system of society is bad, but yours of the South is worse; the cause of social science is advancing, and we are ready to institute a system better than either." We could give many private anecdotes, and quote thousands of authorities, to prove that such is the exact state of opinion with the multitudinous Isms of the North. The correctness of our statement will not be denied. If it is, anyone may satisfy himself of its truth by reading any Abolition or Infidel paper at the North for a single month. The *Liberator*, of Boston, their ablest paper, gives continually the fullest

[1] A visit during the spring of 1855 to New York and Connecticut, to deliver a lecture on 'The Failure of Free Society" at New Haven. Wendell Phillips replied to the lecture from the same platform the following day.

exposé of their opinions, and of their wholesale destructiveness of purpose.

The neglect of the North to take issue with us, or with the Southern Press, in the new positions which we have assumed, our own observations of the working of Northern society, the alarming increase of Socialism, as evinced by its control of many Northern State Legislatures and its majority in the lower house of Congress, are all new proofs of the truth of our doctrine. The character of that majority in Congress is displayed in full relief, by the single fact, which we saw stated in a Northern Abolition paper, that "there are a hundred Spiritual Rappers in Congress." A Northern member of Congress made a similar remark to us a few days since. 'Tis but a copy of the Hiss Legislature of Massachusetts,[2] or the Praise-God-Barebones Parliament of England. Further study, too, of Western European Society, which has been engaged in continual revolution for twenty years, has satisfied us that Free Society every where begets Isms, and that Isms soon beget bloody revolutions. Until our trip to the North, we did not justly appreciate the passage which we are about to quote from Mr. Carlyle's *Latter-Day Pamphlets*. Now it seems to us as if Boston, New Haven, or Western New York had set for the picture:

> To rectify the relation that exists between two men, is there no method, then, but that of ending it? The old relation has become unsuitable, obselete,[3] perhaps unjust; and the remedy is, abolish it; let there henceforth be no relation at all. From the 'sacrament of marriage' downwards, human beings used to be manifoldly related one to another, and each to all; and there was no relation among human beings, just or unjust, that had not its grievances and its difficulties, its necessities on both sides to bear and forbear. But henceforth, be it known, we have changed all that by favor of Heaven; the 'voluntary principle' has come up, which will itself do the business for us; and now let a new sacrament, that of *Divorce*, which we call emancipation,

[2] So-called for Joseph Hiss, a member from Boston, who headed an anti-Catholic committee to investigate nunneries.

[3] Carlyle spelled it "obsolete" in "The Present Time," *Latter-Day Pamphlets*, No. 1 (March, 1850), p. 31.

and spout of on our platforms, be universally the order of the day! Have men considered whither all this is tending, and what it certainly enough betokens? Cut every human relation that has any where grown uneasy sheer asunder; reduce whatsoever was compulsory to voluntary, whatsoever was permanent among us to the condition of the nomadic; in other words, LOOSEN BY ASSIDUOUS WEDGES, in every joint, the whole fabrice[4] of social existence, stone from stone, till at last, all lie now quite loose enough, it can, as we already see in most countries, be overset by sudden outburst of revolutionary rage; and lying as mere mountains of anarchic rubbish, solicit you to sing Fraternity, &c. over it, and rejoice in the now remarkable era of human progress we have arrived at.

Now we plant ourselves on this passage from Carlyle. We say that, as far as it goes, 'tis a faithful picture of the Isms of the North. But the restraints of Law and Public Opinion are less at the North than in Europe. The Isms on each side the Atlantic are equally busy with "assiduous wedges," in "loosening in every joint the whole fabric of social existance"; but whilst they dare invoke Anarchy in Europe, they dare not inaugurate New York Free Love, and Oneida Incest, and Mormon Polygamy. The moral, religious, and social heresies of the North are more monstrous than those of Europe. The pupil has surpassed the master, unaided by the stimulants of poverty, hunger, and nakedness which urge the master forward.

Society need not fail in the Northeast until the whole West is settled, and a refluent population, or excess of immigration, overstocks permanently the labor market on the Atlantic board. Till then, the despotism of skill and capital, in forcing emigration to the West, makes proprietors of those emigrants, benefits them, peoples the West, and by their return trade, enriches the East. The social forms of the North and the South are, for the present, equally promotive of growth and prosperity at home, and equally beneficial to mankind at large, by affording asylums to the oppressed, and by furnishing food and clothing to all. Northern society is a partial failure,

[4] The spelling is "fabric," *ibid.*, p. 32.

but only because it generates Isms which threaten it with overthrow and impede its progress.

Despite of appearing vain and egotistical, we cannot refrain from mentioning another circumstance that encourages us to write. At the very time when we were writing our pamphlet entitled *Slavery Justified*, in which we took ground that Free Society had failed, Mr. Carlyle began to write his *Latter-Day Pamphlets*, whose very title is the assertion of the failure of Free Society. The proof derived from this coincidence becomes the stronger, when it is perceived that an ordinary man on this side the Atlantic discovered and was exposing the same social phenomena that an extraordinary one had discovered and was exposing on the other. The very titles of our works are synonymous – for the "Latter Day" is the "Failure of Society."

Mr. Carlyle, and Miss Fanny Wright (in her *England the Civilizer*) [5] vindicate Slavery by showing that each of its apparent relaxations in England has injured the laboring class. They were fully and ably represented in Parliament by their ancient masters, the Barons. Since the Throne, and the Church, and the Nobility have been stripped of their power, and a House of Commons, representing lands and money, rules despotically, the masses have become outlawed. They labor under all the disadvantages of slavery, and have none of the rights of slaves. This is the true history of the English Constitution, and one which we intend, in the sequel, more fully to expound. This presents another reason why we again appear before the public. Blackstone, which is read by most American gentlemen, teaches a doctrine the exact reverse of this, and that doctrine we shall try to refute.

Returning from the North, we procured in New York a copy of Aristotle's *Politics and Economics*. To our surprise, we found that our theory of the origin of society was identical with his, and that we had employed not only the same

[5] Frances Wright, *England the Civilizer: Her History Developed in its Principles* (London, 1848).

illustrations but the very same words. We saw at once that the true vindication of slavery must be founded on his theory of man's social nature, as opposed to Locke's theory of the Social Contract, on which latter Free Society rests for support. 'Tis true we had broached this doctrine; but with the world at large our authority was merely repulsive, whilst the same doctrine, coming from Aristotle, had, besides his name, two thousand years of human approval and concurrence in its favor; for, without that concurrence and approval, his book would have long since perished.

In addition to all this, we think we have discovered that Moses has anticipated the Socialists, and that in prohibiting "usury of money, and of victuals, and of all things that are lent on usury," and in denouncing "increase" he was far wiser than Aristotle, and saw that other capital or property did not "breed" any more than money, and that its profits were unjust exactions levied from the laboring man. The Socialists proclaim this as a discovery of their own. We think Moses discovered and proclaimed it more than three thousand years ago – and that it is the only true theory of capital and labor, the only adequate theoretical defence of Slavery – for it proves that the profits which capital exacts from labor makes free laborers slaves, without the rights, privileges, or advantages of domestic slaves, and capitalists their masters, with all the advantages, and none of the burdens and obligations of the ordinary owners of slaves.

The scientific title of this work would be best expressed by the conventional French term *"Exploitation."* We endeavor to translate by the double periphrases of "Cannibals All; or, Slaves without Masters." [6]

We have been imprudent enough to write our Introduction first, and may fail to satisfy the expectations which we excite. Our excess of candor must, in that event, in part supply our deficiency of ability.

[6] Carlyle in "The Present Time," p. 53, speaks of "slaves . . . that can find no masters" in describing the working class of Ireland and England. Three pages later he refers to "cannibalism" in County Connaught.

# CANNIBALS ALL!

## I

## THE UNIVERSAL TRADE

We are all, North and South, engaged in the White Slave Trade, and he who succeeds best is esteemed most respectable. It is far more cruel than the Black Slave Trade, because it exacts more of its slaves, and neither protects nor governs them. We boast that it exacts more when we say, "that the *profits* made from employing free labor are greater than those from slave labor." The profits, made from free labor, are the amount of the products of such labor, which the employer, by means of the command which capital or skill gives him, takes away, exacts, or "exploitates" from the free laborer. The profits of slave labor are that portion of the products of such labor which the power of the master enables him to appropriate. These profits are less, because the master allows the slave to retain a larger share of the results of his own labor than do the employers of free labor. But we not only boast that the White Slave Trade is more exacting and fraudulent (in fact, though not in intention) than Black Slavery; but we also boast that it is more cruel, in leaving the laborer to take care of himself and family out of the pittance which skill or capital have allowed him to retain. When the day's labor is ended, he is free, but is overburdened with the cares of family and household, which make his freedom an empty and delusive mockery. But his employer is really free, and may enjoy the profits made by others' labor, without a care, or a trouble, as to their well-being. The negro slave is free, too, when the labors of the day are over, and free in mind as well as body; for the master provides food, raiment, house, fuel, and everything else necessary to the physical well-being of himself and family. The master's labors commence just when the slave's end. No wonder men should prefer white slavery to capital, to negro slavery, since it is more profitable, and is free from all the cares and labors of black slave-holding.

Now, reader, if you wish to know yourself — to "descant on your own deformity" — read on. But if you would cherish self-conceit, self-esteem, or self-appreciation, throw down our book; for we will dispel illusions which have promoted your happiness, and show you that what you have considered and practiced as virtue is little better than moral Cannibalism. But you will find yourself in numerous and respectable company; for all good and respectable people are "Cannibals all" who do not labor, or who are successfully trying to live without labor, on the unrequited labor of other people:— Whilst low, bad, and disreputable people, are those who labor to support themselves, and to support said respectable people besides. Throwing the negro slaves out of the account, and society is divided in Christendom into four classes: the rich, or independent respectable people, who live well and labor not at all, the professional and skillful respectable people, who do a little light work, for enormous wages; the poor hard-working people, who support everybody, and starve themselves; and the poor thieves, swindlers, and sturdy beggars, who live like gentlemen, without labor, on the labor of other people. The gentlemen exploitate, which being done on a large scale and requiring a great many victims, is highly respectable — whilst the rogues and beggars take so little from others that they fare little better than those who labor.

But, reader, we do not wish to fire into the flock. "Thou

art the man!" You are a Cannibal! and if a successful one, pride yourself on the number of your victims quite as much as any Fiji chieftain, who breakfasts, dines, and sups on human flesh — and your conscience smites you, if you have failed to succeed, quite as much as his, when he returns from an unsuccessful foray.

Probably, you are a lawyer, or a merchant, or a doctor, who has made by your business fifty thousand dollars, and retired to live on your capital. But, mark! not to spend your capital. That would be vulgar, disreputable, criminal. That would be, to live by your own labor; for your capital is your amassed labor. That would be to do as common working men do; for they take the pittance which their employers leave them to live on. They live by labor; for they exchange the results of their own labor for the products of other people's labor. It is, no doubt, an honest, vulgar way of living, but not at all a respectable way. The respectable way of living is to make other people work for you, and to pay them nothing for so doing — and to have no concern about them after their work is done. Hence, white slave-holding is much more respectable than negro slavery — for the master works nearly as hard for the negro as he for the master. But you, my virtuous, respectable reader, exact three thousand dollars per annum from white labor (for your income is the product of white labor) and make not one cent of return in any form. You retain your capital, and never labor, and yet live in luxury on the labor of others. Capital commands labor, as the master does the slave. Neither pays for labor; but the master permits the slave to retain a larger allowance from the proceeds of his own labor, and hence "free labor is cheaper than slave labor." You, with the command over labor which your capital gives you, are a slave owner — a master, without the obligations of a master. They who work for you, who create your income, are slaves, without the rights of slaves. Slaves without a master! Whilst you were engaged in amassing your capital, in seeking to become independent, you were in the White Slave Trade. To become independent is to be able to make other people support you, without being obliged to labor for *them.* Now, what man in society is not seeking to attain this situation? He who attains it is a slave owner, in the worst sense. He who is in pursuit of it is engaged in the slave trade. You, reader, belong to the one or other class. The men without property, in free society, are theoretically in a worse condition than slaves. Practically, their condition corresponds with this theory, as history and statistics everywhere demonstrate. The capitalists, in free society, live in ten times the luxury and show that Southern masters do, because the slaves to capital work harder and cost less than negro slaves.

The negro slaves of the South are the happiest, and, in some sense, the freest people in the world. The children and the aged and infirm work not at all, and yet have all the comforts and necessaries of life provided for them. They enjoy liberty, because they are oppressed neither by care nor labor. The women do little hard work, and are protected from the despotism of their husbands by their masters. The negro men and stout boys work, on the average, in good weather, not more than nine hours a day. The balance of their time is spent in perfect abandon. Besides, they have their Sabbaths and holidays. White men, with so much of license and liberty, would die of ennui; but negroes luxuriate in corporeal and mental repose. With their faces upturned to the sun, they can sleep at any hour; and quiet sleep is the greatest of human enjoyments. "Blessed be the man who invented sleep." 'Tis happiness in itself — and results from contentment with the present, and confident assurance of the future. We do not know whether free laborers ever sleep. They are fools to do so; for, whilst they sleep, the wily and watchful capitalist is devising means to ensnare and exploitate them. The free laborer must work or starve. He is more of a slave than the negro, because he works longer and harder for less allowance than the slave, and has no holiday, because the cares of life with him begin when its labors end. He has no liberty, and not a single right. We know, 'tis often said, air and water are common property, which all have equal right to participate and enjoy; but this is utterly false. The appropriation of the lands carries with it the appropriation of all on or above the lands, *usque ad cœlum, aut ad inferos.*[1] A man cannot breathe the air without a place to breathe it from, and all places are appropriated. All water is private property "to the middle of the stream," except the ocean, and that is not fit to drink.

Free laborers have not a thousandth part of the rights and liberties of negro slaves. Indeed, they have not a single liberty, unless it be the right or liberty to die. But the reader may think that he and other capitalists and employers are freer than negro slaves. Your capital would soon vanish, if you dared indulge in the liberty and abandon of negroes. You hold your wealth and position by the tenure of constant watchfulness, care, and circumspection. You never labor; but you are never free.

Where a few own the soil, they have unlimited power over the balance of society, until domestic slavery comes in to compel them to permit this balance of society to draw a sufficient and comfortable living from *terra mater*. Free society asserts the right of a few to the earth – slavery maintains that it belongs, in different degrees, to all.

But, reader, well may you follow the slave trade. It is the only trade worth following, and slaves the only property worth owning. All other is worthless, a mere *caput mortuum*,[2] except in so far as it vests the owner with the power to command the labors of others – to enslave them. Give you a palace, ten thousand acres of land, sumptuous clothes, equipage, and every other luxury; and with your artificial wants you are poorer than Robinson Crusoe, or the lowest working man, if you have no slaves to capital, or domestic slaves. Your capital will not bring you an income of a cent, nor supply

[1] "Even to heaven or to hell."
[2] "Worthless residue."

one of your wants, without labor. Labor is indispensable to give value to property, and if you owned every thing else, and did not own labor, you would be poor. But fifty thousand dollars means, and is, fifty thousand dollars worth of slaves. You can command, without touching on that capital, three thousand dollars' worth of labor per annum. You could do no more were you to buy slaves with it, and then you would be cumbered with the cares of governing and providing for them. You are a slaveholder now, to the amount of fifty thousand dollars, with all the advantages, and none of the cares and responsibilities of a master.

"Property in man" is what all are struggling to obtain. Why should they not be obliged to take care of man, their property, as they do of their horses and their hounds, their cattle and their sheep. Now, under the delusive name of liberty, you work him "from morn to dewy eve" – from infancy to old age – then turn him out to starve. You treat your horses and hounds better. Capital is a cruel master. The free slave trade, the commonest, yet the cruellest of trades.

# II

# LABOR, SKILL, AND CAPITAL

Nothing written on the subject of slavery from the time of Aristotle is worth reading until the days of the modern Socialists. Nobody, treating of it, thought it worth while to enquire from history and statistics whether the physical and moral condition of emancipated serfs or slaves had been improved or rendered worse by emancipation. None would condescend to compare the evils of domestic slavery with the evils of liberty without property. It entered no one's head to conceive a doubt as to the actual freedom of the emancipated. The relations of capital and labor, of the property-holders to the non-property-holders were things about which no one had thought or written. It never occurred to either the enemies or the apologists for slavery that if no one would employ the free laborer, his condition was infinitely worse than that of actual slavery — nor did it occur to them that if his wages were less than the allowance of the slave, he was less free after emancipation than before. St. Simon, Fourier, Owen, Fanny Wright, and a few others, who discovered and proclaimed that property was not only a bad master but an intolerable one, were treated as wicked visionaries. After the French and other revolutions in Western Europe in 1830, all men suddenly discovered that the social relations of men were false, and that social, not political, revolutions were needed. Since that period, almost the whole literature of free society is but a voice proclaiming its absolute and total failure. Hence the works of the socialists contain the true defence of slavery.

Most of the active intellect of Christendom has for the last twenty years been engaged in analyzing, detecting, and exposing the existing relations of labor, skill, and capital, and in vain efforts to rectify those relations. The philosophers of Europe who have been thus engaged have excelled all the moral philosophers that preceded them in the former part of their pursuit, but suggested nothing but puerile absurdities in the latter. Their destructive philosophy is profound, demonstrative, and unanswerable — their constructive theories, wild, visionary, and chimerical on paper, and failures in practice. Each one of them proves clearly enough that the present edifice of European society is out of all rule and proportion, and must soon tumble to pieces — but no two agree as to how it is to be rebuilt. "We must (say they all) have a new world, if we are to have any world at all!" and each has a little model Utopia or Phalanstery for his new and better world, which, having already failed on a small experimental scale, the inventor assures us, is, therefore, the very thing to succeed on a large one. We allude to the socialists and communists, who have more or less tinged all modern literature with their doctrines. In analyzing society, in detecting, exposing, and generalizing its operations and its various phenomena, they are but grammarians or anatomists, confining philosophy to its proper sphere, and employing it for useful purposes. When they attempt to go further — and having found the present social system to be fatally diseased, propose to originate and build up another in its stead — they are as presumptuous as the anatomist who should attempt to create a man. Social bodies, like human bodies, are the works of God, which man may dissect, and sometimes heal, but which he cannot create. Society was not always thus diseased, or socialism would have been as common in the past as it is now. We think these presumptuous philosophers had best compare it in its healthy state with what it is now, and supply deficiencies or lop off excrescencies, as the comparison may suggest. But our present business is to call attention to some valuable discoveries in the *terra firma* of social science, which these socialists have made in their vain voyages in search of an ever receding and illusory Utopia. Like the alchemists, although they have signally failed in the objects of their pursuits, they have incidentally hit upon truths, unregarded and unprized by themselves, which will be valuable in the hands of more practical and less sanguine men. It is remarkable, that the political economists, who generally assume labor to be the most just and correct measure of value, should not have discovered that the profits of capital represent no labor at all. To be consistent, the political economists should denounce as unjust all interests, rents, dividends, and other profits of capital. We mean by rents that portion of the rent which is strictly income. The amount annually required for repairs and ultimately to rebuild the house is not profit. Four per cent will do this. A rent of ten per cent is in such case a profit of six per cent. The four per cent is but a return to the builder of his labor and capital spent in building. "The use of a thing is only a fair subject of change in so far as the article used is consumed in the use; for such consumption is the consumption of the labor or capital of the owner, and is but the exchange of equivalent amounts of labor."

These socialists, having discovered that skill and capital, by means of free competition, exercise an undue mastery over labor, propose to do away with skill, capital, and free competition altogether. They would heal the diseases of society by destroying its most vital functions. Having laid down the broad proposition that equal amounts of labor, or their results, should be exchanged for each other, they get at the conclusion that as the profits of capital are not the results of labor, the capitalist shall be denied all interest or rents, or other profits on his capital, and be compelled in all cases to exchange a part of the capital itself for labor or its results. This would prevent accumulation, or at least limit it to the procurement of the coarsest necessaries of life. They say, "The lawyer and the artist do not work so hard and continuously as the ploughman, and should receive less wages than he — a bushel of wheat represents as much labor as a speech or portrait, and should be exchanged for the one or the other." Such a system of trade and exchange would equalize conditions, but would banish civilization. Yet do these men show that, by means of the taxation and oppression which capital and skill exercise over labor, the rich, the professional, the trading and skillful part of society have become the masters of the laboring masses, whose condition, already intolerable, is daily becoming worse. They point out distinctly the character of the disease under which the patient is laboring, but see no way of curing the disease except by killing the patient.

In the preceding chapter, we illustrated their theory of capital by a single example. We might give hundreds of illustrations, and yet the subject is so difficult that few readers will take the trouble to understand it. Let us take two well-known historical instances: England became possessed of two fine islands, Ireland and Jamaica. Englishmen took away, or defrauded, from the Irish their lands, but professed to leave the people free. The people, however, must have the use of land, or starve. The English charged them, in rent, so much that their allowance, after deducting that rent, was not half that of Jamaica slaves. They were compelled to labor for their landlords by fear of hunger and death — forces stronger than the overseer's lash. They worked more, and did not get half so much pay or allowance as the Jamaica negroes. All the reports to the French and British Parliaments show that the physical wants of the West India slaves were well supplied. The Irish became the subjects of capital — slaves, with no masters obliged by law, self-interest, or domestic affections to provide for them. The freest people in the world, in the loose and common sense of words, their condition, moral, physical, and religious, was far worse than that of civilized slaves ever has been or ever can be — for at length, after centuries of slow starvation, three hundred thousand perished in a single season for want of food. Englishmen took the lands of Jamaica also, but introduced negro slaves, whom they were compelled to support at all seasons, and at any cost. The negroes were comfortable, until philanthropy taxed the poor of England and Ireland a hundred millions to free them. Now, they enjoy Irish liberty, whilst the English hold all the good lands. They are destitute and savage, and in all respects worse off than when in slavery.

Public opinion unites with self-interest, domestic affection, and municipal law to protect the slave. The man who maltreats the weak and dependent, who abuses his authority over wife, children, or slaves is universally detested. That same public opinion which shields and protects the slave encourages the oppression of free laborers – for it is considered more honorable and praiseworthy to obtain large fees than small ones, to make good bargains than bad ones (and all fees and profits come ultimately from common laborers) – to live without work, by the exactions of accumulated capital, than to labor at the plough or the spade for one's living. It is the interest of the capitalist and the skillful to allow free laborers the least possible portion of the fruits of their own labor; for all capital is created by labor, and the smaller the allowance of the free laborer, the greater the gains of his employer. To treat free laborers badly and unfairly, is universally inculcated as a moral duty, and the selfishness of man's nature prompts him to the most rigorous performance of this cannibalish duty. We appeal to political economy, the ethical, social, political, and economic philosophy of free society, to prove the truth of our doctrines. As an ethical and social guide, that philosophy teaches that social, individual, and national competition is a moral duty, and we have attempted to prove that all competition is but the effort to enslave others without being encumbered with their support. As a political guide, it would simply have government "keep the peace," or, to define its doctrine more exactly, it teaches "that it is the whole duty of government to hold the weak whilst the strong rob them" – for it punishes crimes accompanied with force, which none but the weak-minded commit, but encourages the war of the wits, in which the strong and astute are sure to succeed in stripping the weak and ignorant.

It is time, high time, that political economy was banished from our schools. But what would this avail in free society, where men's antagonistic relations suggest to each one, without a teacher, that "he can only be just to himself, by doing wrong to others." Aristotle, and most other ancient philosophers and statesmen, held the doctrine "that as money would not breed, interest should not be allowed." Moses, no doubt, saw as the modern socialists do that all other capital stood on the same grounds with money. None of it is self-creative, or will "breed." The language employed about "usury" and "increase" in 25th Leviticus, and 23d Deuteronomy is quite broad enough to embrace and prohibit all profits of capital. Such interest or "increase," or profits, might be charged to the Heathen, but not to the Jews. The whole arrangements of Moses were obviously intended to prevent competition in the dealings of the Jews with one another, and to beget permanent equality of condition and fraternal feelings.

The socialists have done one great good. They enable us to understand and appreciate the institutions of Moses, and to see that none but Divinity could have originated them.* The situation of Judea was, in many respects, anomalous, and we are not to suppose that its political and social relations were intended to be universal. Yet, here it is distinctly asserted that, under certain circumstances, all profits on capital are wrong.

* Not only does Moses evince his knowledge of the despotism of capital, in forbidding its profits, but also in his injunction, not to let emancipated slaves "go away empty." Deuteronomy xv. 13, 14.

"And when thou sendest him out free from thee, thou shalt not let him go away empty. Thou shalt furnish him liberally out of thy flock, and out of thy floor, and out of thy wine-press: of that wherewith the Lord thy God hath blessed thee thou shalt give unto him."

People without property exposed to the unrestricted exactions of capital are infinitely worse off after emancipation than before. Moses prevented the exactions of capital by providing property for the new free man.

The reformers of the present day are all teetotalists, and attempt to banish evil altogether, not to lessen or restrict it. It would be wiser to assume that there is nothing, in its essence, evil, in the moral or physical world, but only rendered so by the wrongful applications which men make of them. Science is every day discovering that the most fatal poisons when properly employed become the most efficacious medicines. So, what appear to be the evil passions and propensities of men, and of societies, under proper regulation, may be made to minister to the wisest and best of purposes. Civilized society has never been found without that competition begotten by man's desire to throw most of the burdens of life on others, and to enjoy the fruits of their labors without exchanging equivalent labor of his own. In all such societies (outside the Bible) such selfish and grasping appropriation is inculcated as a moral duty; and he who succeeds best, either by the exercise of professional skill or by accumulation of capital, in appropriating the labor of others without laboring in return is considered most meritorious. It would be unfair, in treating of the relations of capital and labor, not to consider its poor-house system, the ultimate resort of the poor.

The taxes or poor rates which support this system of relief, like all other taxes and values, are derived from the labor of the poor. The ablebodied, industrious poor are compelled by the rich and skillful to support the weak, and too often, the idle poor. In addition to defraying the necessary expenses and the wanton luxuries of the rich, to supporting government, and supporting themselves, capital compels them to support its poor houses. In collection of the poor rates, in their distribution, and in the administration of the poor-house system, probably half the tax raised for the poor is exhausted. Of the remainder, possibly another half is expended on unworthy objects. Masters, in like manner, support the sick, infant, and aged slaves from the labor of the strong and healthy. But nothing is wasted in collection and administration, and nothing given to unworthy objects. The master having the control of the objects of his bounty takes care that they shall not become burdensome by their own crimes and idleness. It is contrary to all human customs and legal analogies that those who are dependent, or are likely to become so, should not be controlled. The duty of protecting the weak involves the necessity of enslaving them – hence, in all countries, women and children, wards and apprentices, have been essentially slaves, controlled, not by law, but by the will of a superior. This is a fatal defect in the poor-house system. Many men become paupers from their own improvidence or misconduct, and masters alone can prevent such misconduct and improvidence. Masters treat their sick, infant, and helpless slaves well, not only from feeling and affection, but from motives of self-interest. Good treatment renders them more valuable. All poor houses are administered on the penitentiary system, in order to deter the poor from resorting to them. Besides, masters are always in place to render needful aid to the unfortunate and helpless slaves. Thousands of the poor starve out of reach of the poor houses, or other public charity.

A common charge preferred against slavery is that it induces idleness with the masters. The trouble, care, and labor of providing for wife, children, and slaves, and of properly governing and administering the whole affairs of the farm is usually borne on small estates by the master. On larger ones, he is aided by an overseer or manager. If they do their duty, their time is fully occupied. If they do not, the estate goes to ruin. The mistress, on Southern farms, is usually more busily, usefully, and benevolently occupied than any one on the farm. She unites in her person the offices of wife, mother, mistress, housekeeper, and sister of charity. And she fulfills all these offices admirably well. The rich men, in free society, may, if they please, lounge about town, visit clubs, attend the theatre, and have no other trouble than that of collecting rents, interest, and dividends of stock. In a well-constituted slave society, there should be no idlers. But we cannot divine how the capitalists in free society are to be put to work. The master labors for the slave, they exchange industrial value. But the capitalist, living on his income, gives nothing to his subjects. He lives by mere exploitation.

It is objected that slavery permits or induces immorality and ignorance. This is a mistake. The intercourse of the house-servants with the white family, assimilates, in some degree, their state of information, and their moral conduct, to that of the whites. The house-servants, by their intercourse with the field hands, impart their knowledge to them. The master enforces decent morality in all. Negroes are never ignorant of the truths of Christianity, all speak intelligible English, and are posted up in the ordinary occurrences of the times. The reports to the British Parliament show that the agricultural and mining poor of England scarce know the existence of God, do not speak intelligible English, and are generally depraved and ignorant. They learn nothing by intercourse with their superiors, as negroes do. They abuse wives and children, because they have no masters to control them, and the men are often dissipated and idle, leaving all the labor to be done by the women and children — for the want of this same control.

Slavery, by separating the mass of the ignorant from each other, and bringing them in contact and daily intercourse with the well-informed, becomes an admirable educational system — no doubt a necessary one. By subjecting them to the constant control and supervision of their superiors, interested in enforcing morality, it becomes the best and most efficient police system, so efficient that the ancient Romans had scarcely any criminal code whatever.

The great objections to the colonial slavery of the latter Romans, to serfdom, and all forms of prædial slavery are: that the slaves are subjected to the cares as well as the labors of life; that the masters become idlers; that want of intercourse destroys the affectionate relations between master and slave, throws the mass of ignorant slaves into no other association but that with the ignorant, and deprives them as well of the instruction as [of] the government of superiors living on the same farm. Southern slavery is becoming the best form of slavery of which we have any history, except that of the Jews. The Jews owned but few slaves, and with them the relation of master and slave was truly affectionate, protective, and patriarchal. The master, wife, and children were in constant intercourse with the slaves, and formed, in practice as well as theory, affectionate, well-ordered families.

As modern civilization advances, slavery becomes daily more necessary, because its [modern civilization's] tendency to accumulate all capital in a few hands cuts off the masses from the soil, lessens their wages and their chances of employment, and increases the necessity for a means of certain subsistence, which slavery alone can furnish when a few own all the lands and other capital.

Christian morality can find little practical foothold in a community so constituted that to "love our neighbor as ourself" or "to do unto others as we would they should do unto us" would be acts of suicidal self-sacrifice. Christian morality, however, was not preached to free competitive society, but to slave society, where it is neither very difficult nor unnatural to practice it. In the various family relations of husband, wife, parent, child, master, and slave, the observance of these Christian precepts is often practiced, and almost always promotes the temporal well being of those who observe it. The interests of the various members of the family circle, correctly understood, concur and harmonize, and each member best promotes his own selfish interest by ministering to the wants and interests of the rest. Two great stumbling blocks are removed from the acceptance of Scripture, when it is proved that slavery, which it recognizes, approves and enjoins, is promotive of men's happiness and well-being, and that the morality which it inculcates, although wholly impracticable in free society, is readily practiced in the form of society to which it was addressed.

We do not conceive that there can be any other moral law in free society than that which teaches "that he is most meritorious who most wrongs his fellow beings"; for any other law would make men martyrs to their own virtues. We see thousands of good men vainly struggling against the evil necessities of their situation, and aggravating by their charities the evils which they would cure, for charity in free society is but the tax which skill and capital levy from the working poor, too often to bestow on the less deserving and idle poor. We know a man at the North who owns millions of dollars, and would throw every cent into the ocean to benefit mankind. But it is capital, and, place it where he will, it becomes an engine to tax and oppress the laboring poor.

It is impossible to place labor and capital in harmonious or friendly relations, except by the means of slavery, which identifies their interests. Would that gentleman lay his capital out in land and negroes, he might be sure, in whatever hands it came, that it would be employed to protect laborers, not to oppress them; for when slaves are worth near a thousand dollars a head, they will be carefully and well provided for. In any other investment he may make of it, it will be used as an engine to squeeze the largest amount of labor from the poor for the least amount of allowance. We say allowance, not wages; for neither slaves nor free laborers get wages, in the popular sense of the term: that is, the employer or capitalist pays them from nothing of his own, but allows them a part, generally a very small part, of the proceeds of their own labor. Free laborers pay one another, for labor creates all values, and capital, after taking the lion's share by its taxing power, but pays the so-called wages of one laborer from the proceeds of the labor of another. Capital does not breed, yet remains undiminished. Its profits are but its taxing power. Men seek to become independent in order to cease to pay labor, in order to become masters, without the cares, duties, and responsibilities of masters. Capital exercises a more perfect compulsion over free laborers than human masters over slaves; for free laborers must at all times work or starve, and slaves are supported whether they work or not. Free laborers have less liberty than slaves, are worse paid and provided for, and have no valuable rights. Slaves, with more of actual practical liberty, with ampler allowance, and constant protection, are secure in the enjoyment of all the rights which provide for their physical comfort at all times and under all circumstances. The free laborer must be employed or starve, yet no one is obliged to employ him. The slave is taken care of, whether employed or not. Though each free laborer has no particular master, his wants and other men's capital make him a slave without a master, or with too many masters, which is as bad as none. It were often better that he had an ascertained master, instead of an irresponsible and unascertained one.

There are some startling social phenomena connected with this subject of labor and capital, which will probably be new to most of our readers. Legislators and philosophers often puzzle their own and other people's brains, in vain discussions as to how the taxes shall be laid so as to fall on the rich rather than the poor. It results from our theory that as labor creates all values, laborers pay all taxes, and the rich, in the words of Gerrit Smith, "are but the conduits that pass them over to government."

Again, since labor alone creates and pays the profits of capital, increase and accumulation of capital but increase the labor of the poor, and lessen their remuneration. Thus the poor are continually forging new chains for themselves. Proudhon cites a familiar instance to prove and illustrate this theory: a tenant improves a farm or house, and enhances their rents; his labor thus becomes the means of increasing the tax, which he or some one else must pay to the capitalists. What is true in this instance is true of the aggregate capital of the world: its increase is but an increased tax on labor. A., by trade or speculation, gets hold of an additional million of dollars to the capital already in existence. Now his million of dollars will yield no profit, unless a number of pauper laborers, sufficient to pay its profits, are at the same time brought into existence. After supporting their families, it will require a thousand of laborers to pay the interest or profits of a million of dollars. It may, therefore, be generally assumed as true that where a country has gained a millionaire, it has by the same process gained a thousand pauper laborers, provided it has been made by profits on foreign trade, or by new values created at home – that is, if it be an *addition* of a million to the capital of the nation.

A nation borrows a hundred millions, at six per cent, for a hundred years. During that time it pays, in way of tax, called interest, six times the capital loaned, and then returns the capital itself. During all this time, to the amount of the interest, the people of this nation have been slaves to the lender. He has commanded, not paid, for their labor; for his capital is returned intact. In the abstract, and according to equity, "the use of an article is only a proper subject of charge when the article is consumed in the use; for this consumption is the consumption of the labor of the lender or hirer, and is the exchange of equal amounts of labor for each other."

A., as a merchant, a lawyer, or doctor, makes twenty dollars a day, that is, exchanges each day of his own labor for twenty days of the labor of common working men, assuming that they work at a dollar a day. In twenty years, he amasses fifty thousand dollars, invests it, and settles it on his family. Without any labor, he and his heirs, retaining all his capital, continue, by its means, to levy a tax of three thousand dollars from common laborers. He and his heirs now pay nothing for labor, but command it. They have nothing to pay except their capital, and that they retain. (This is the exploitation or despotism of capital, which has taken the place of domestic slavery, and is, in fact, a much worse kind of slavery.

Hence arises socialism, which proposes to reconstruct society.) Now, this capitalist is considered highly meritorious for so doing, and the poor, self-sacrificing laborers, who really created his capital, and who pay its profits, are thought contemptible, if not criminal. In the general, those men are considered the most meritorious who live in greatest splendor, with the least, or with no labor, and they most contemptible who labor most for others, and least for themselves. In the abstract, however, that dealing appears most correct where men exchange equal amounts of labor, bear equal burdens for others, with those that they impose on them. Such is the golden rule of Scripture, but not the approved practice of mankind.

"The worth of a thing is just what it will bring" is the common trading principle of mankind. Yet men revolt at the extreme applications of their own principle, and denunciate any gross and palpable advantage taken of the wants, position, and necessities of others as *swindling*. But we should recollect, that in all instances where unequal amounts of labor are exchanged at par, advantage is really taken by him who gets in exchange the larger amount of labor, of the wants, position, and necessities of him who receives the smaller amount.

We have said that laborers pay all taxes, but labor being capital in slave society, the laborers or slaves are not injured by increased taxes, and the capitalist or master has to retrench his own expenses to meet the additional tax. Capital is not taxed in free society, but *is taxed* in slave society, because, in such society, labor is capital.

The capitalists and the professional can, and do, by increased profits and fees, throw the whole burden of taxation on the laboring class. Slaveholders cannot do so; for diminished allowance to their slaves would impair their value and lessen their own capital.

Our exposé of what the socialists term the exploitation of skill and capital will not, we know, be satisfactory to slaveholders even; for although there be much less of such exploitation or unjust exaction in slave society, still, too much of it remains to be agreeable to contemplate. Besides, our analysis of human nature and human pursuits is too dark and sombre to meet with ready acceptance. We should be rejoiced to see our theory refuted. We are sure, however, that it never can be, but equally sure that it is subject to many modifications and limitations that have not occurred to us. We have this consolation, that in rejecting as false and noxious all systems of moral philosophy we are thrown upon the Bible, as containing the only true system of morals. We have attempted already to adduce three instances in which the justification of slavery furnished new and additional evidence of the truth of Christianity. We will now add others.

It is notorious that infidelity appeared in the world, on an extensive scale, only cotemporaneously with the abolition of slavery, and that it is now limited to countries where no domestic slavery exists. Besides, abolitionists are commonly infidels, as their speeches, conventions, and papers daily evince. Where there is no slavery, the minds of men are unsettled on all subjects, and there is, emphatically, faith and conviction about nothing. Their moral and social world is in a chaotic and anarchical state. Order, subordination, and adaptation have vanished; and with them, the belief in a Deity, the author of all order. It had often been urged that the order observable in the moral and physical world furnished strong evidence of a Deity, the author of that order. How vastly is this argument now strengthened by the new fact, now first developed, that the destruction of social order generates universal scepticism. Mere political revolutions affect social order but little, and generate but little infidelity. It remained for social revolutions, like those in Europe in 1848, to bring on an infidel age; for, outside of slave society, such is the age in which we live.

If we prove that domestic slavery is, in the general, a natural and necessary institution, we remove the greatest stumbling block to belief in the Bible; for whilst texts, detached and torn from their context, may be found for any other purpose, none can be found that even militates against slavery. The distorted and forced construction of certain passages, for this purpose, by abolitionists, if employed as a common rule of construction, would reduce the Bible to a mere allegory, to be interpreted to suit every vicious taste and wicked purpose.

But we have been looking merely to one side of human nature, and to that side rendered darker by the false, antagonistic, and competitive relations in which so-called liberty and equality place man.

Man is, by nature, the most social and gregarious, and, therefore, the least selfish of animals. Within the family there is little room, opportunity, or temptation to selfishness — and slavery leaves but little of the world without the family. Man loves that nearest to him best. First his wife, children, and parents, then his slaves, next his neighbors and fellow-countrymen. But his unselfishness does not stop here. He is ready and anxious to relieve a famine in Ireland, and shudders when he reads of a murder at the antipodes. He feels deeply for the sufferings of domestic animals, and is rendered happy by witnessing the enjoyments of the flocks, and herds, and caroling birds that surround him. He sympathizes with all external nature. A parched field distresses him, and he rejoices as he sees the groves, and the gardens, and the plains flourishing, and blooming, and smiling about him. All men are philanthropists, and would benefit their fellow-men if they could. But we cannot be sure of benefiting those whom we cannot control. Hence, all actively good men are ambitious, and would be masters, in all save the name.

Benevolence, the love of what is without, and the disposition to incur pain or inconvenience to advance the happiness and well-being of what is without self, is as universal a motive of human conduct as mere selfishness — which is the disposition to sacrifice the good of others to our own good.

The prevalent philosophy of the day takes cognizance of but half of human nature — and that the worst half. Our happiness is so involved in the happiness and well-being of everything around us that a mere selfish philosophy, like political economy, is a very unsafe and delusive guide.

We employ the term Benevolence to express our outward affections, sympathies, tastes, and feelings, but it is inadequate to express our meaning; it is not the opposite of selfishness, and unselfishness would be too negative for our purpose. Philosophy has been so busy with the worst feature of human nature that it has not even found a name for this, its better feature. We must fall back on Christianity, which embraces man's whole nature, and though not a code of philosophy, is something better; for it proposes to lead us through the trials and intricacies of life, not by the mere cool calculations of the head, but by the unerring instincts of a pure and regenerate heart. The problem of the Moral World is too vast and complex for the human mind to comprehend; yet the pure heart will, safely and quietly, feel its way through the mazes that confound the head.

## III

## SUBJECT CONTINUED — EXPLOITATION OF SKILL

The worth of a thing is just what it will bring." The professional man who charges the highest fees is most respected, and he who undercharges stands disgraced. We have a friend who has been, and we believe will continue to be, one of the most useful men in Virginia. He inherited an independent patrimony. He acquired a fine education, and betook himself laboriously to an honorable profession. His success was great, and his charges very high. In a few years he amassed a fortune, and ceased work. We expounded our theory to him. Told him we used to consider him a good man, and quite an example for the rising generation; but that now he stood condemned under our theory. Whilst making his fortune, he daily exchanged about one day of his light labor for thirty days of the farmer, the gardener, the miner, the ditcher, the sewing woman, and other common working people's labor. His capital was but the accumulation of the results of their labor; for common labor creates all capital. Their labor was more necessary and useful than his, and also harder and more disagreeable. It should be considered more honorable and respectable. The more honorable because they were contented with their situation and their profits, and not seeking to exploitate by exchanging one day of their labor for many of other people's. To be exploitated ought to be more creditable than to exploitate. They were "slaves without masters," the little fish who were food for all the larger. They stood disgraced, because they would not practice cannibalism, rise in the world by more lucrative, less useful and less laborious pursuits, and live by exploitation rather than labor. He, by practicing cannibalism more successfully than others, had acquired fame and fortune. 'Twas the old tune – "Saul has slain his thousands, and David his tens of thousands." The more scalps we can show, the more honored we are.

We told him he had made his fortune by the exploitation of skill, and was now living by the still worse exploitation of capital. Whilst working, he made thirty dollars a day – that is, exploitated or appropriated the labor of thirty common working men, and gave in exchange his own labor, intrinsically less worthy, than any one of theirs. But now he was doing worse. He was using his capital as a power to compel others to work for him – for whom he did not work at all. The white laborers who made his income, or interests and dividends, were wholly neglected by him, because he did not know even who they were. He treated his negro slaves much better. It was true, he appropriated or exploitated much of the results of their labor, but he governed them and provided for them, with almost parental affection. Some of them we knew, who feigned to be unfit for labor, he was boarding expensively. Our friend at first ridiculed our theory. But by degrees began to see its truth, and being sensitively conscientious, was disposed to fret whenever the subject was introduced.

One day he met us, with a face beaming with smiles, and said, "I can explain and justify that new theory of yours. This oppression and exaction of skill and capital which we see continually practiced and which is too natural to man ever to cease is necessary in order to disperse and diffuse population over the globe. Half the good lands of the world are unappropriated and invite settlement and cultivation. Most men who choose can become proprietors by change of residence. They are too much crowded in many countries, and exploitation that disperses them is a blessing. It will be time enough to discuss your theory of the despotism of skill and capital, when all the world is densely settled, and the men without property can no longer escape from the exactions of those who hold property."

Our friend's theory is certainly ingenious and novel, and goes far to prove that exploitation is not an unmitigated evil. Under exceptional circumstances, its good effects on human happiness and well-being may greatly over-balance its evil influences. Such, probably, is the case at the North. There, free competition and the consequent oppressions of skill and capital are fiercer and more active than in any other country. But in forty-eight hours, laborers may escape to the West, and become proprietors. It is a blessing to them to be thus expelled, and a blessing to those who expel them. The emigration to the West rids the East of a surplus population, and enriches it by the interchanges of trade and commerce which the emigration immediately begets. As an exceptional form of society, we begin to think that at the North highly useful. It will continue to be good and useful until the Northwest is peopled. Then, and not till then, it will be time for Mr. Greeley to build phalansteries, and for Gerrit Smith to divide all the lands. We find that we shall have to defend the North as well as the South against the assaults of the abolitionist – still, we cannot abate a jot or tittle of our theory: "Slavery is the natural and normal condition of society." The situation of the North is abnormal and anomalous. So in desert or mountainous regions, where only small patches of land can be cultivated, the father, wife, and children are sufficient for the purpose, and slavery would be superfluous.

In order to make sure that our reader shall comprehend our theory, we will give a long extract from *The Science of Society* by Stephen Pearl Andrews of New York.[1] He is, we think, far the ablest writer on moral science that America has produced. Though an abolitionist, he has not a very bad

[1] Stephen Pearl Andrews, *The Science of Society* (New York, 1851).

opinion of slavery. We verily believe, there is not one intelligent abolitionist at the North who does not believe that slavery to capital in free society is worse than Southern negro slavery; but like Mr. Andrews, they are all perfectionists, with a Utopia in full view:

I. Suppose I am a wheelwright in a small village, and the only one of my trade. You are travelling with certain valuables in your carriage, which breaks down opposite my shop. It will take an hour of my time to mend the carriage. You can get no other means of conveyance, and the loss to you, if you fail to arrive at the neighboring town in season for the sailing of a certain vessel, will be $500, which fact you mention to me, in good faith, in order to quicken my exertions. I give one hour of my work and mend the carriage. What am I in equity entitled to charge — what should be the *limit of price* upon my labor?

Let us apply the different measures, and see how they will operate. If Value is the limit of price, then the price of the hour's labor should be $500. That is the equivalent of the value of the labor to you. If cost is the limit of price, then you should pay me a commodity, or commodities, or a representative in currency, which will procure me commodities having in them one hour's labor equally as hard as the mending of the carriage, without the slightest reference to the degree of benefit which that labor has bestowed on you; or, putting the illustration in money, thus: assuming the twenty-five cents to be an equivalent for an hour's labor of an artizan in that particular trade, then, according to the *Cost Principle*, I should be justified in asking only twenty-five cents, but according to the *Value Principle*, I should be justified in asking $500.

The *Value Principle*, in some form of expression, is, as I have said, the only *recognized* principle of trade throughout the world. "A thing is worth what it will bring in the market." Still, if I were to charge you $500, or a fourth part of that sum, and, taking advantage of your necessities, force you to pay it, everybody would denounce me, the poor wheelwright, as an extortioner and a scoundrel. Why? Simply because this is an *unusual* application of the principle. Wheelwrights seldom have a chance to make such a "speculation," and therefore it is not according to the "established usages of trade." Hence its manifest injustice shocks, in such a case, the common sense of right. Meanwhile you, a wealthy merchant, are daily rolling up an immense fortune by doing business upon the same principle which you condemn in the wheelwright, and nobody finds fault. At every scarcity in the market, you immediately raise the price of every article you hold. It is your *business* to take advantage of the necessities of those with whom you deal, by selling to them according to the *Value* to them, and not according to the *Cost* to you. You go further. You, by every means in your power, create those necessities, by buying up particular articles and holding them out of the market until the demand becomes pressing, by circulating false reports of short crops, and by other similar tricks known to the trade. This is the same in principle, as if the wheelwright had first dug the rut in which your carriage upset, and then charged you the $500.

Yet hitherto no one has thought of seriously questioning the principle, namely, that *"Value is the limit of price,"* or, in other words, that *"it is right to take for a thing what it is worth."* It is upon this principle or maxim, that all *honorable* trade professes now to be conducted, until instances arise in which its oppressive operation is so glaring and repugnant to the moral sense of mankind, that those who carry it out are denounced as rogues and cheats. In this manner a sort of conventional limit is placed upon the application of a principle which is equally *the principle* of every swindling transaction, and of what is called legitimate commerce. The discovery has not hitherto been made, that the principle itself is essentially vicious, and that in its infinite and all-pervading variety of applications, this vicious principle is *the source* of the injustice, inequality of condition, and frightful pauperism and wretchedness which characterize the existing state of our so-called civilization. Still less has the discovery been made, that there is another simple principle of traffic which, once understood and applied in practice, will effectually rectify all those monstrous evils, and introduce into human society the reign of absolute equity in all property relations, while it will lay the foundations of universal harmony in the social and moral relations as well.

II. Suppose it costs me ten minutes' labor to concoct a pill which will save your life when nothing else will; and suppose, at the same time, to render the case simple, that the knowledge of the ingredients came to me by accident, without labor or *cost*. It is clear that your life is worth to you more than your fortune. Am I, then, entitled to demand of you for the nostrum the whole of your property, more or less? Clearly so, if *it is right to take for a thing what it is worth*, which is theoretically the highest ethics of trade.

Forced, on the one hand, by the impossibility, existing in the nature of things, of ascertaining and measuring positive values, or of determining, in other words, what a thing *is really worth*, and rendered partially conscious by the obvious hardship and injustice of every unusual or extreme application of the principle that it is either no rule or a bad one, and not guided by the knowledge of any true principle out of the labyrinth of conflicting rights into which the false principle conducts, the world has practically abandoned the attempt to combine Equity with Commerce, and lowered its standard of morality to the inverse statement of the formula, namely, that, "*A thing is worth what it will bring*"; or, in other words, that it is fitting and proper to take for a thing when sold whatever can be got for it. This, then, is what is denominated the Market Value of an article, as distinguished from its actual value. Without being more equitable as a measure of price, it certainly has a great practical advantage over the more decent theoretical statement, in the fact that it *is* possible to ascertain by experiment how much you can force people, through their necessities, to give. The principle, in this form, measures the price by the degree of *want* on the part of the purchaser, that is, by what he supposes will prove to be the value or benefit to him of the commodity purchased, in comparison with that of the one with which he parts in the transaction. Hence it becomes immediately and continually the interest of the seller to place the purchaser in a condition of as much want as possible; "to corner" him, as the phrase is in Wall Street, and force him to buy at the dearest rate. If he is unable to increase his actual necessity, he resorts to every means of creating an imaginary want by false praises bestowed upon the qualities and uses of his goods. Hence the usages of forestalling the market, of confusing the public knowledge of Supply and Demand, of advertising and puffing worthless commodities, and the like, which constitute the existing commercial system — a system which, in our age, is ripening into putrefaction, and coming to offend the nostrils of good taste no less than the innate sense of right, which, dreadfully vitiating as it is, it has failed wholly to extinguish.

The Value Principle in this form, as in the other, is therefore *felt*, without being distinctly understood, to be essentially diabolical, and hence it undergoes again a kind of sentimental modification wherever the *sentiment* for honesty is most potent. This last and highest expression of the doctrine of honesty, as now known in the world, may be stated in the form of the hortatory precept, "Don't be *too* bad," or, "Don't gouge *too* deep." No Political Economist, Financier, Moralist, or Religionist, has any more definite standard of right in commercial transactions than that. It is not too much to affirm that neither Political Economist, Financier, Moralist, nor Religionist knows at this day, nor ever has known, what it *is* to be honest. The religious teacher, who exhorts his hearers from Sabbath to Sabbath to be *fair* in their dealings with each other and with the outside world, does not know, and could not for his life tell, how much he is, in fair dealing or equity, bound to pay his washerwoman or his housekeeper for any service whatever which they may render. The *sentiment* of honesty exists, but the *science* of honesty is wanting. The sentiment is first in order. The science must be an outgrowth, a consequential development of the sentiment. The precepts of Christian Morality deal properly with that which is the soul of the other, leaving to intellectual investigation the discovery of its scientific complement.

It follows from what has been said, that the Value Principle is the commercial embodiment of the essential element of conquest and war — war transferred from the battlefield to the counter — none the less opposed, however, to the spirit of Christian Morality, or the sentiment of human brotherhood. In bodily conflict, the physically strong conquer and subject the physically weak. In the conflict of trade, the intellectually astute and powerful conquer and subject those who are intellectually feeble, or whose intellectual development is not of the precise kind to fit them for the conflict of wits in the matter of trade. With the progress of civilization and development we have ceased to think that superior physical strength gives the *right* of conquest and subjugation. We have graduated, in idea, out of the period of physical dominion. We remain, however, as yet in the period of intellectual conquest or plunder. It has not been questioned hitherto, as a general proposition, that the man who has superior intellectual endowments to others, has a right resulting therefrom to profit thereby at the cost of others. In the extreme applications of the admission only is the conclusion ever denied. In the whole field of what are denominated the legitimate operations of trade, there is no other law recognized than the relative "smartness" or shrewdness of the parties, modified at most by the sentimental precept stated above.

The intrinsic wrongfulness of the principal axioms and practice of existing commerce will appear to every reflecting mind from the preceding analysis. It will be proper, however, before dismisisng the consideration of the Value Principle, to trace out a little more in detail some of its specific results.

The principle itself being essentially iniquitous, all the fruits of the principle are necessarily pernicious.

Among the consequences which flow from it are the following:

I. *It renders falsehood and hypocrisy a necessary concomitant of trade.* Where the object is to buy cheap and sell dear, the parties find their interest in mutual deception. It is taught, in theory, that "honesty is the best policy," in the long run; but in practice the merchant discovers speedily that he must starve if he acts upon the precept —

in the short run. Honesty — even as much honesty as can be arrived at — is *not* the best policy under the present unscientific system of commerce; if by the best policy is meant that which tends to success in business. Professional merchants are sharp to distinguish their true policy for that end, and they do not find it in a full exposition of the truth. Intelligent merchants know the fact well, and conscientious merchants deplore it; but they see no remedy. The theory of trade taught to innocent youths in the retired family, or the Sunday school, would ruin any clerk, if adhered to behind the counter, in a fortnight. Hence it is uniformly abandoned, and a new system of morality acquired the moment a practical application is to be made of the instruction. A frank disclosure, by the merchant, of all the secret advantages in his possession, would destroy his reputation for sagacity as effectually as it would that of the gambler among his associates. Both commerce and gambling, as professions, are systems of strategy. It is the business of both parties to a trade to over-reach each other — a fact which finds its unblushing announcement in the maxim of the Common Law, *Caveat emptor* (let the purchaser take care).

II. *It makes the rich richer and the poor poorer.* — Trade being, under this system, the intellectual correspondence to the occupation of the cutthroat or conqueror under the reign of physical force — the stronger consequently accumulating more than his share at the cost of the destruction of the weaker — the consequence of the principle is that the occupation of trade, for those who possess intellectual superiority, with other favorable conditions, enables them to accumulate more than their share of wealth, while it reduces those whose intellectual development — of the precise kind requisite for this species of contest — and whose material conditions are less favorable — to wretchedness and poverty.

III. *It creates trade for trade's sake, and augments the number of non-producers, whose support is chargeable upon Labor.* As trade under the operation of this principle, offers the temptation of illicit gains and rapid wealth at the expense of others, it creates trade where there is no necessity for trade — not as a beneficent interchange of commodities between producers and consumers, but as a means of speculation. Hence thousands are withdrawn from actual production and thrust unnecessarily into the business of exchanging, mutually devouring each other by competition, and drawing their subsistence and their wealth from the producing classes, without rendering any equivalent service. Hence the interminable range of intermediates between the producer and consumer, the total defeat of organization and economy in the distribution of products, and the intolerable burden of the unproductive classes upon labor, together with a host of the frightful results of pauperism and crime.

IV. *It degrades the dignity of Labor.* Inasmuch as trade, under the operation of this principle, is more profitable, or at any rate is liable to be, promises to be, and in a portion of cases *is* more profitable than productive labor, it follows that the road to wealth and social distinction lies in that direction. Hence "Commerce is King." Hence, again, productive labor is depreciated and contemned. It holds the same relation to commerce in this age — under the reign of intellectual superiority — that commerce itself held a few generations since — under the reign of physical force — to military achievement, personal or hereditary. Thus the degradation of labor, and all the innumerable evils which follow in its train, in our existing civilization, find their efficient cause in this same false principle of exchanging products. The next stage of progress will be the inauguration of Equity — equality in the results of every species of industry according to burdens, and the consequent accession of labor to the highest rank of human estimation. Commerce will then sink to a mere brokerage, paid, like any other species of labor, according to its repugnance, as the army is now sinking to a mere police force. It will be reduced to the simplest and most direct methods of exchange, and made to be the merest servant of production, which will come, in its turn, to be regarded as conferring the only true patents of nobility.

V. *It prevents the possibility of a scientific Adjustment of Supply to Demand.* It has been already shown that speculation is the cause why there has never been, and cannot now be any scientific Adaptation of Supply to Demand. It has also been partially shown, at various points, that speculation, or trading in chances and fluctuations in the market has its root in the Value Principle, and that the Cost Principle extinguishes speculation. It will be proper, however, in this connection to define exactly the limits of speculation, and to point out more specifically how the Value Principle creates it, and how the Cost Principle extinguishes it.

By speculation is meant, in the ordinary language of trade, risky and unusual enterprises entered upon for the sake of more than ordinary profits, and in that sense there is attached to it, among merchants, a slight shade of imputation of dishonesty or disreputable conduct. As we are seeking now, however, to employ language in an exact and scientific way, we must find a more precise definition of the term. The line between ordinary and more than ordinary profits is too vague for a scientific treatise. At one extremity of the long succession of chance-dealing and advantage-taking transactions stands gambling, which is denounced by the common verdict of mankind as merely a more specious form of robbery. It holds the same relation to robbery itself that duelling holds to murder. Where is the other end of this succession? At what point does a man begin to take an undue advantage of his fellow man in a commercial transaction? It clearly appears, from all that has been shown, that he does so from the moment that he receives from him more than an exact equivalent of cost. But it is the constant endeavor of every trader, upon any other than the Cost Principle, to do that. The business of the merchant is profit-making. *Profit* signifies, etymologically, *something made over and above*, that is, something beyond an *equivalent*, or, in its simplest expression, *something for nothing*.

It is clear, then, that there is no difference between profit-making in its mildest form, speculation in its opprobrious sense as the middle term, and gambling as the ultimate, except in degree. There is simply the bad gradation of rank which there is between the slaveholder, the driver on the slave plantation, and the slave dealer, or between the man of pleasure, the harlot, and the pimp.

The philanthropy of the age is moving heaven and earth to the overthrow of the institution of slavery. But slavery has no scientific definition. It is thought to consist in the feature of chattelism; but an ingenious lawyer would run his pen through every statute upon slavery in existence, and expunge that fiction of the law, and yet leave slavery, for all practical purposes, precisely what it is now. It needs only to appropriate the services of the man by operation of law, instead of the man himself. The only distinction, then, left between his condition and that of the laborer who is robbed by the operation of a false commercial principle, would be in the fact of the oppression being more tangible and undisguisedly degrading to his manhood.

If, in any transaction, I get from you some portion of your earnings without an equivalent, I begin to make you my slave — to confiscate you to my uses; if I get a larger portion of your services without an equivalent, I make you still further my slave; and, finally, if I obtain the whole of your services without an equivalent — except the means of keeping you in working condition for my own sake, I make you completely my slave. Slavery is merely one development of a general system of human oppression, for which we have no comprehensive term in English, but which the French Socialists denominate *exploitation* — the abstraction, directly or indirectly, from the working classes of the fruits of their labor. In the case of the slave, the instrument of that abstraction is force and legal enactments. In the case of the laborer, generally, it is speculation in the large sense, or *profit-making*. The slaveholder will be found, therefore, upon a scientific analysis, to hold the same relation to the trader which the freebooter holds to the blackleg. It is a question of taste which to admire most, the daredevil boldness of the one, or the oily and intriguing propensities and performances of the other.

# IV

# INTERNATIONAL EXPLOITATION

As individuals possessing skill or capital exploitate, or compel other individuals in the same community to work for them for nothing, or for undue consideration, precisely in the same way do nations possessed of those advantages exploitate other nations with whom they trade, who are without them.

England lends, say, five hundred millions of dollars to governments and individuals in America. In a hundred years, she will have withdrawn from us, in interest, six times the amount loaned or advanced, and at the expiration of that time she withdraws the principal itself. We pay England a tax of at least three thousand millions of dollars in a century; for her loans to us are probably even larger than the amount assumed. She commands the results of our labor to that extent, and gives us not a cent of the results of her labor in return — for her principal loaned represents her labor, and that we return to her intact. We are, to that extent, her slaves — "slaves without masters"; for she commands and enjoys our labor, and is under none of the obligations of a master — to protect, defend, and provide for us.

Her superior skill in the mechanic arts, by means of free trade, taxes or exploitates us quite as much as her capital. She exchanges her comparatively light and skillful labor for our hard, exposed, and unintellectual labor; and, in the general, compels us to labor three hours for her, when she labors one for us. Thus, after deducting the cost of the material, a yard of her cloth will exchange for an amount of our cotton, corn, or meat that cost three times as much labor to produce as her yard of cloth.

As in society, the skillful and professional tax or exploitate the common laborer by exchanging one hour of their light labor for many of the common workingman's hard labor, as lawyers, doctors, merchants, and mechanics deal with day laborers, so England and New England treat us of the South. This theory, and this alone, accounts for England's ability to pay the interest on her national debt, and yet increase her wealth. She effects it all by the immense profits of the exploitation of her skill and capital, by the power which they give her to command labor, and appropriate its results, without consideration, or for a very partial consideration. She trades with the world, and exploitates it all, except France. France sets the fashion, and this enables her to exploitate England. England, in her trade with France, has to pay for French fashions as well as French labor. In other words, France possesses superior skill, and exploitates England by means of it. Labor, not skill, is the just and equitable measure of values.

America sends her cotton, her surplus grain and meats, and other agricultural products, and her California gold to England, and gets worse than nothing in return; for if she were compelled to produce at home what she procures from England, she must cultivate a thousand skillful and intellectual pursuits, instead of being, as she too much is, confined to the coarse drudgery of common labor. The Southern States of this Union are exploitated of their labor and their brains, in their trade with England and New England. They produce nothing which we had not better produce at home. Northern trade exploitates us. Trade further South would enrich us and enlighten us; for we would manufacture for the far South. We should become exploitators, instead of being exploitated.

When we were in New Haven, a distinguished abolitionist boasted to us that mechanics received two dollars per day for their labor, and, by their China trade, exchanged the products of one day's labor for twenty days' labor of the Chinese, who worked for ten cents a day. The New England mechanic was thus the master of twenty Chinese laborers, whose labor he commanded for one of his own day's labor. Here was an instance of individual, not of national exploitation. Well might China dread free trade. It gives her taskmasters, who impoverish her people and depress her civilization; for they, by their machinery and superior skill, withdraw her people from a thousand mechanical pursuits that promoted civilization.

In *Sociology*, we explained this subject synthetically; we have tried now to expound it analytically.

V

# FALSE PHILOSOPHY OF THE AGE

The moral philosophy of our age (which term we use generically to include Politics, Ethics, and Economy, domestic and national) is deduced from the existing relations of men to each other in free society, and attempts to explain, to justify, to generalize and regulate those relations. If that system of society be wrong, and its relations false, the philosophy resulting from it must partake of its error and falsity. On the other hand, if our current philosophy be true, slavery must be wrong, because that philosophy is at war with slavery. No successful defence of slavery can be made, till we succeed in refuting or invalidating the principles on which free society rests for support or defence. The world, however, is sick of its philosophy; and the Socialists have left it not a leg to stand on. In fact, it is, in all its ramifications, a mere expansion and application of Political Economy — and Political Economy may be summed up in the phrase, "Laissez Faire," or "Let Alone." A system of unmitigated selfishness pervades and distinguishes all departments of ethical, political, and economic science. The philosophy is partially true, because selfishness, as a rule of action and guide of conduct, is necessary to the existence of man, and of all other animals. But it should not be, with man especially, the only rule and guide; for he is, by nature, eminently social and gregarious. His wants, his weakness, his appetites, his affections compel him to look without, and beyond self, in order to sustain self. The eagle and the owl, the lion and the tiger are not gregarious, but solitary and self-supporting. They practice political economy because 'tis adapted to their natures. But men and beavers, herds, bees, and ants require a different philosophy, another guide of conduct. The Bible (independent of its authority) is [by] far man's best guide, even in this world. Next to it, we would place Aristotle. But all books written four hundred or more years ago, are apt to yield useful instruction, whilst those written since that time will generally mislead. We mean, of course, books on moral science. We should not be far out in saying that no book on physics written more than four hundred years ago is worth reading, and none on morals written within that time. The Reformation, which effected much of practical good, gave birth to a false philosophy, which has been increasing and ramifying until our day, and now threatens the overthrow of all social institutions. The right of Private Judgment led to the doctrine of Human Individuality, and a Social Contract to restrict that individuality. Hence, also, arose the doctrines of Laissez Faire, free competition, human equality, freedom of religion, of speech and of the press, and universal liberty. The right of Private Judgment, naturally enough, leads to the right to act on that judgment, to the supreme sovereignty of the individual, and the abnegation of all government. No doubt the Reformation resulted from the relaxation of feudalism and the increased liberties of mind and body which men had begun to relish and enjoy. We have no quarrel with the Reformation, as such, for reform was needed, nor with all of the philosophy that has been deduced from it; but it is the excess of reform, and the excessive applications of that philosophy, to which we object. Man is selfish, as well as social; he is born a part and member of society, born and lives a slave of society; but he has also natural individual rights and liberties. What are his obligations to society, what his individual rights, what position he is entitled to, what duties he should fulfill depend upon a thousand ever-changing circumstances, in the wants and capacities of the individual, and in the necessities and well-being of the society to which he belongs. Modern philosophy treats of men only as separate monads or individuals; it is, therefore, always partly false and partly true; because, whilst man is always a limb or member of the Being, Society, he is also a Being himself, and does not bear to society the mere relation which the hand or the foot does to the human body. *We* shall propose no new philosophy, no universal and unerring principles or guide in place of those which we assail. A Moral Pathology, which feels its way in life, and adapts itself to circumstances as they present themselves, is the nearest approach to philosophy which it is either safe or wise to attempt. All the rest must be left to Religion, to Faith, and to Providence. This inadequacy of philosophy has, in all ages and nations, driven men to lean on religious faith for support. Though assailing all common theories, we are but giving bold and candid expression to the commonest of thoughts. The universal admiration of the passage we are about to cite proves the truth of our theory, whilst it debars us of all claim to originality:

SOLOMON, melancholy, gloomy, dissatisfied, and tossed upon a sea of endless doubt and speculation, exclaims, "Vanity of vanities, saith the Preacher; all is vanity." But, at length, he finds rest from the stormy ocean of philosophy, in the calm haven of faith. How beautiful and consoling, and how natural, too, his parting words:

> Let us hear the conclusion of the whole matter: Fear God and keep his commandments, for this is the whole duty of man.
>
> For God shall bring every work into judgment, with every secret thing, whether it be good, or whether it be evil.

In his Tenth, or Golden Satire, JUVENAL comes to a like conclusion, after having indulged in like speculations:

> Nil ergò optabunt homines? Si consilium vis,
> Permittes ipsis expendere numinibus, quid
> Conveniat nobis, rebusque sit utile nostris.
> Nam pro jucundis aptissama quæque dabunt diis
> Carior est illis homo, quàm sibi.[1]

[1] "Is there nothing then for which men shall pray? If you ask my counsel,

The Epicurean HORACE, in his first Satire, sees the same difficulty, but gives a less satisfactory solution:

> Est modus in rebus; sunt certi denique fines,
> Quos ultra citraque nequit consistere rectum.[2]

BURKE's beautiful words, "What shadows we are, and what shadows we pursue!" convey the same thought, without attempting a solution.

SHAKSPEARE employs the profoundest philosophy, to assail all philosophy:

> There are more things in heaven and earth,
> Horatio, than are dreamt of in your philosophy.

The infidel, VOLTAIRE, admits that "philosophy had ascertained few truths, done little good"; and when he sums up that little, satisfies the reader that it has done nothing – unless it be to perplex and mislead.

He, Voltaire, also, in another connection, exclaims, mournfully:

> I now repeat this confession, still more emphatically, since the more I read, the more I meditate, and the more I acquire, the more I am enabled to affirm, that I know nothing.

NEWTON, admitting his own ignorance, is a standing monument of the inadequacy and futility of moral researches and speculations.

PINDAR –

> Man, the frail being of a day,
> Uncertain shadow of a dream,
> Illumined by the heavenly beam,
> Flutters his airy life away.

---

you will leave it to the gods themselves to provide what is good for us, and what will be serviceable for our state; for, in place of what is pleasing, they will give us what is best. Man is dearer to them than he is to himself." Juvenal, *Satires*, X, 346–350.

[2] "There is measure in all things. There are, in short, fixed bounds, beyond and short of which, right can find no place." Horace, *Satires*, I, i, 106–107.

ÆSCHYLUS —

Vain thy ardor, vain thy grace,
They, nor force, nor aid repay;
Like a dream, man's feeble race,
Short-lived reptiles of a day.

SOPHOCLES —

'Tis said to think, but me the farce of life persuades,
That men are only spectral forms, or hollow shades.

ARISTOPHANES —

Come now, ye host of fading lives, like the race of withering leaves,
Who live a day, creatures of clay, tribes that flit like shadows away;
Ephemeral, wingless insects, dreamy shapes, that death expects
Soon to bind in phantom sheaves.

We will conclude our citations, which we might continue to the crack of doom (for all who have written well and much have indulged similar reflections), with Doctor Johnson's *Rasselas*, which is intended to expand and apply what others had concisely and tersely stated. The Doctor's is an elaborate failure.

Philosophy can neither account for the past, comprehend the present, nor foresee and provide for the future. "I'll none of it."

## VI

# FREE TRADE, FASHION, AND CENTRALIZATION

Liberty and political economy beget and encourage free trade, as well between different localities and different nations as between individuals of the same towns, neighborhoods, or nations. The nations possessed of most skill and capital, and commercial enterprise, and cunning gradually absorb the wealth of those nations who possess less of those qualities. The effect of international free trade, aided by the facilities of the credit system, of the mail, and speedy steam communication, is to centralize wealth in a few large cities, such as New York, Paris, and London; and of social free trade to aggregate wealth in a few hands in those cities. Theoretically, the disparities of shrewdness, of skill and business capacity, between nations and individuals, would, in the commercial and trading war of the wits, rob the weak and simple, and enrich the strong and cunning. The facts of history, and of the increasing inequalities of social, individual, and national wealth, under the system of free trade, stimulated by political economy, correspond with the theory. Every month brings forth its millionaire, and every day its thousands of new paupers. New York and London grow richer rapidly on the fruits of a trade that robs the less commercial and skillful people who traffic with them.

But the worst effect of free trade is that it begets centers of opinion, thought, and fashions, robs men of their nationality, and impairs their patriotism by teaching them to ape foreign manners, affect foreign dress and opinions, and despise what is domestic. Paris, as the center of thought and fashion, wields as much power, and makes almost as much money as London, by being the center of trade and capital. An American or Englishman will give five prices for an article because it is made in Paris. Thus the want of true self-respect in America and England makes labor produce more in Paris than elsewhere. A Virginian thinks it a disgrace to be dressed in homespun, because homespun is unfashionable. The Frenchman prides himself on being a Frenchman; all other people affect the cosmopolitan.

The tendency of all this is to transfer all wealth to London, New York, and Paris, and to reduce the civilization of Christendom to a miserable copy of French civilization, itself an indifferent copy of Roman civilization, which was an imitation but a falling off from that of Greece.

We pay millions monthly for French silks, French wines, French brandy, and French trinkets, although we can and do make as comfortable articles for dress, and as good liquors, at home. But we despise ourselves, and admire the French, and give four hours of American labor for one of French labor, just to be in the fashion. And what is our fashion? To treat whatever is American with contempt. People who thus act are in a fair way to deserve and meet with from others that contempt which they feel for themselves. The little States of Greece each had its dialect, and cultivated it, and took pride in it. Now, dialects are vulgar and provincial. We shall have no men like the Greeks, till the manners, dress, and dialect of gentlemen, betray, like the wines of Europe, the very neighborhood whence they come. So thought Mr. Calhoun, and talked South Carolina dialect in the Senate. But for all that, it was the best English of the day. Its smack of provincialism gave it a higher flavor.

We of the South teach political economy, because it is taught in Europe. Yet political economy, and all other systems of moral science which we derive from Europe are tainted with abolition, and at war with our institutions. We must build up centers of trade, of thought, and fashion at home. We must become national, nay, provincial, and cease to be imitative cosmopolitans. We must, especially, have good colleges and universities, where young men may learn to admire their homes, not to despise them.

The South feels the truth of all this, and after a while will begin to understand it. She has been for years earnestly and actively engaged in *promoting* the exclusive and protective policy, and preaching free trade, non-interference of government and Let Alone. But she does not let alone. She builds roads and canals, encourages education, endows schools and colleges, improves river navigation, excludes, or taxes heavily foreign showmen, foreign pedlars, sellers of clocks, &c., tries to build up by legislation Southern commerce, and by State legislation to multiply and encourage industrial pursuits. Protection by the State Government is her established policy – and that is the only expedient or constitutional protection. It is time for her to avow her change of policy and opinion, and to throw Adam Smith, Say, Ricardo & Co. in the fire.

We want American customs, habits, manners, dress, manufactures, modes of thought, modes of expression, and language. We should encourage national and even State peculiarities; for there are peculiarities and differences in the wants and situations of all people that require provincial and national, not cosmopolitan, institutions and productions. Take language, for instance. It is a thing of natural growth and development, and adapts itself naturally to the changes of time and circumstance. It is never ungrammatical as spoken by children, but always expressive, practical and natural. Nature is always grammatical, and language, the child of nature, would continue so but for the grammarians, who, with their Procrustean rules, disturb its proportions, destroy its variety and adaptation, and retard its growth. They are to language what dentists are to teeth: they more often injure it than improve it.

Grammar, lexicography, and rhetoric, applied to language,

destroys its growth, variety, and adaptability — stereotype it, make it at once essentially a dead language, and unfit for future use; for new localities, and changes of time and circumstances beget new ideas, and require new words and new combinations of words. Centralization and cosmopolitanism have precisely the same effect. They would furnish a common language from the center, which is only fully expressive and comprehensive at that center. Walking and talking are equally natural, and talking masters and walking masters equally useless. Neither can foresee and provide for the thousands of new circumstances which make change of language or varieties of movement necessary. Nature is never at a loss, and is the only reliable dancing master and grammar teacher. She is always graceful and appropriate, and always ready to adapt herself to changes of time, situation, and circumstances.

Paris is becoming the universal model and grammar of Christendom; nothing is right unless it be à la Parisienne. Now, in truth, nothing can be right, natural, appropriate, or in good taste outside of Paris that is Parisienne. When will our monkey imitative world cease to sacrifice millions of money, cease to show its want of good sense and propriety, and cease to render itself ridiculous by aping what, in the nature of things, is unsuitable, inappropriate, and unnatural? Fashion, aided by free trade and centralization, is subjecting us to the dominion of Parisian thought; and commerce, by means of the same agencies, makes us tributaries to London. Trade and fashion conquer faster than arms.

After the Romans had conquered Greece, Athens became the school and center of thought for the civilized world. Men had but one set of ideas, but one set of models to imitate in the whole range of the fine arts. Inventiveness and originality ceased, and genius was subdued. The rule of Horace, *Nullius addictus in verba magistri jurare*,[1] was [re]versed, and men ceased to think for themselves, but looked to the com-

[1] "Not compelled to swear to the opinions of any master."

mon fountain of thought at Athens, where the teachers of mankind borrowed all their ideas from the past. Improvement and progress ceased, and imitation, chaining the present to the car of the past, soon induced rapid retrogression. Thus, we think centralization of thought occasioned the decline of civilization. Northern invaders introduced new ideas, broke up centralization, arrested imitation, and begot originality and inventiveness. Thus a start was given to a new and Christian civilization. Now, a centralization occasioned by commerce and fashion threatens the overthrow of our civilization, as arms and conquest overthrew the ancient.

The ill effect of centralization of thought, whether its center be the past or some locality of the present, is apparent in the arts and literature of the Latin nations of Europe. France, Spain, and Italy, though possessed of more genius, have displayed less originality than England and Germany. French art is a mere rehash of Roman art, and very inferior to its original. The natural growth, changes and adaptation of language, are admirably described by Horace in his *De Arte Poetica.* He makes a great blunder in advising the forming and compounding words from the Greek, however; for the very want that occasions new words shows that they cannot be supplied from the past. In the passage we are about to quote, he seems to have seen and deplored the advent of that age of rule and criticism that was to stereotype language, thought, art itself, prevent progress, and inaugurate decline. From Horace's day, criticism ruled, language and art were stereotyped, and the world declined:

> Dixeris egregie, notum si callida verbum,
> Reddiderit junctura novum: si forte necesse est
> Indiciis monstrare recentibus abdita rerum,
> Fingere cinctutis non exaudita Cethegis
> Continget; dabiturque licentia sumpta pudenter;
> Et nova fictaque nuper habebunt verba fidem, si
> Græco fonte cadant, parce detorta. Quid autem
> Cæcilio, Plantoque dabit Romanus, ademptum
> Virgilio, Varioque? ego cur acquirere pauca

Si possum, invideor; cum lingua Catonis et Enni
Sermonem patrium ditaverit, et nova rerum
Nomina protulerit? Licuit, semperque licebit
Signatum præsente nota producere nomen.
Ut silvæ foliis pronos mutantur in annos,
Prima cadunt; ita verborum vetus interit ætas,
Et juvenum ritu florent modo nata, vigentque.[2]

Italy, of the middle ages, imbided more of the Christian and chivalric element, threw off for a while imitation and subserviency to the past, and shone forth with brilliant originality in all the works of art. But she, like France, has relapsed into imitation of the antique, and falls far below either Roman or mediæval art. With the age of Cervantes, Spanish genius expired. His happy ridicule expelled the absurdities of Knight Errantry, but unfortunately expelled, at the same time, the new elements of thought which Christianity and Chivalry had introduced into modern literature. They were its only progressive elements in the Latin nations of Europe, who in all else were mere Romans.

Fénelon's *Télémaque* is a servile imitation of Virgil's, *Æneid,* and that is an equally servile imitation of Homer. Each copy falls below the original.

Nothing shows so strongly the want of originality and want of independence of taste and thought among these Latin nations as their contempt for Shakspeare. He violates all the rules of Greek and Roman art, and erects a higher art of his

[2] "You will express yourself most happily, if a skilful setting makes a familiar word new. If haply one must betoken abstruse things by novel terms, you will have a chance to fashion words never heard of by the kilted Cethegi, and license will be granted, if used with modesty; while words, though new and of recent make, will win acceptance, if they spring from a Greek fount and are drawn therefrom but sparingly. Why indeed shall Romans grant this license to Caecilius and Plautus, and refuse it to Vergil and Varius? And why should I be grudged the right of adding, if I can, my little fund, when the tongue of Cato and of Ennius has enriched our mother-speech and brought to light new terms for things? It has ever been, and ever will be, permitted to issue words stamped with the mint-mark of the day. As forests change their leaves with each year's decline, and the earliest drop off: so with words, the old race dies, and, like the young of human kind, the new-born bloom and thrive." Horace, *Ars Poetica,* 47–62.

own; but Frenchmen, Italians, and Spaniards have no tastes and no ideas differing from, or in advance of, the ancients, and can neither understand nor appreciate the genius of Shakspeare. In Germany, he is almost as much read and admired as in England.

Imitation, grammar, and slavery suit the masses. Liberty and Laissez Faire, the men of genius, and the men born to command. Genius, in her most erratic flights, represents a higher Grammar than Dr. Blair or Lindlay Murray [3] – the grammar of progressive nature. To secure true progress, we must unfetter genius, and chain down mediocrity. Liberty for the few – Slavery, in every form, for the mass!

The rules of art destroy art. Homer never could have produced the *Iliad*, had he learned grammar and rhetoric and criticism. 'Tis well for the world, he lived before Longinus. Euripides, Sophocles, and Aristophanes, and the Greek Masters in Sculpture and Painting knew nothing of the rules of art and canons of criticism. Without the modern helps to art, Grecian art so far excelled ours that it is a popular theory that they possessed an Ideal that has been lost. Early in the days of the Roman Empire, the rhetoricians, by attempting to teach eloquence by rule, so corrupted it that the Emperors found it necessary to banish them from Rome.

We are no doubt indebted to the ignorance of the ancients for the invention of Gothic architecture. No one taught to reverence Greek architecture would have violated its rules by imitating the Gothic.

When about the time of the Reformation, the study of the ancients was revived, each Gothic spire stopped half way in its course towards heaven. Mediæval art expired – and now the world has no art, but basely copies the past.

Had Shakspeare been as learned as Ben Jonson, he would have written no better than Ben Jonson. The lofty genius of Milton would have created a glorious English epic, had he not

[3] Lindlay Murray (1745–1826), prolific grammarian and Quaker, who was strong for decorum and propriety.

travelled too much abroad, and dwelt too much with the past. The *Paradise Lost* is a splendid piece of Mosaic, made up of bits of Greek and Roman mythology, Hebrew theology, Christian morality, Mediæval romance, set in the purest Anglo-Saxon, twisted into Latin collocation. 'Tis the song of the mockingbird.

What then? Shall we not in boyhood sojourn and linger at Athens and at Rome, nor in manhood travel into France and Italy?

*Est modus in rebus.*[4] Study the past, but be careful not to copy it, and never travel abroad until age has matured your love and respect for your native land.

[4] "There is measure in all things."

# VII

# THE WORLD IS *TOO LITTLE* GOVERNED

Whether with reason or with instinct blest,
All enjoy that power that suits them best;
Order is Heaven's first law, and this confessed,
Some are, and must be greater than the rest —
More rich, more wise; but who infers from hence
That such are happier, shocks all common sense.
Heaven to mankind impartial, we confess,
If all are equal in their happiness;
But mutual wants this happiness increase,
All nature's difference, keeps all nature's peace:
Condition, circumstance, is not the thing;
Bliss is the same, in subject, or in king!

POPE.

Mobs, secret associations, insurance companies, and social and communistic experiments are striking features and characteristics of our day, outside of slave society. They are all attempting to supply the defects of regular governments, which have carried the Let Alone practice so far that one-third of mankind are let alone to indulge in such criminal immoralities as they please, and another third to starve. Mobs (*vide* California) supply the deficiencies of a defective police, and insurance companies and voluntary unions and associations afford that security and protection which government, under the lead of political economy, has ceased to render.

A lady remarked to us, a few days since, "that society was like an army, in which the inferior officers were as necessary as the commander-in-chief. Demoralization and insubordination ensue if you dispense with sergeants and corporals in an army, and the same effects result from dispensing with guardians, masters, and heads of families in society." We don't know whether she included the ladies in her ideas of the heads of families; protesting against such construction of her language, we accept and thank her for her illustration. Rev'd Nehemiah Adams has a similar thought in his admirable work, *A South-side View of Slavery*,[1] which we regret is not before us. On some public occasion in Charleston, he was struck with the good order and absence of all dissipation, and very naively asked where was their mob. He was informed that "they were at work." He immediately perceived that slavery was an admirable police institution, and moralizes very wisely on the occasion. Slavery is an indispensable police institution – especially so to check the cruelty and tyranny of vicious and depraved husbands and parents. Husbands and parents have, in theory and practice, a power over their subjects more despotic than kings; and the ignorant and vicious exercise their power more oppressively than kings. Every man is not fit to be king, yet all must have wives and children. Put a master over them to check their power, and we need not resort to the unnatural remedies of woman's rights, limited marriages, voluntary divorces, and free love, as proposed by the abolitionists.

Mr. Carlyle says, "Among practical men the idea prevails that government can do nothing but 'keep the peace.' They say all higher tasks are unsafe for it, impossible for it, and, in fine, not necessary for it or for us. Truly, it is high time that same beautiful notion of No-Government should take itself away. The world is daily rushing towards wreck whilst it lasts. If your government is to be a constituted anarchy, what issue can it have? Our own interest in such government is, that it would be kind enough to cease and go its way before the inevitable wreck."

The reader will excuse us for so often introducing the thoughts and words of others. We do so not only for the sake

[1] Nehemiah Adams, *A South-side View of Slavery* (Boston, 1854).

of their authority, but because they express our own thoughts better than we can express them ourselves. In truth, we deal out our thoughts, facts, and arguments in that irregular and desultory way in which we acquired them. We are no regular built scholar – have pursued no "royal road to mathematics," nor to anything else. We have, by observation and desultory reading, picked up our information by the wayside, and endeavored to arrange, generalize, and digest it for ourselves. To learn "to forget" is almost the only thing we have labored to learn. We have been so bored through life by friends with dyspeptic memories, who never digest what they read because they never forget it, who retain on their intellectual stomachs in gross, crude, undigested, and unassimilated form everything that they read, and retail and repeat it in that undigested form to every good-natured listener; we repeat, that we have been so bored by friends with good memories that we have resolved to endeavor to express what was useful out of facts, and then to throw the facts away. A great memory is a disease of the mind, which we are surprised no medical writer has noticed. The lunatic asylum should make provision for those affected with this disease; for, though less dangerous, they are far more troublesome and annoying than any other class of lunatics. Learning, observation, reading are only useful in the general, as they add to the growth of the mind. Undigested and unforgotten, they can no more have this effect, than undigested food on the stomach of a dyspeptic can add to his physical stature. We thought once this thing was original with us, but find that Say pursued this plan in writing his Political Economy. He first read all the books he could get hold of on this subject, and then took time to forget them, before he began to write.

We will not trouble the reader further, for the present, with our egotisms or our arguments, but refer him to the whole of Carlyle's *Latter-Day Pamphlets* to prove that "the world is too little governed," and, therefore, is going to wreck. We say to the whole of those pamphlets, for that is their one, great leading idea. We also add an extract from the speech of Ulysses, in the play of *Troilus and Cressida*, that beautifully illustrates and enforces our thought. We give the extract because it is a play that few read, it being, on the whole, far inferior to Shakspeare's other plays, and by few considered as wholly, if at all, his work:

> The heavens themselves, the planets and this centre,
> Observe degree, priority, and place,
> Insisture, course, proportion, season, form,
> Office and custom, in all line of order:
> And, therefore, is the glorious planet, Sol,
> In nobler eminence enthron'd and spher'd,
> Amidst the other; whose med'cinable eye
> Corrects the ill aspects of planets evil,
> And posts, like the commandment of a king,
> Sans check, to good and bad: But, when the planet
> In evil mixture, to disorder wander,
> What plagues, and what portents? what mutiny?
> What raging of the sea? shaking of earth?
> Commotion in the winds? frights, changes, horrors,
> Divert and crack, rend and deracinate,
> The unity and married calm of states
> Quite from their fixture? O, when degree is shak'd,
> Which is the ladder of all high designs,
> The enterprise is sick! How could communities,
> Degrees in schools, and brotherhoods in cities,
> Peaceful commerce from dividable shores,
> The primogenitive and due of birth,
> Prerogative of ages, crowns, sceptres, laurels,
> But by degree, stand in authentic place?
> Take but degree away, untune that string,
> And, hark, what discord follows! each thing meets
> In mere oppugnancy: The bounded waters
> Should lift their bosoms higher than the shores,
> And make a sop of all this solid globe:
> Strength should be lord of imbecility,
> And the rude son should strike his father dead:
> Force should be right; or, rather, right and wrong.
> (Between whose endless jar justice resides,)
> Should lose their names, and so should justice too.

We promised to write no more in this chapter; but, like Parthos, when "we have an idea," we want to give others the benefit of it. We agree with Mr. Jefferson that all men have natural and inalienable rights. To violate or disregard such rights, is to oppose the designs and plans of Providence, and cannot "come to good." The order and subordination observable in the physical, animal, and human world show that some are formed for higher, others for lower stations – the few to command, the many to obey. We conclude that about nineteen out of every twenty individuals have "a natural and inalienable right" to be taken care of and protected, to have guardians, trustees, husbands, or masters; in other words, they have a natural and inalienable right to be slaves. The one in twenty are as clearly born or educated or some way fitted for command and liberty. Not to make them rulers or masters is as great a violation of natural right as not to make slaves of the mass. A very little individuality is useful and necessary to society – much of it begets discord, chaos and anarchy.

NOTE. – Since writing this chapter, we have received our copy of Mr. Adams's work. We congratulate ourselves on our success in "learning to forget." Here is the passage to which we refer:

> One consequence of the disposal of the colored people, as to individual control, is the absence of mobs. That fearful element in society, an irresponsible and low class, is diminished at the South. Street brawls and conflicts between two races of laboring people, or the ignorant and more excitable portions of different religious denominations, are mostly unknown within the bounds of slavery. Our great source of disturbance at the North, jealousy and collisions between Protestant and Irish Roman Catholic laborers, is obviated there.
>
> When the remains of Mr. Calhoun were brought to Charleston, a gentleman from a free State in the procession said to a southern gentleman, "Where is your underswell?" referring to the motley crowd of men and boys of all nations which gather in most of our large places on public occasions. He was surprised to learn that those respectable, well-dressed, well-behaved colored men and boys on the sidewalks, were a substitute for that class of population which he

had elsewhere been accustomed to see with repugnant feelings on public occasions.

As we are on the subject of Mr. Adams's book, we will give another extract from it, confirmatory of our doctrines:

> There is another striking peculiarity of Southern society which is attributable to slavery, and is very interesting to a Northerner at the present day. While the colored people are superstitious and excitable, popular delusions and fanaticisms do not prevail among them. That class of society among us in which these things get root, has a substitute in the colored population. Spiritual rappings, biology, second-adventism, Mormonism, and the whole spawn of errors which infest us, do not find subjects at the South. There is far more faith in the South, taken as a whole, than with us. Many things which we feel called to preach against here are confined to the boundaries of the Free States; yet the white population are readers of books, though not of newspapers, perhaps more generally than we. That vast amount of active but uninstructed mind with us, which seizes every new thing, and follows brilliant or specious error, and erects a folly into a doctrine with a sect annexed, and so infuses doubt or contempt of things sacred into many minds, is no element in Southern life. This is one reason why there is more faith, less infidelity, at the South, than at the North. The opinions of a lower class on moral and religious subjects, have a powerful effect on the classes above them; more than is generally acknowledged; and hence we derive an argument in favor of general education, in which moral and religious principles shall have their important place.

# VIII

## LIBERTY AND SLAVERY

Effugit imago,
Par livibus [*sic*] ventis, volucrique simillima somno.[1]

It seems to us that the vain attempts to define liberty in theory, or to secure its enjoyment in practice, proceed from the fact that man is naturally a social and gregarious animal, subject, not by contract or agreement, as Locke and his followers assume, but by birth and nature, to those restrictions of liberty which are expedient or necessary to secure the good of the human hive, to which he may belong. There is no such thing as *natural human* liberty, because it is unnatural for man to live alone and without the pale and government of society. Birds and beasts of prey, who are not gregarious, are naturally free. Bees and herds are naturally subjects or slaves of society. Such is the theory of Aristotle, promulged more than two thousand years ago, generally considered true for two thousand years, and destined, we hope, soon again to be accepted as the only true theory of government and society.

Modern social reformers, except Mr. Carlyle, proceeding upon the theory of Locke, which is the opposite of Aristotle, propose to dissolve and disintegrate society, falsely supposing that they thereby follow nature. There is not a human tie that binds man to man that they do not propose to cut "sheer asunder." 'Tis true, after their work of destruction is finished, they see the necessity of society; but instead of

[1] "The form fled, even as light winds, and most like a winged dream." Virgil, *Aeneid*, II, 793–794.

that natural and historical society, which has usually existed in the world, with its gradations of rank and power, its families, and its slaves, they propose wholly to disregard the natural relations of mankind, and profanely to build up states, like Fourierite Phalansteries, or Mormon and Oneida villages, where religion shall be banished, and in which property, wife and children shall be held somewhat in common. These social establishments, under a self-elected despotism like that of Joe Smith, or Brigham Young, become patriarchal, and succeed so long as such despotism lasts. That is, when the association loses the character intended by its founders, and acquires a despotic head like other family associations, it works well, because it works naturally. But this success can only be temporary; for nothing but the strong rule of a Cromwell or Joe Smith can keep a society together that wants the elements of cohesion in the natural ties that bind man to man; and Cromwells and Joe Smiths are not to be found every day.

'Tis an historical fact that this family association, this patriarchal government, for purposes of defence against enemies from without, gradually merges into larger associations of men under a common government or ruler. This latter is the almost universal and, we may thence infer, natural and normal condition of civilized man. In this state of society there is no liberty for the masses. Liberty has been exchanged by nature for security.

What is falsely called Free Society is a very recent invention. It proposes to make the weak, ignorant, and poor, free, by turning them loose in a world owned exclusively by the few (whom nature and education have made strong, and whom property has made stronger) to get a living. In the fanciful state of nature, where property is unappropriated, the strong have no weapons but superior physical and mental power with which to oppress the weak. Their power of oppression is increased a thousand fold when they become the exclusive owners of the earth and all the things thereon. They are masters without the obligations of masters, and the poor are slaves without the rights of slaves.

It is generally conceded, even by abolitionists, that the serfs of Europe were liberated because the multitude of laborers and their competition as freemen to get employment, had rendered free labor cheaper than slave labor. But, strange to say, few seem to have seen that this is in fact asserting that they were less free after emancipation than before. Their obligation to labor was increased; for they were compelled to labor more than before to obtain a livelihood, else their free labor would not have been cheaper than their labor as slaves. They lost something in liberty, and everything in rights—for emancipation liberated or released the masters from all their burdens, cares, and liabilities, whilst it increased both the labors and the cares of the liberated serf. In our chapter on the Decay of English Liberty, we show that the whole struggle in England has been to oppress the working man, pull down the powers, privileges, and prerogatives of the throne, the nobility, and the church, and to elevate the property-holding class. The extracts from the *Era* and *Northern Churchman*, in another chapter, will further elucidate this subject. We promised to confirm our doctrine of the illusory and undefinable character of liberty and slavery, by extracts from standard authors.

PALEY on Civil Liberty:

To do what we will, is natural liberty: to do what we will, consistently with the interest of the community to which we belong, is civil liberty; that is to say, the only liberty to be desired in a state of civil society.

I should wish, no doubt, to be allowed to act, in every instance, as I pleased; but I reflect, that the rest also of mankind would then do the same; in which state of universal independence and self-direction, I should meet with so many checks and obstacles to my own will, from the interference and opposition of other men's, that not only my happiness, but my liberty, would be less than whilst the whole community were subject to the dominion of equal laws.

The boasted liberty of a state of nature exists only in a state of solitude. In every kind and degree of union and intercourse with his species, it is possible that the liberty of the individual may be augmented by the very laws which restrain it; because he may gain more from the limitation of other men's freedom than he suffers by the diminution of his own. Natural liberty is the right of common upon a waste; civil liberty is the safe, exclusive, unmolested enjoyment of a cultivated enclosure.

The definitions which have been framed of civil liberty, and which have become the subject of much unnecessary altercation, are most of them adapted to this idea. Thus, one political writer makes the essence of the subject's liberty to consist in his being governed by no laws but those to which he hath actually consented; another is satisfied with an indirect and virtual consent; another, again, places civil liberty in the separation of the legislative and executive offices of government; another in the being governed by *law*; that is, by known, preconstituted, inflexible rules of action and adjudication; a fifth, in the exclusive right of the people to tax themselves by their own representatives; a sixth, in freedom and purity of elections of representatives; a seventh, in the control which the democratic part of the constitution possesses over the military establishment.

### Montesquieu on Liberty:

There is no word that has admitted of more various significations, and has made more different impressions on human minds, than that of *liberty*. Some have taken it for a faculty of deposing a person on whom they had conferred a tyrannical authority; others, for the power of choosing a person whom they are obliged to obey; others, for the right of bearing arms, and of being thereby enabled to use violence; others, for the privilege of being governed by a native of their own country, or by their own laws. A certain nation for a long time thought that liberty consisted in the privilege of wearing a long beard.

Some have annexed this name to one form of government, in exclusion of others; those who had a republican taste applied it to this government; those who like a monarchical state, gave it to monarchies. Thus, they all have applied the name of liberty to the government most conformable to their own customs and inclinations; and as in a republic, people have not so constant and so present a view of the institutions they complain of, and likewise as the laws there seem to speak more, and the executors of the laws least, it is generally attributed to republics, and denied to monarchies. In fine, as in democracies, the people seem to do very near whatever they please, liberty has been placed in this sort of government, and the power of the people has been confounded with their liberty.

It is true, that in democracies the people seem to do what they please; but political liberty does not consist in an unrestrained freedom. In governments, that is, in societies directed by laws, liberty can consist only in the power of doing what we ought to will, and in not being constrained to do what we ought not to will.

We must have continually present to our minds the difference between independence and liberty. Liberty is a right of doing whatever the laws permit; and if a citizen could do what they forbid, he would no longer be possessed of liberty, because all his fellow citizens would have the same power.

## Blackstone on Liberty:

The absolute right of man, considered as a free agent, endowed with discernment to know good from evil, and with power of choosing those measures which appear to him to be most desirable, are usually summed up in one general appellation, and denominated the natural liberty of mankind.

This national liberty consists properly in a power of acting as one thinks fit, without any restraint or control, unless by the law of nature; being a right inherent in us by birth, and one of the gifts of God to man at his creation, when he endued him with the faculty of free will. But every man, when he enters into society, gives up a part of his natural liberty, as the price of so valuable a purchase; and, in consideration of receiving the advantages of mutual commerce, obliges himself to conform to those laws which the community has thought proper to establish. And this species of legal obedience and conformity is infinitely more desirable than that wild and savage liberty which is sacrificed to obtain it. For, no man that considers a moment would wish to retain the absolute, uncontrolled power of doing what he pleases; the consequence of which is, that every other man would also have the same power; and then there would be no security to individuals in any of the enjoyments of life. Political, therefore, or civil liberty, which is that of a member of society, is no other than natural liberty, so far restrained by human laws (and no farther) as is necessary and expedient for the general advantage of the public. Hence, we may collect that the law, which restrains a man from doing mischief to his fellow citizens, though it diminishes the natural, increases the civil liberty of mankind; but that every wanton and causeless restraint of the will of the subject, whether practiced by a monarch, a nobility, or a popular assembly, is a degree of tyranny: nay, that even laws themselves, whether made with or without our consent, if they regulate and constrain our conduct in matters of mere indifference, without any good end in view, are regulations destructive of liberty; whereas, if any public advantage can arise from observing such precepts, the control of our private inclinations, in one or two particular points, will conduce to preserve our general freedom in others of more importance, by supporting that state of society which can alone secure our independence. Thus the statute of King Edward IV, which forbade the fine gentlemen of those times (under the degree of a lord) to wear pikes upon their shoes or boots of more than two inches in length, was a law that savored of oppression; because, however ridiculous the fashion then in use might appear, the restraining it by pecuniary penalties, could serve no purpose of common utility. But the statute of King Charles II, which prescribes a thing seemingly as indifferent (a dress for the dead, who are all ordered to be buried in woollen), is a law consistent with public liberty; for it encourages the staple trade, on which, in great measure, depends the universal good of the nation. So that laws, when prudently framed, are by no means subversive, but rather introductive of liberty; for (as Mr. Locke has well observed) where there is no law, there is no freedom. But then, on the other hand, that constitution or frame of government — that system of laws, is alone calculated to maintain civil liberty, which leaves the subject entire master of his own conduct, except in those points wherein the public good requires some direction or restraint.

The idea and practice of this political or civil liberty, flourish in their highest vigor in those kingdoms where it falls little short of perfection, and can only be lost or destroyed by the folly or demerits of its owner: the legislature, and of course the laws of England, being peculiarly adapted to the preservation of this inestimable blessing even in the meanest subject.

Very different from the modern constitutions of other States on the continent of Europe, and from the genius of the imperial law, which, in general, are calculated to vest an arbitrary and despotic power of controlling the actions of the subject, in the prince or in a few grandees. And this spirit of liberty is so deeply implanted in our constitution, and rooted even in our very soil, that a slave, or a negro, the moment he lands in England, falls under the protection of the laws, and so far becomes a freeman, though the master's right to his service may possibly still continue.

Next to personal security, the law of England regards, asserts and preserves the personal liberty of individuals. This personal liberty consists in the power of locomotion, of changing situation, or removing one's person to whatever place one's inclinations may direct, without imprisonment or restraint, unless by due course of law. Concerning which, we may make the same observations as upon the preceding article; that it is a right strictly natural; that the laws of England have never abridged it without sufficient cause; and, that in this kingdom, it can never be abridged at the mere discretion of the magistrate, without the explicit permission of the laws.

Now, let the reader examine and study these definitions of Liberty by Paley, Montesquieu, and Blackstone, and he will see that they are in pursuit of an *ignis fatuus* that eludes their grasp. He will see more, that their liberty is a mere modification of slavery. That each of them proposes that degree of restraint, restriction, and control that will redound to the general good. That each is in pursuit of good government, not liberty. Government presupposes that liberty is surrendered as the price of security. The degree of government must depend on the moral and intellectual condition of those to be governed. Take, for instance, Blackstone's definition of civil liberty, and our negro slaves enjoy liberty, because the restrictions on their free will and free agency not only redound to public good, but are really necessary to the protection and government of themselves. We mean to involve ourselves in no such absurdities. Negroes, according to Blackstone, Paley, and Montesquieu, although slaves, are free, because their liberty is only so far restricted as the public interest and their own good require. Our theory is that they are not free, because God and nature, and the general good and their own good, intended them for slaves. They enjoy all the rights calculated to promote their own interests, or the public good. They are, at the South, well governed and well protected. These are the aims of all social institutions, and of all governments. There can be no liberty where there is government; but there may be security for good government. This the slave has in the selfish interest of the master and in his domestic affection. The free laborer has no such securities. It is the interest of employers to kill them off as fast as possible; and they never fail to do it.

We do not mean to say that the negro slave enjoys liberty. But we do say that he is well and properly governed, so as best to promote his own good and that of society. We do mean to say further that what we have quoted from these great authors is all fudge and nonsense. Liberty is unattainable; and if attainable, not desirable.

Liberty of locomotion, which Blackstone boasts of as one of the rights of Englishmen, belongs to the mass of them less than to other people. For five hundred years the poor laws have confined the poor to their parishes, denied them the right to bargain for their own wages, and as late as 1725, set them up in stalls and shambles for hire, like cattle. Liberty in England, as in Rome and Greece, has been, and is now, the privilege of the few – not the right of the many. But in Rome, Greece, and the Southern States of America, the many have gained in protection what they lost in liberty. In England, the masses have neither liberty nor protection. They are slaves without masters. This right of locomotion, of choosing or changing their domicil, is not only denied to the mass of the poor, but in all countries as well as in England, to wives, to children, to wards, apprentices, soldiers, sailors, convicts, lunatics, and idiots. Take, then, this test of liberty, and how little of it is there in England! But, in fact, there is a very large nomadic class of beggars, rogues, and journeymen workmen, who are always wandering, and yet, who are the most wretched members of society and its greatest pests. So much for locomotion.

Great as the difficulty is to determine what is Liberty, to ascertain and agree on what constitutes Slavery is still greater. Slavery, in its technical form, has been almost universal, yet not exactly alike in all its circumstances and all its regulations in any two ages, or in any two countries. In very many ancient States, the power of life and death was vested in the master. In most countries, the slave cannot acquire or hold property legally. In all, he holds more or less by the permission. In many, his legal right to separate property is protected by law. Even in Cuba, he can compel his master to emancipate him, upon offering an adequate price, and in some cases of irreconcilable disagreement, force his master to sell him to another master. It is remarkable at first view that in Cuba, where the law attempts to secure mild treatment to the slave, he is inhumanly treated; and in Virginia, where there is scarce any law to protect him, he is very humanely governed and provided for. In Cuba, many of the slaves are savages, and do not elicit the domestic affection of the master, who sees in them little more than brutes. The master is, besides, often an absentee, and tho' overseers be far more humane than Irish rent-collectors, they have neither the interests nor feelings of resident masters. But the most efficient cause of cruelty and neglect, is the African slave trade, which makes it cheaper to buy than to rear slaves. In Virginia, the slaves have advanced much in morality, religion, and intelligence, and their masters and mistresses, living on the farm with them, naturally become attached to them. Self-interest, however, is everywhere the strongest motive to human conduct. Negroes are immensely valuable, and increase rapidly in value and in numbers when well treated. The law of self-interest secures kind and humane treatment to Southern slaves. All the legislative ingenuity in the world will never enact so efficient a law in behalf of free laborers.

During the decline of the Roman Empire, slavery became colonial or prædial. The slaves occupied the place of tenants or serfs, were *adscripti soli*, and could only be sold with the farm. Many antiquarians consider the colonial slavery of the Romans as the true origin of the feudal system. This kind of slavery was universal in Europe till a few centuries since, and now prevails to a great extent. The serfs of Russia, Poland, Turkey, and Hungary, are happier and better provided for than the free laborers of Western Europe. They have homes, and lands to cultivate. They work but little, because their wants are few and simple. They are not overworked and under-fed, as are the free laborers of Western Europe. Hence, they never rise in riots and insurrections, burn houses, commit strikes – nor do they emigrate.

This form of slavery, however, makes the master an idle absentee, depriving the slaves of his guardianship, his government, and his protection. By throwing large masses of the ignorant into exclusive association with each other, it promotes and increases ignorance, negligence, and idleness. Men will not improve their condition who have no examples to emulate and no teachers to instruct. Were their farms conducted as ours of the South, the wealthy would have ample employment, and the slaves or serfs find in their masters examples, governors, teachers, and protectors.

The right to sell one's children, or one's self, into slavery has been very common, and is now practiced in China. The ancient Germans used to even stake their liberty at games of hazard. This would never have been done, nor would the laws have permitted it, if the situation of the slave had been greatly inferior to that of the free. But how shall we class wives, children, wards, apprentices, prisoners, soldiers and sailors? They are not free, because their personal liberty is controlled by the will of a superior, not by mere law. They are liable to confinement and punishment by their superiors, whose will stands in place of law as to them. They have no right of locomotion like that enjoyed by the free. They have no liberty secured by law – they are not free. Are they, therefore, slaves?

Paley defines slavery to be, "An obligation to labor for the benefit of the master, without the contract or consent of the servant." The sick, the superannuated, the infirm, and the infant slaves are under no such obligation in theory or practice. The master is under an obligation, legally, theoretically, and practically, to labor for them. Therefore, the master of twenty slaves is always a slave himself. If he be a good man, he is the happier for performing his duties as slave to those classes of his slaves. But what becomes of that slavery of the ancients and of China, where the slave, by actual contract, sells himself? This is not slavery according to Paley.

The great and glaring defect, however, of Paley's definition is that he omits the obligation on the master to provide for and protect the slave. 'Tis but half of a definition, and that half false. It does often happen that the *obligations* of the master are more onerous than those of the slave. Yet Paley omits those obligations altogether. The slave, when capable to do so, must work for the master; but the master, at all times, must provide for the slave. If incapable of doing so, the law gives the slave a new master and protector. His situation is less honorable, but far more secure than that of the master. Definitions are perilous attempts. We never read one that a seventy-four with all sail set might not drive through. We shall define nothing ourselves, for we know that this is the business of Omnipotence, that alone knows "all things in heaven and on earth."

We proceed to examine the attempted definitions of Montesquieu and Blackstone. Blackstone objects to the right to sell one's self that the consideration enures to the buyer. This may or may not be so, according to the laws of the State where the contract is made. It is not a necessary feature of slavery, and cannot fairly be employed as an objection to it. In fact, the slaves of the South, in their houses, gardens, fruit, vegetables, pigs, and fowls, hold more property than the peasantry of Europe, and are far better secured in its possession by their masters, than that peasantry is by the law. He further objects, that in case of absolute slavery, not only the liberty but the life of the slave is at the master's disposal. This objection is false and puerile. In no civilized country has the master the right to kill his slave.

The protection or support to which the slave is entitled

would be an ample consideration of itself for the sale of his liberty. A much larger one than the capitalists of Europe would be willing to give; for they all say that free labor is cheapest.

Montesquieu thus defines slavery: "Slavery, properly so called, is the establishment of a right which gives to one man such a power over another as renders him absolute master of his life and fortune." This is French liberty under the rule of the republican Bonapartes, and English liberty under Cromwell – not Southern slavery. France is always happy and prosperous with a master, and the masses in England look back to the Protectorate with fond regret. These despots played the part of Southern masters. They forced the strong to support the weak, the rich to take care of the poor. The nations became two farms or families. Western Europe will soon have to choose between domestic slavery and universal slavery.

Democracy and liberty are antagonistic; for liberty permits and encourages the weak to oppress the strong, whilst democracy proposes, so far as possible, to equalize advantages, by fairly dividing the burdens of life and rigidly enforcing the performance of every social duty by every member of society, according to his capacity and ability.

# IX

# PALEY ON EXPLOITATION

Paley maintains, to its fullest extent, the doctrine of exploitation which we have endeavored to expound and illustrate in the last three chapters. Yet, neither Paley nor any of his readers were ever aware of its tremendous consequences. It is only when those consequences are pointed out that the mind revolts at the theory.

He saw and said that capital paid labor nothing, yet discovered no iniquity in the transaction. He saw that labor produced everything — capital nothing, and "all that the capitalist does is to distribute what others produce." He should have added, after retaining the "lion's share" himself. Our whole theory is to be found in a single paragraph of Paley, and if there be nothing strange or monstrous in his theory, there can be nothing of the kind in ours; for our theories are identical. Chapter 2, Book 3d of his philosophy, under the head of "The Treatment of Our Domestics and Dependents," he employs the following language: "Another reflection of a like tendency with the former is, that our obligation to them is much greater than theirs to us. It is a mistake to suppose that the rich man maintains his servants, tradesmen, tenants and laborers: the truth is, they maintain him. It is their industry which supplies his table, furnishes his wardrobe, builds his houses, adorns his equipage, provides his amusements. It is not the estate, but the labor employed on it, that pays his rents. *All that he does is, to distribute what others produce; which is the least part of the business.*" He should have added, "but far the most profitable part."

A few additional truths, and this paragraph of Paley's would be an admirable description of "Cannibals" above, and "Slaves without Masters" below.

His servants are obliged to work as our slaves, not for pay, but for an allowance out of the proceeds of their own labor. His employers, like our masters, only distribute something of their earnings to the laborers, giving them far less than masters give to slaves, retaining more to themselves – and hence "free labor is cheaper than slave labor."

But Paley did not comprehend what he wrote. We, aided by the Socialists, will try to make it understood by others.

Philosophy cannot justify the relation between the free laborer and the idle, irresponsible employer. But, 'tis easy to justify that between master and slave. Their obligations are mutual and equal; and if the master will superintend and provide for the slave in sickness, in health, infancy, and old age – if he will feed and clothe and house him properly, guard his morals, and treat him kindly and humanely, he will make his slaves happy and profitable, and be himself a worthy, useful, and conscientious man.

# X

# OUR BEST WITNESSES AND MASTERS IN THE ART OF WAR

> I think few worth damnation, save their kings;
> And these but as a kind of quit-rent, to
> Assert my right as lord.
>
> VISION OF JUDGMENT.

We intend this chapter as our trump card, and have kept it in reserve, because it is rash to "lead trumps." We could produce a cloud of witnesses, but should only protract the trial thereby. We call into court Horace Greeley, Wm. Goodell, Gerrit Smith, Wm. Lloyd Garrison, and Stephen Pearl Andrews, and propose to prove by them (the actual leaders and faithful exponents of abolition) that their object, and that of their entire party, is not only to abolish Southern slavery, but to abolish also, or greatly to modify, the relations of husband and wife, parent and child, the institution of private property of all kinds, but especially separate ownership of lands, and the institution of Christian churches as now existing in America. We further charge that whilst actively engaged in attempts to abolish Southern slavery, they are busy, with equal activity and more promise of success, in attempts to upset and reorganize society at the North.

In convening these gentlemen as witnesses, and also arraigning them on trial, we are actuated by no feelings of personal ill will or disrespect. We admire them all, and have had kindly intercourse and correspondence with some of them. They are historical characters, who would seek notoriety in order to further their schemes of setting the world to rights. We have no doubt of their sincere philanthropy, and as little doubt that they are only "paving hell with good intentions." We speak figuratively. We shall try their cause in the most calm and judicial temper. We would address each of them in language borrowed from Lord Byron:

> Why,
> My good old friend, for such I deem you,
> Though our different parties make us fight so shy,
> I ne'er mistake you for a *personal* foe;
> Our difference is political, and I
> Trust that whatever may occur,
> You know my great respect for you, and this
> Makes me regret whatever you do amiss.

Indeed, we should be ungrateful and discourteous in the extreme, if we did not entertain kindly remembrance and make gentlemanly return for the generous reception and treatment we received, especially from leading abolitionists, when we went north to personate Satan by defending Slavery. Though none agreed with us, none were made converts by us:

> Yet still between his darkness and his brightness,
> There passed a mutual glance of great politeness.

We will first call Mr. Wm. Goodell to the stand. His position as one of the most active leaders of the Gerrit Smith or Syracuse wing of abolition, would entitle his admissions and assertions of the failure of his own society to the greatest credence, since such admissions and assertions weaken his assaults on the South, and must be reluctantly drawn from him; but, independent of his peculiar position, his high character as a man and his distinction as an author should enlist attention and command respect for what he says. In his *Democracy of Christianity*,[1] vol. 2d, page 197, he thus writes:

[1] William Goodell, *The Democracy of Christianity*, 2 vols. (New York, 1849).

And what is this pride of wealth, after all, growing up into the aristocracy of wealth, the usurpations of wealth, the oppressions of wealth, grinding the masses of humanity into the dust to-day, throughout our modern Christendom, in the middle of our nineteenth century civilization and progress, with a hoof more flinty, more swinish, and MORE MURDEROUS [capitals ours — G.F.] than that of semi-barbarous feudalism in its bloodiest days.

He understands the intolerable exploitation of capital better than we do, for he lives in a country where slavery has not stepped in to shield the laborer. He, the laborer, is a "slave without a master," and his oppressors, "cannibals all."

Mr. Goodell's book appears to us to carry the doctrine of human equality to a length utterly inconsistent with the power and control which ordinary Christian marriage gives to the husband over the wife; yet he assures us he is the unflinching friend of Christian marriage. The purity of his sentiments revolt at the conclusions to which his abstract doctrines inevitably lead. Yet his idea of Christian marriage may differ, so far as the power of the husband is concerned, widely from ours. We are sure he would do nothing, designedly, to impair the purity and sacredness of the relation.

Mr. Goodell is a Christian socialist, and looks to a proximate millennium to rectify the false relations of men and property in his own society, and to the arm of the Federal Government to set things right in the South. Why not leave all to Providence, especially since the right of the Government to abolish Southern slavery is denied by all respectable authority outside of abolition, and also by the Garrisonians, who are the most thorough-going of all abolitionists, and of all disorganizers. Mr. Goodell's plan of "rectifying human relations" at the North, by a millennium, is quite as common as that of Mr. Greeley, Andrews, and Owen, each of whom has discovered a new social science that they are sure will fit the world, because it won't fit a village.

We really think that a man of Mr. Goodell's nice sense of

justice and propriety should have hesitated long ere he invoked a God to do that which he would be ashamed to do himself. If it be wrong to strip the rich of their possessions, why hope or expect that God will perpetrate a wrong at which human conscience revolts when it is proposed to be done by human agency.

After an elaborate argument, to prove the advent of a millennial state of society, through the instrumentality of Christianity, Mr. Goodell, on page 510, vol. 2d, of his *Democracy of Christianity,* thus sums up and concludes:

> Glance over, again, the items included in these predictions: — The general and permanent prevalence of peace, — the result of justice, *equity*, SECURITY, and the actual *possession*, [italics his — G. F.] by each and every one of "his vine and fig tree" — that is, of soil sufficient to produce the needful fruits of the earth, or, in some way, a supply for his physical wants.
>
> Add to this, the general diffusion and great increase of knowledge, especially moral and religious knowledge, which includes the knowledge of social relations, duties and rights, — the knowledge that implies "wisdom," and that wisdom which begins with 'the fear of the Lord.' Next the application of all this knowledge, wisdom and fear of the Lord, to the concerns of civil government, insomuch that "the kingdoms of this world shall become the kingdoms of Christ," and the dominion be given to THE PEOPLE, who at that period, shall have become purified and instructed by him, — who shall all be righteous, who "shall all know the Lord, from the least to the greatest," and even "the feeble among them shall be as David." To this, add general contentment and enjoyment, facilities of social and international intercourse, the general prevalence of the spirit of benevolence and brotherly love, and the absence of those maddening and satanic temptations, delusions and prejudices, that have so long decieved, enslaved and embroiled the nations; — all this cemented by the true spiritual worship, protection, and love of the Common Father of all men.
>
> Is any thing wanting to complete the picture, and to ratify the assurance of a state of liberty, equality, common brotherhood, common interests, common sympathy, and common participancy in social rights, immunities, privileges, and arrangements? Must we need be told in addition to all this, that "the thrones of despotism shall be cast down," that the "beast" of civil and ecclesiastical tyranny and usurpation, the persecutor "of the holy apostles and people," shall be given "to

the burning flames," that the yoke of domination "shall be dashed into pieces as a potter's vessel," that "subversion" shall tread upon the heels of subversion, and one despotism overturn another, till He, "whose right it is, shall rule." That the masses shall be elevated, the exclusives brought low, that the "lofty" shall be "humbled," and the "haughty bowed down" — *in such a period of general possession, general justice, equality and contentment as has been already and previously described?*

Now, Mr. Goodell deplores that the condition of his society is so bad, that it becomes necessary to upset and reverse it by a millennium. Is not this, considering his high position and authority, strong evidence to prove "the failure of Free Society." We should add that his whole book teems with evidence of his uncompromising hostility to existing Church institutions, and the existing Priesthood, as abuses and interpolations that have been engrafted improperly on Christianity. He obviously belongs, in faith, to those early Christians, who resembled the Essenes in their social relations, and who daily expected the advent of the millennium. Their error in the last respect shows that it is the Bible, and not their construction of it, that should be our rule of faith and guide of conduct.

The next witness we call up is Gerrit Smith, a man who has a national reputation as an orator, a philanthropist, and a gentleman, who writes better than he speaks, and whose active charity and benevolence are only exceeded in the greatness of their amount by the grossness of their misapplication. He is a zealous Christian, yet edits, or did edit the *Progressive Christian*, which proposed to abolish Christianity as now understood. He builds churches to keep out the clergy, and heads Christian conventions to put down Christian institutions, and agrees with Wendell Phillips that the pulpit of the North stands in the way of reform — *et delenda est Carthago* [2] — the pulpit should be destroyed!

Like Mr. Goodell, he seems to look to an approaching millennium. But he is a man of restless activity and energy,

[2] "Carthage must be destroyed."

and of incalculable daring, and would put his shoulder to the wheel, and inaugurate the millennium at once. He assumes the responsibility, declares continually in speeches, lectures, and essays that land monopoly is an intolerable evil, that lands should be as common and as free for use to all, as air and water, and proposes to divide them at once. He is one of the largest owners of real estate at the North, and yet the most uncompromising agrarian in the world. His disinterestedness is only exceeded by his rashness and destructiveness:

> The mildest-manner'd man,
> That ever cut a throat or scuttled ship.

His amiableness of disposition and evenness of temper never desert him, because he has not to "screw his courage to the sticking-place." 'Tis always there. The "red right arm of Thundering Jove" could not shake his tenacity of purpose; and, in a case of conscience, he would let the world or the Union slide with equal equanimity:

> Si fractus illabitur [*sic*] orbis,
> Impavidum ferient ruinœ [*sic*]! [3]

He gives a forty thousand or so to Kansas emigrants from the North, because, as a gentleman, he feels it his duty to stick to his country, right or wrong; and abolitionists are *his* country. His gross eccentricities and intellectual aberrations are but the natural outgrowth of the social system which surrounds him, and which reminds him and every other ingenuous and candid mind,

> That whatever is, is *wrong!*

He is only seemingly eccentric and erratic. He feels the difficulty of disposing of his immense wealth without making it an engine of oppression and exaction. He understands the theory of capital and labor, as his speeches show — knows

[3] "Were the vault of heaven to break and fall upon him, its ruins would smite him undismayed." Horace, *Odes*, III, iii, 7–8.

that labor produces everything, and that capital is the whip that forces it to work, and also the exploitator that robs it of most of the proceeds of its industry. "La propriété c'est le vol!" [4] he sees is true, save in the impurity of motive which it seems to attribute to its owners. If he endows colleges, or gives his money in large sums to individuals, in the one case it is used to rear up exploitators, who rob labor by professional skill, and in the other, to those who use it at once as an engine of exaction and oppression. If he gives it in smaller sums to the poor, he is generally giving to the idle the labor of the industrious, and offering a premium to continued idleness; for he can neither control the conduct nor expenditure of his beneficiaries. He is too good, and too proud, to spend his income in pomp and luxury. Too good thus to waste the proceeds of labor (as all public or private luxury does) and thus increase the burdens of the working class. Too proud to derive reflected importance and standing from extraneous glitter and costly show and equipage. He has (no doubt, in vain) attempted to ameliorate the condition of a great many slaves, by purchasing them and emancipating them. Could he retain them as slaves, he might see that his charity was not misapplied, by educating them and controlling their conduct. To us, it occurs that a large capital can only be safely invested in slaves and lands, if the owner wishes to be sure that it shall not be used as an engine of oppression, or as a persuasive to idleness and dissipation.

We should do injustice to Mr. Smith were we not to add that he is quite as busy in abducting negroes as in buying them. The underground railroad is one of his favorite pets and beneficiaries. His restless energy is not satisfied with the slow proceedings of this road, and hence he buys negroes, as well as aids the abducting of them. He has been severely censured for buying them by those whom he supplies with the means to steal them, or whom he rescues from the fangs

[4] "Property is theft."

of the law, when caught in abortive efforts to abduct them.

He had the education and has the feelings and bearing of the Southerner. His father owned slaves and a territory full of Indians, and he was reared as playmate and prince in their midst; hence, he has the proud humility of the Southerner, not the exacting and supercilious arrogance of the Northerner. He does not demand deference and respect, because it has, from boyhood, been yielded to him, as his due, by admitted inferiors.

The value of his testimony, establishing, if true, the utter and entire failure of free society, cannot be overestimated. He is learned, candid, honest, well-informed, and has always lived in free society. Its subversion, which he proposes, and actively attempts, would strip him of millions of wealth. He is the leading champion of slave abolition, and, by admitting the failure of free society, blunts and neutralizes all his arguments against slavery. In every way, then, pride of opinion, seeming consistency, and pecuniary interest tempt him to extol, not to condemn free society. It is true, he thinks slavery also a failure, and a greater failure; but he knows little practically about slave society, and cannot admit for us, although he may for himself and his section. — *En passant*, we would say to him, that air and water are the subjects of more exclusive appropriation in free society than land. — He is a lawyer, and knows that the ownership of the soil carries with it the ownership of everything, *ad inferos, et usque ad cœlum.* In fact, in cities where the poor most do congregate, their food and raiment differ not half so much from that of the rich as their enjoyment of pure air and water. Men must get a place to breathe and drink from; and all places are appropriated.

Yes, Mr. Smith, you are vainly trying to grasp The Right! The Right is connected with, affected by, and affects all the Past, all the Present, and all the Future. God knows the Right — man only the Expedient.

Our next witness is Horace Greeley, Editor of the Tribune,

and Napoleon of the Press. His first distinction was won by his espousing and elaborately propagating the Social Philosophy of Charles Casimir Fourier. This he did, some twenty years since, in a long controversy with the *Courier & Enquirer*, the latter paper sustaining the conservative side. The correspondence was afterwards published in book form, and we regret that we have not been able to possess ourselves of a copy. The whole edition, we learn, was burnt at the Harpers'. Consigned by Providence, not by a human censor, to the flames. Should we misrepresent our witness, it will be because we have tried in vain to get this book. We think he was the first, in America, to assert, and maintain by arguments and proofs, the inadequacy and injustice of the whole social and governmental organization at the North. He, not ourselves, is the American author of the theory of the Failure of Free Society. His remedies, though not as radical and scientific as those of Proudhon and Mr. Andrews, did very well for a beginning. He, we think, proposed at once to coop mankind up in Phalansteries, where, in a few generations, all the distinctions of separate property, and of separate wives and children, would be obliterated and lost, and society would gradually and gently be fused and crystalized into a system of pure and perfect Communism. The *Tribune* has to minister to a variety of tastes, all agreeing in their destructive tendencies, but differing widely as to the manner in which they shall attain their conclusions; hence, it is hard to deduce any well defined system of philosophy from its columns. Mr. Andrews intimates that our witness is no philosopher at all. Be it so. Yet all must admit that no man of the age has the organ or faculty of Destructiveness so fully developed. The *Tribune* has been, from the time of the controversy of which we have spoken, to the present day, the great Organ of Socialism, of Free Love, and of all the other Isms which propose to overthrow and rebuild society and government, or to dispense with them altogether. Steadily pursuing this destructive course, the *Tribune* has for years become the most popular paper in the North, and, 'tis said, has more readers in Europe and America than any paper in the world; and yet its only peculiar thought, its whole intellectual, moral, social, and political stock in trade, consists of the one idea, variously expressed, illustrated and enforced, "The Failure of Free Society"; or, as Carlyle phrases it, "We must have a new world, if we are to have any world at all."

What a striking illustration of our theory that "a mere verbal formula often distinguishes a truism from a paradox." *We* assert a theory bluntly and plainly, and attempt to prove it by facts and arguments, and the world is ready to exclaim, "Oh, what shocking heresy." Mr. Greeley, for twenty years, maintains the same theory, in different language, and elicits the admiration and gratitude of the world. Oh, *Le Pauvre Peuple*! how long will it permit its flatterers to deceive and betray it? Mr. Greeley and ourselves agree in our destructive philosophy, but are wide asunder as the poles in what is constructive. Each proposes to protect the weak. He promises "protection without control or abridgment of liberty." We tell those who ask for or require protection and support that "they must submit to be controlled, for that the price of security has ever been, and ever will be, the loss of liberty."

The popularity of the *Tribune* shows that the world is prepared to upset existing social systems. When that is done, it will have to choose between Free Love and Slavery, between more of government and no government. We think, like Carlyle, more of government is needed. We, too, are a Socialist (for free society), but we would screw up the strings of society, not further relax them, much less cut them "sheer asunder"!

We wish to display the truth, and nothing but truth, to the public, on the subjects of Abolition and Socialism; and, for fear of misrepresentation, have written letters to Mr. Greeley and Mr. Garrison, copies of which we shall append to this chapter. Should they be silent, the letters will at least show our solicitude to arrive at truth.

We have written enough about Mr. Andrews, and quoted enough from his book already, to show that he is the great philosopher of his party, and the comprehensive and truthful expositor of its doctrines, its tendencies, and ultimate results. His co-laborers, less scientific and far-sighted than he, might be ready to exclaim on reading his book, "Thinkest thou they servant a dog, that he shall do this thing!" But Mr. Andrews is right. To this complexion must they come at last. A plunge into the soft and sensual waters of the lake of Free Love — then a sudden and violent exit into the keen and shivering atmosphere of despotism.

We know less of Mr. Garrison than of either of the other gentlemen. He heads the extreme wing of the Socialist, Infidel, Woman's-Right, Agrarian and Abolition party, who are called Garrisonians. He edits the *Liberator*, which is conducted with an ability worthy of a better cause. He and his followers seem to admit that the Bible and the Constitution recognize and guarantee Slavery, and therefore denounce both, and propose disunion and no priests or churches as measures to attain abolition. Mr. Garrison usually presides at their meetings, and we infer, in part, their principles and doctrines, from the materials that compose those meetings. A Wise-Woman will rise and utter a philippic against Marriage, the Bible, and the Constitution — and will be followed by negro Remond, who "spits upon Washington," and complains of the invidious distinction of calling whites Anglo-Saxons, and negroes Africans. And now, Phillips arises,

> Armed with hell-flames and fury,

and gently begins, in tones more dulcet, and with action more graceful than Belial, to

> Pour the sweet milk of concord into hell!
> Uproar the universal peace —
> Destroy all unity on earth.

Then Mr. Parker will edify the meeting by stirring up to bloody deeds in Kansas or in Boston — in which, as becomes his cloth, he takes no part — and ends by denouncing things in general, and the churches and parsons in particular. And, probably, the whole will conclude with a general indulgence and remission of sins, from Mr. Andrews, who assumes, for the nonce, the character of Father Confessor, and assures the tender conscience that it is right and incumbent to take the oath to sustain the Constitution with the deliberate purpose of violating it, because such oaths are taken under moral duress. These Garrisonians are as intellectual men as any in the nation. They lead the Black Republican party, and control the politicians. Yet are they deadly enemies of Northern as well as of Southern institutions.

Now, gentlemen, all of you are philosophers, and most zealous philanthropists, and have for years been roaring, at the top of your voice, to the Oi Polloi rats, that the old crazy edifice of society, in which they live, is no longer fit for human dwelling, and is imminently dangerous. The rats have taken you at your word, and are rushing headlong, with the haste and panic of a *sauve qui peut*,[5] into every hole that promises shelter — into "any port in a storm." Some join the Rappists and Shakers; thousands find a temporary shelter in Mr. Greeley's Fourierite Phalansteries; many more follow Mr. Andrews to Trialville, to villages in the far West, or to Modern Times; [6] and a select few to the saloons of Free Love; and hundreds of thousands find shelter with Brigham Young, in Utah; whilst others, still more frightened, go to consult the Spiritual Telegraph, that raps hourly at the doors of heaven and of hell, or quietly put on their ascension robes to accompany Parson Miller in his upward flight. But the greater number are waiting (very impatiently) for Mr. Andrews to establish his New

[5] "Let him save himself who can."

[6] "Modern Times" was a free-love and free-thought settlement established on Long Island in 1851 by the philosophical anarchist, Josiah Warren.

and Better World, or for Mr. Garrison and Mr. Goodell to inaugurate their Millennium.

Why, Gentlemen! none of these worse than Cassandra vaticinations – why none of this panic, terror, confusion, and flight in Slave Society? Are we suffering, and yet contented? Is our house tumbling about our heads, and we sitting in conscious security amidst the impending ruin? No! No! Our edifice is one that never did fall, and never will fall; for Nature's plastic hand reared it, supports it, and will forever sustain it.

Have we not shown, in this single chapter, that the North has as much to apprehend from abolition as the South, and that it is time for conservatives everywhere to unite in efforts to suppress and extinguish it?

We add hereto a letter we addressed to the public as to "Our Trip to the North," and our reply to a Mr. Hogeboom, a New York abolitionist. Also, our letters to Garrison and Greeley. We do this to show that we intend not to mislead, misrepresent, or deceive. In truth, the leading Abolitionists are our pets and favorites. We have an inveterate and perverse penchant of finding out good qualities in bad fellows. Robespierre and Milton's Satan are our particular friends.

---

## MY TRIP TO THE NORTH

*To the Editors of the* Enquirer:

GENTLEMEN, – I hesitated long before resolving to address you this letter. I feel that I shall be amenable to the charge of egotism; but I have written a book, in which I undertake to defend and justify Slavery, and to advise the South as to its future policy. In that I am egotistical, as everyone is who writes a book. I have "stepped in so far, that returning were more tedious than go o'er." I will not do things by halves. When I wrote that book, I believed that Government, Law, Religion, and Marriage were victims bound and filleted for sacrifice by Northern abolition. What was then matter of doubtful opinion, inference and speculation, has become, since my trip to the North, subject of fixed faith and conviction. I enjoyed the warm and elegant hospitality of some of the Liberty party of the North. I was in social intercourse with many of them. I have received many pamphlets, books and speeches from them. I have no private confidences to betray, because I heard no secrets. This party is conscientious, believes itself right, and courts discussion and notoriety. I, besides, conversed freely with strangers, in public conveyances and at hotels. I think, with my previous study on the subject of Slavery and Abolition, I may be able to make some useful suggestions to the South and the North.

It seemed to me that in attempting to prove "Free Society a failure" in my lecture at New Haven, I was "but carrying coals to New Castle." The Liberty party, at least, discovered that long before I did, and are as intent on subverting and reconstructing society at home as on abolishing slavery with us. A part of them, I will not undertake to say how large a portion, are infidels, who find the Bible no impediment to their schemes of social reform, because they assert that it is false. This wing of the Liberty party is in daily expectation of discovering a new Social Science, that will remedy all the ills that human flesh is heir to. They belong to the schools of Owen, Louis Blanc, Fourier, Comte, and the German and French Socialists and Communists. The other wing, and probably the most numerous wing of the party, is composed of the Millennial Christians – men who expect Christ, either in the flesh or in the spirit, soon to reign on earth; the lion to lie down with the lamb; every man to sit down under his own vine and fig tree; all to have an interest in lands; marrying and giving in marriage to cease; war to be abolished, and peace and good will to reign among men. They are as intent on abolishing all Church government and authority, as the infidels. They would, equally with them, trample on all law and government, because "liberty is," say they, "an inalienable right," and law, religion, and government continue to protect slavery. Marriage, Christian marriage, which requires the obedience of the wife, is slavery; and they would modify it, or destroy it. Land monopoly, they say, gives to property or capital a greater power over labor than masters have over slaves; hence, they very wisely and logically conclude that land, like air and water, should be common property.

The Liberty party is composed of very able men – of philosophers and philanthropists. They have demonstrated, beyond a doubt, that slavery is necessary, unless they can get up a Millennium or discover a new Social Science. The increasing crime and poverty of mankind, and the utter failure of all social experiments like those of Owen and others, indicate neither the advent of the one, nor the discovery of the other.

This Liberty party are the best allies of the South, because they admit, and continually expose, the utter failure of Free Society.

One of the most distinguished of this party thus writes to Wendell Phillips, Esq.: "I cannot refrain from expressing, in this connection, my grief that many abolitionists have allowed their faith in the Bible to be shaken."

In my short trip to the North, I was struck with nothing so much as the avowed infidelity of many, and the Christianity melting into infidelity of the great mass of the balance with whom I conversed. I have no doubt, however, that although such a state of things is too common at the North, yet my peculiar associations made the evil appear greater than it really is. The religious and conservative, like the lily of the valley, are silent and secluded. As a specimen of this religion melting, as I think, into infidelity, I will give another extract from the letter to Wendell Phillips:

> You have been much censured for holding that the anti-slavery cause can reach success only over the ruins of the American government and the American church. Nevertheless, you are right. The religion which

tolerates — nay, sanctifies — slavery, must necessarily be conquered ere the devotees and dupes of that religion will suffer slavery to be abolished. Again, so long as the actual government is on the side of slavery, the bloodless abolition of slavery is impracticable.

The author of the letter from which I quote and Mr. Phillips to whom it is addressed are gentlemen, scholars, and Christians. They are, besides, historical characters. We violate no privacy in holding up their opinions to public view and general criticism. Is their's not Christianity melting into infidelity? I have lately received a book, in two volumes, entitled *The Democracy of Christianity*, from its author – William Goodell of New York, a member of the Liberty Party. The author evinces much ability, ingenuity, and research. He is one of the millennial Christians – obviously pious and sincere. He sees no exodus from the appalling evils of Free Society, except that state of perfect equality, peace, happiness, and security, that he, like the men of Cromwell's day, thinks is promised and predicted in the Bible. I cite the following passage from the conclusion of his work:

> Glance over again the items included in these predictions: — The general and permanent prevalence of peace — the result of justice, equity, security, and the actual possession, by each and every one, of "his vine and fig tree," i.e. of soil sufficient to produce the needful fruits of the earth, or in some way, a supply of his physical wants.

If this state of things ever occurs, God will bring it about without the help of abolitionists.

We do not deem it necessary to quote from the infidel agrarians and abolitionists, because their splendid promises and bloody and disastrous failures, have been matters of every day's history and of every day's occurrence, from the times of Marat and the guillotine to those of Lamartine and Cavaignac.

The Proletariat of France, the nomadic Pauper Banditti of England, the starving tenantry of Ireland, the Lazzaroni of Italy, and the half-savages of Haiti, are the admitted results of practical abolition. But, say the Liberty party, abolition has stopped half-way; abolish churches, law, government, marriage, and separate property in lands, and then the scheme will work charmingly.

Well, possibly it will; but as we are very happy, comfortable, and contented in slave society, suppose you try the *experimentum in vile corpus.*[7] Begin at home, and if the experiment works well, we of the South will follow your example. You have a little Eden now near Lake Oneida. Some hundreds of Oneida perfectionists, living in primitive simplicity, among whom there is no "marrying or giving in marriage," no separate property, all things enjoyed in common; and we suppose, neither priest nor officer to disturb or mar the harmony of millennial society. "We but tell the tale as 'twas told to us." Does it work well? If so, why not form all your institutions on that model?

You of the Liberty party seem to think that "passional attraction" and "attractive labor" will keep all men up to their duties, and dispense with the necessity of Church and State, Law and Religion, Priest and Officer. You think you follow nature, but in truth you are superficial observers of nature. Man, it is true, is a social and gregarious animal, but like all animals of that kind, he is, by nature, law-making and law-abiding. The ants and bees are ruled by despotic and exacting governments, and by laws and regulations, wise and less changeable than those of the Medes and Persians. But man is not only a law-making animal, but a religious one also. In remitting him to a state of anarchy and infidelity, you would not remit him to a state of nature, but one of continuous, exterminating warfare, such as France witnessed during the reign of terror.

I find, Messrs. Editors, that I am somewhat wandering from the subject with which I commenced, and will conclude — for the present, at least.

Very respectfully, your ob't serv't.

G. F.

[7] "Experiment on a worthless body."

## LETTER TO MR. HOGEBOOM

*Port Royal, Va.*, Jan. 14th, 1856.

To A. Hogeboom, Esq., Sheds Corners, Madison County, N. Y.

Dear Sir: — Your letter reached this office during my absence from home. I embrace the earliest opportunity of replying to it, because I rejoice that public attention at the North may, by this means, be excited to the subject of my book. I am sure I should not have been honored with your correspondence had you read the book and known its subject. That subject is the "Failure of Free Society." You have only read extracts from it, you say, in the Northern papers. Those papers will be slow to notice the facts, authorities, and admissions which it cites to prove the failure of their form of society. I send you the book and refer you particularly to the preface, to the second and third chapters, and to the "summing up" in the concluding chapter.

If this does not satisfy you that free society is a cruel failure, read the history of the English Poor Laws, and you will find that the laboring class of England have, every day since the emancipation of the villeins, been in a worse condition, morally and physically, than any slaves ever were. Read, also, two articles, the one in the *North British Review*, and the other in *Blackwood* for December, depicting the demoralized and starving condition of the whole laboring class of Great Britain. Read, also, Carlyle's *Latter-Day Pamphlets*. If this does not convince you that the *Little Experiment* (for it is a very little one, both in time and space) is a disastrous and cruel failure, look at home! How comes it that your distinguished neighbor, Gerrit Smith, proposes to make land as free for the enjoyment of all as air and water? Confessedly, because the despotism of capital over labor is *intolerable*. Confessedly, because your form of society is found to be a failure in practice! Why does another distinguished abolitionist, Mr. Goodell of New York, in his book, on the Democracy of Christianity, declare that wealth now is more cruel, oppressive, and *murderous*, than Feudal masters? Why does Mr. Greeley advocate the doctrines of Fourier, and propose to subvert your society and reconstruct it from top to bottom, making a sort of common property of women and children, as well as of lands and houses? Why does, much your ablest philosopher, Stephen Pearl Andrews, propose plans of reform still more sweeping? And, why are his doctrines popular with the "higher classes" in New York? Why, in fine, are the larger number of the abolitionists, millennial Christians, in daily expectation of the advent of Christ, who is to divide all property equally, and give to each one his "vine and fig tree"? And why are the others, Atheists, like Owen and Fourier, attempting to invent new and better forms of society?

Why have you Bloomer's and Women's Right's men, and strong-minded women, and Mormons, and anti-renters, and "vote myself a farm" men, Millerites, and Spiritual Rappers, and Shakers, and Widow Wakemanites, and Agrarians, and Grahamites, and a thousand other superstitious and infidel Isms at the North? Why is there faith in nothing, speculation about everything? Why is this unsettled, half-demented state of the human mind coextensive in time and space with free society? Why is Western Europe now starving? And why has it been fighting and starving for seventy years? Why all this, except that free society is a failure? Slave society needs no defence till some other permanently practicable form of society has been discovered. None such has been discovered. Nobody at the North who reads my book will attempt to reply to it; for all the learned abolitionists had unconsciously discovered and proclaimed the failure of free society long before I did.

I am indebted for the honor of your correspondence, to your ignorance of what my book contains. I reply through the Press, because I intend to use your letter merely as an occasion to challenge the North, to dispute or deny my assertion that "free society is a failure!"

In conclusion, I propose to you, and through you to the whole North, these questions.

Do not the past history and present condition of Free Society in Western Europe (where alone the experiment has been fully tried,) prove that it is attended with greater evils, moral and physical, than Slave Society?

Do not the late writers on society in Western Europe, and in our free States, generally admit that those evils are intolerable, and that Free Society requires total subversion and re-organization?

Should you not, therefore, abolish your form of society, and adopt ours, until Mr. Greeley, or Brigham Young, or Mr. Andrews, or Mr. Goodell, or some other socialist of Europe or America, invents and puts into successful practice, a social organization better than either, or until the millennium does actually arrive?

With the assurance that I am quite as intent on abolishing Free Society as you are on abolishing slavery, and with the confidence that all of divine authority and almost all of human authority is on my side, I remain, your co-philanthropist, and

Obedient servant,

GEO. FITZHUGH.

---

### LETTER TO MR. GARRISON

*Port Royal, Va.*, July 18, 1856.

DEAR SIR — I am about to publish a work entitled *Cannibals All; or, Slaves Without Masters.* I shall, in effect, say, in the course of my argument, that every theoretical abolitionist at the North is a Socialist or Communist, and proposes or approves radical changes in the organization of society. I shall cite Mr. Greeley, Mr. Goodell, S. P. Andrews, Gerrit Smith, yourself, and other distinguished and leading abolitionists, of both sexes, as proof of my assertion. I shall also endeavor to show that all the literary mind of Western Europe concurs with you. You, I perceive, have read a work already written by me, and will not mistake my object. We live in a dangerous crisis, and every patriot and philanthropist should set aside all false delicacy in the earnest pursuit of truth. I believe Slavery natural, necessary, indispensable. You think it inexpedient, immoral, and criminal. Neither of us should withhold any facts that will enable the public to form correct opinions. Should you not reply to this letter, I shall publish a copy of it in my book, and insist that your silence is an admission of the truth of my charges. I regret that your very able paper reaches me irregularly.

Your obedient servant,

GEO. FITZHUGH.

LLOYD GARRISON, Esq., Boston, Mass.

---

### LETTER TO MR. GREELEY

*Port Royal, Va.*, July 20, 1856.

DEAR SIR — I am writing a work entitled *Cannibals All; or, Slaves Without Masters.* I shall state, as a matter of fact, that all theoretical abolitionists assert the failure of free society, and each proposes some plan for its reorganization. I shall cite particularly yourself, Gerrit Smith, S. P. Andrews, Mr. Goodell, and Mr. Garrison. I shall rely on your discussion with the *Courier* and *Enquirer*, which has been burnt, chiefly as my proof of your opinion.

I wish to afford you, and other distinguished gentlemen, an opportunity of correcting me if I have come to erroneous conclusions. I have, therefore, written to Mr. Garrison, and I now write to you, to afford you an opportunity to correct me if I am wrong. I know you all think our society a greater failure than your own; but you can *admit* for yourselves, not for us. I shall publish a copy of this letter in my book if you do not reply, and possibly if you reply, both this letter and your answer.

'Tis not possible that our two forms of society can long coexist. All Christendom is one republic, has one religion, belongs to one race, and is governed by one public opinion. Social systems, formed on opposite principles, cannot co-endure.

With much respect,
Your obedient servant,
GEO. FITZHUGH.

Before parting with our "Masters in the Art of War," we must abate a little of the honors we have lavished on them. We have said that they discovered and proclaimed the failure of Free Society before we did. So they did; but they mistook it for the failure of all society. Their little world of Western Europe and Yankeedom was, in their eyes, the whole world. Hence, exclaims Mr. Carlyle, "We must have a new world, if we are to have any world at all." And Andrews takes up the cry, all the North joins in chorus, and sends the sad knell echoing back to Europe. Not so fast, gentlemen. Your world is not one-tenth of the whole world, and all is peace, quiet, and prosperity outside of it. We of the South, and all slave countries, want no new world.

Now we were the first to discover and proclaim that Free Society *alone* had failed, and failed because it was free. We occupied vantage ground, a good standpoint, saw both forms of society, and thus discovered what our masters had overlooked. Everybody sees it now, and gives us no more credit for the discovery, than his cotemporaries gave Columbus – *At mihi plaudo*!

> ITALIAM! primus conclamat Achates;
> Italiam, cœto [*sic*] socii clamore salutant.[8]

[8] "Italy! first Achates shouts aloud; Italy the crews hail with joyful cry." *Aeneid*, III, 523–524.

# XI

# DECAY OF ENGLISH LIBERTY, AND GROWTH OF ENGLISH POOR LAWS

Blackstone, whose Commentaries have been, for half a century, a common school-book, and whose opinions on the rise, growth, and full development of British liberty are generally received as true, as well in America as in Europe, maintains a theory the very opposite of that for which we are about to contend.

He holds that the appearance of the House of Commons, about the reign of Henry the Third, was the dawn of approaching liberty. We contend that it was the origin of the capitalist and moneyed interest government, destined finally to swallow up all other powers in the State, and to bring about the most selfish, exacting, and unfeeling class despotism. He thinks the emancipation of the serfs was another advance towards equality of rights and conditions. We think it aggravated inequality of conditions, and divested the liberated class of every valuable, social, and political right. A short history of the English Poor Laws, which we shall annex, will enable the reader to decide between us on this head. He thinks the Reformation increased the liberties of the subject. We think that, in destroying the noblest charity fund in the world, the church lands, and abolishing a priesthood, the efficient and zealous friends of the poor, the Reformation tended to diminish the liberty of the mass of the people, and to impair their moral, social, and physical well-being. He thinks that the Revolution, by increasing the power of the House of Commons, and lessening the prerogative of the Crown, and the influence of the Church, promoted liberty. We think the Crown and the Church the natural friends, allies, and guardians of the laboring class; the House of Commons, a moneyed firm, their natural enemies; and that the Revolution was a marked epoch in the steady decay of British liberty.

He thinks that the settlement of 1688 that successfully asserted in theory the supreme sovereignty of Parliament, but particularly the supreme sovereignty of the House of Commons, was the consummation or perfection of British liberty. We are sure that that settlement, and the chartering of the Bank of England which soon succeeded it united the landed and moneyed interests, placed all the powers of government in their hands, and deprived the great laboring class of every valuable right and liberty. The nobility, the church, the king were now powerless; and the mass of the people, wholly unrepresented in the government, found themselves exposed to the grinding and pitiless despotism of their natural and hereditary enemies. Mr. Charles Dickens, who pities the condition of the negro slaves, thus sums up, in a late speech, the worse condition of the "Slaves Without Masters" in Great Britain: "Beneath all this, is a *heaving* mass of poverty, ignorance, and crime." Such is English liberty for the masses. Thirty thousand men own the lands of England, three thousand those of Scotland, and fewer still those of Ireland. The great mass of the people are cut off from the soil, have no certain means of subsistence, and are trespassers upon the earth, without a single valuable or available right. Contrast their situations with that of the old villeins, and see then whether our theory of British liberty and the British constitution be true, or that of Blackstone.

All writers agree there were no beggars or paupers in England until the liberation of the serfs; and moreover admit that slaves, in all ages and in all countries, have had all their physical wants sufficiently supplied. They also concur in stating that crime was multiplied by turning loose on society a class of men who had been accustomed to and still needed the control of masters.

Until the liberation of the villeins, every man in England had his appropriate situation and duties, and a mutual and adequate interest in the soil. Practically the lands of England were the common property of the people of England. The old Barons were not the representatives of particular classes in Parliament, but the friends, and faithful and able representatives of all classes; for the interests of all classes were identified. Monteil,[1] a recent French author, who has written the most accurate and graphic description of social conditions during the Feudal ages, describes the serfs as the especial pets and favorites of the Barons. They were the most dependent, obedient, and useful members of the feudal society, and like younger children, became favorites. The same class now constitute the Proletariat, the Lazzaroni, the Gypsies, the Parias, and the Pauper Banditti of Western Europe, and the Leperos of Mexico. As slaves, they were loved and protected; as pretended freemen, they were execrated and persecuted.

Mr. Lester, a New York abolitionist, after a long and careful observation and study of the present condition of the English laboring class, solemnly avers, in his *Glory and Shame of England*,[2] that he would sooner subject his child to Southern slavery, than have him to be a free laborer of England.

But it is the early history of the English Poor Laws that proves most conclusively that the liberation of the villeins was a sham and a pretence and that their situation has been worse, their rights fewer, and their liberties less, since emancipation than before. The Poor Laws, from the time of Edward the Third to that of Elizabeth, were laws to punish the poor, and to keep them at work for low wages. Not till

[1] Probably Amans-Alexis Monteil, who published social studies of French history during the middle ages and later.

[2] Charles Edwards Lester, *The Glory and Shame of England*, 2 vols. (London, 1841).

late in the reign of Elizabeth was any charitable provision made for them. Then, most of them would have starved, as the confiscation and sales of the church lands had deprived them of their only refuge, but for the new system of charity. The rich must have labor, and could not afford to let them *all* starve, although they were ready to attempt the most stringent means to prevent their increase.

In the *Edinburgh Review*, October, 1841, on Poor Law Reform, we find the following admirable history and synopsis of the English Poor Laws:

The great experiment of Poor Law amendment, which has now for seven years been in progress among our southern neighbors, appears to us to have been insufficiently attended to, and therefore to have been imperfectly understood in this part of the island. We do not believe that many of our Scottish readers are fully aware of the origin of the English Poor Laws, of the changes which they underwent, of the abuses which they created, of the remedy which has been applied; or of the obstacles which have diminished the success of that great measure, and now threaten its efficiency. And yet these are subjects of the deepest interest, even to those who study legislation merely as a science. A series of laws are exhibited, persevered in for centuries, by a nation always eminent for practical wisdom; of which the result has almost invariably been failure, or worse than failure; which in scarcely a single instance have attained their objects, and in most cases have produced effects precisely opposite to the intentions of their framers;—have aggravated whatever they were intended to prevent. From us, as Scotchmen, they merit peculiar attention, not only from the resemblance of our poor laws to the earlier English statutes; but from the probability that, as the connection between the two countries becomes more intimate, we shall at no distant period follow the example, whatever it may be, of the larger country to which we are united; and participate in the evils and advantages of the system which she may finally adopt. This fate already threatens Ireland. It is scarcely probable that Scotland can avoid it.

Each of the subjects to which we have alluded, would require a volume for its complete development; but we are constrained to give to them such consideration as is admissible within the limits of an article of moderate length.

The Committee of the House of Commons which considered the Poor Laws in 1817, commence their able Report by stating, that "the principle of a compulsory provision for the impotent, and for setting to work the able-bodied, originated, without doubt, in motives of the purest humanity." From this statement, plausible as it is, we utterly dissent. We believe that the English poor laws originated in selfishness, ignorance, and pride. Better motives, without doubt, though misdirected by almost equal ignorance, dictated the changes which were made in those laws during the 18th century — the fourth which elapsed from their commencement; but we are convinced that their origin was an attempt substantially to restore the expiring system of slavery. The evils of slavery are now understood; it is admited that it destroys all the nobler virtues, both moral and intellectual; that it leaves the slave without energy, without truth, without honesty, without industry, without providence; in short, without any of the qualities which fit men to be respected or even esteemed. But mischievous as slavery is, it has many plausible advantages, and freedom many apparent dangers. The subsistence of a slave is safe; he cannot suffer from insufficient wages, or from want of employment; he has not to save for sickness or old age; he has not to provide for his family; he cannot waste in drunkenness the wages by which they were to be supported; his idleness or dishonesty cannot reduce them to misery; they suffer neither from his faults nor his follies. We believe that there are few of our Highland parishes in which there is not more suffering from poverty than would be found in an equal Russian population. Again, the master thinks that he gains by being able to proportion the slave's subsistence to his wants. In a state of freedom, average wages are always enough to support, with more or less comfort, but still to support, an average family. The unmarried slave receives merely his own maintenance. A freeman makes a bargain; he asks whatever his master can afford to pay. The competition among employers forces them to submit to these terms; and the highly paid workman often wastes his extra wages in idleness and debauchery. And when employment is abundant; that is, when his services are most wanted, he often tries to better himself by quitting his master. All this is disagreeable to masters who have been accustomed to the apparent economy of servile labor, and to its lethargic obedience.

The great motive of the framers of the earlier English poor laws was to remedy the latter class of inconveniences; those which affect, or appear to affect the master. The motive of the framers of the later acts again, beginning with George I., was to remedy the first class of evils: those which affect the free laborer and his family.

The first set of laws were barbarous and unskillful, and their failure is evident from their constant re-enactment or amendment, with different provisions and severer penalties. The second set had a different fate — they ultimately succeeded, in many districts, in giving to the laborer and to his family the security of servitude. They succeeded in relieving him and those who, in a state of real freedom, would have been dependent on him, from many of the penalties imposed by nature on idleness, improvidence, and misconduct. And by doing this, they in a great measure effected, though certainly against the intentions of the legislature, the object which had been vainly attempted by the earlier laws. They confined the laborer to his parish; they dictated to him who should be his master; and they proportioned his wages, not to his services, but to his wants. Before the poor law amendment act, nothing but the power of arbitrary punishment was wanting in the pauperized parishes to a complete system of praedial slavery.

Our limits will not allow us to do more than to state very briefly the material parts of the numerous statutes, beginning by the statute of laborers, 23d Edward III., (1349) and ending by the 39th Eliz. cap. 4 (1597), which were passed for the supposed benefit of masters.

The 23d Ed. III. requires all servants to accept the wages which were usually given five or six years before, and to serve by the year, not by the day; it fixes a positive rate in many employments; forbids persons to quit the places in which they had dwelt in the winter, and search employment elsewhere in the summer; or to remove, in order to evade the act, from one county to another. A few years after, in 1360, the 34th Ed. III. confirmed the previous statute, and added to the penalties, which it imposed on laborers or artificers absenting themselves from their services, that they should be branded on the forehead with the letter F. It imposed also a fine of £10 on the mayor and bailiffs of a town which did not deliver up a laborer or artificer who had left his service.

Twenty-eight years after, in 1388, was passed the 12th Rich. II., which has generally been considered as the origin of the English poor laws. By that act the acts of Ed. III. are confirmed — laborers are prohibited, on pain of imprisonment, from quitting their residences in search of work, unless provided with testimonials stating the cause of their absence, and the time of their returning, to be issued by justices of the peace at their discretion. And, "because laborers will not, nor, for a long season, would not, serve without extrageous and excessive hire," prices are fixed for their labor; and punishments awarded against the laborer who receives more, and the master who gives more. Persons who have been employed in husbandry until twelve years of age, are prohibited from becoming artisans. Able-bodied beggars are to be treated as laborers wandering without passports. Impotent beggars are to remain where they are at the time of the proclamation of the act; or, if those places are unwilling or unable to support them, they are, within forty days, to repair to the places where they were born, and there dwell during their lives.

We have said that this act has been treated as the origin of the English poor laws. It has been so considered in consequence of the last clause, which is the first enactment recognizing the existence of the impotent poor. But this enactment makes no provision for them; though, by requiring them to be stationary in a given spot for the rest of their lives, it seems to assume that they would be supported there. It gives them, however, no claim, nor is there a clause in the whole act intended to benefit any persons except the employers of labor, and principally of agricultural labor — that is to say, the landowners who made the law. If the provisions of the act could have been enforced, the agricultural laborers, and they formed probably four-fifths of the population of England, though nominally free, would have been as effectually *ascripti glebae* [3] as any Polish serf. And, to make a nearer approximation to slavery, in the next year (1389), the 13th Rich. II. was passed; which directs the justices of every county to make proclamation every half year, at their discretion, according to the price of food, what wages every artificer and laborer shall receive by the day. This act, with some intervals, during which the legislature attempted itself to fix the prices of labor, remained substantially in force until the present century. A further attempt to reduce husbandry laborers to a hereditary caste of serfs, was made by the 7th Hen. IV. cap. 17 (1405), which, after reciting that the provisions of the former acts were evaded by persons apprenticing their children to crafts in towns — so that there is such a scarcity of husbandry laborers that *gentlemen* are impoverished — forbids persons not having 20s. a-year in land to do so, under penalty of a year's imprisonment.

It appears, however, that the laborers did not readily submit to the villenage to which the law strove to reduce them; for from this time the English statute book is deformed by the enactment against able-bodied persons leaving their homes, or refusing to work at the wages offered to them, or loitering, (that is to say, professing to be out of work,) which, to use the words of Dr. Burn, "make this part of English history look like the history of the savages in America. Almost all the severities have been inflicted, except scalping."[*] A new class of criminals, designated by the terms "sturdy rogues" and "vagabonds," was

[3] "Bound to the soil."

[*] *History of the Poor Laws*, p. 120.

created. Among these were included idle and suspect persons, living suspiciously.† Persons having no land or craft whereby they get their living.‡ Idle persons calling themselves serving-men, having no masters. Persons who, after having been sent home, absent themselves from such labor as they shall be appointed to.§ Able-bodied poor persons who do not apply themselves to some honest labor or other; or serve even for meat and drink, if nothing more is to be obtained.* Persons able to labor, not having land or master, nor using any lawful employment. Laborers using loitering, and refusing to work for reasonable wages.†

The first attempt on the part of a person dependent on his labor for his support to assert free agency, by changing his abode, or by making a bargain for his services, or even by refusing to work for "bare meat and drink," rendered him liable to be whipped and sent back to his place of birth, or last residence, for three years; or, according to some statutes, for one year, there to be at the disposal of the local authorities. The second attempt subjected him, at one time, to slavery for life, "to be fed on bread and water and refuse meat, and caused to work by beating, chaining, or otherwise;" and for the third, he was to suffer death as a felon.

We have seen that the 12th Rich. II. required the impotent poor to remain for life where they were found at the proclamation of the act, or at the places of their birth. The subsequent statutes require them to proceed either to their places of birth, or last places of residence, for three years. The law assumed, as we have already remarked, that they would be supported there by voluntary alms; and as respects the able-bodied, it assumed that an able-bodied slave, for such the laborer given up to the local authorities was, could always be made worth his maintenance; that maintenance being, of course, the lowest that could keep him in working order. It appears, however, that casual alms were found an insufficient, or an inconvenient provision for the impotent; that the local authorities were not sufficiently severe taskmasters of the able-bodied; and that the keeping them at work required some fund, by way of capital. The 27th Hen. VIII. cap. 25 (1536), therefore, requires the parishes to which the able-bodied should be sent, "to keep them to continual labor in such wise that they may get their own living by the continual labor of their own hands"; on pain that every parish making default shall forfeit twenty shillings a-month. It directs the

† 11 Hen. VII. cap. 2.
‡ 22 Hen. VIII. cap. 12.
§ 27 Hen. VIII. cap. 25.
* 1 Ed. VI. cap. 3.
† 3 and 4 Ed. VI. cap. 16; 14 Eliz. cap. 5; 30 Eliz. cap. 4.

churchwardens, and two others of every parish, to collect alms and broken meat, to be employed in supporting the impotent poor, and "setting and keeping to work the sturdy vagabonds"; and forbids other almsgiving, on pain of forfeiting ten times the amount. This is the first attempt at making charity legal and systematic; and it was obviously a part of the scheme for confining the laboring population to their own parishes. It seems to have been supposed that voluntary alms, systematically distributed, would provide wholly for the impotent, and form a fund which, aided by the fruits of their forced labor, would support the "sturdy vagabonds;" and, therefore, that no one could have an excuse for changing his residence.

In the early part of Elizabeth's reign was passed a statute, 5th Eliz. cap. 3 (1562), inflicting the usual penalties, whipping, slavery, and death, on sturdy vagabonds; that is to say, on those who, having no property but their labor, presumed to act as if they had a right to dispose of it; and containing the usual provisions for confining the impotent poor to their parishes. In one respect, however, it was a great step in advance; for it contains for the first time a provision enabling the justices to tax, at their discretion, those who refused to contribute to the relief of the impotent and the keeping at work the able-bodied. Concurrently with this statute, and indeed as a part of it, for it is the next chapter on the roll of parliament, was passed the 5th Eliz. cap. 4. This statute requires all persons brought up to certain specified trades, at that time the principal trades of the country, and not possessed of property, or employed in husbandry, or in a gentleman's service, to continue to serve in such trades; and orders that all other persons, between twelve years old and sixty, not being gentlemen, or students in a school or university, or entitled to property, and not engaged in maritime or mining operations, be compelled to serve in husbandry with any person that will require such person to serve, within the same county. Females, in corporate towns, between the ages of twelve and forty, and unmarried, are to be disposed of in service by the corporate authorities, at such wages, and in such sort and manner, as the authorities think meet. The hours of work are fixed by the statute; and the justices are, twice a-year, after "conferring together respecting the plenty or scarcity of the time," to fix the wages. Persons directly or indirectly paying more, are to be punished by imprisonment and fine; persons receiving more, by imprisonment. No person is to depart from one parish to another, or from one hundred or county to serve in another hundred or county, without a license from the local authorities.

When we recollect that disobedience to these enactments exposed a man or woman to be included in the proscribed class of vagabonds, punishable by whipping, branding, slavery, and death, it must be admitted that, whatever might be the practice, the *law* gave little freedom to the laboring classes.

The 14th Eliz. cap. 5, (1572) carried on the same legislation against the able-bodied, merely aggravating the penalty, by subjecting the offenders (that is, all persons who would not work for what the justices should think reasonable wages) to whipping and burning for the first offence, and to the penalties of felony for the second. It made a further approach to the present system, by directing the fund "for setting to work the rogues and vagabonds," and relieving the impotent, to be raised by a general assessment.

Twenty-five years afterwards, the two acts of the 39th Eliz. cap. 3 and 4, were passed, which for the first time divided into separate statutes the punishment of the able-bodied, and the relief of the impotent. By the second of these acts, vagabonds (including, we repeat, persons able to labor, having no lord or master, not using any lawful employments, and laborers refusing to work for common wages) are to be whipped, but not branded, and sent back to their parishes: if they appear to be such as will not be reformed, they are to be transported, or adjudged perpetually to the galleys.

The other act, the 39th Eliz. cap. 3, differs so slightly from the 43d Eliz. cap. 2 that it requires no further attention.

The 43d of Eliz. directs that the churchwardens and two or more householders, to be appointed by the justices, shall take order, with the consent of the justices, for setting to work children, and all persons having no means to maintain themselves, and using no ordinary or daily trade of life to get their living by; and to raise a fund by taxation of the inhabitants for such setting to work, and for the necessary relief of the lame, impotent, old, and blind poor not able to work. And the justices are directed to send to the House of Correction, or common jail, "such as shall not employ themselves to work, being appointed thereunto as aforesaid."

It appears from this statement, that the 43d of Elizabeth deserves neither the praise nor the blame which have been lavished on it. So far from having been prompted by benevolence, it was a necessary link in one of the heaviest chains in which a people calling itself free has been bound. It was part of a scheme prosecuted for centuries, in defiance of reason, justice, and humanity, to reduce the laboring classes to serfs, to imprison them in their parishes, and to dictate to them their employments and their wages. Of course, persons confined to certain districts by penalties of whipping, mutilation, and death, must be supported; and, if they were capable of labor, it was obvious that they ought to be made to contribute to the expense of their maintenance. Thence arose the provisions for relieving the impotent, and setting to work the able-bodied. But these provisions do not, on the other hand, deserve the censure passed on them by the Committee of the House of Commons in 1817. They were not of a nature to induce the industrious to relax their efforts. They held out no temptations to idleness. The able-bodied, who were the objects of the 43d Elizabeth, were those "who, having no means to maintain themselves, used no ordinary and daily trade of life to get their living by;" such persons were, by the previous acts, criminals; the work to which they were to be put was forced work; and if they did not employ themselves in it "being thereunto appointed as aforesaid," the justices were to commit them to jail. The industrious laborer was not within the spirit or the words or the act. This was, indeed, the complaint of Lord Hale: "The plaster," says his Lordship, "is not so large as the sore. There are many poor who are able to work if they had it, and had it at reasonable wages, whereby they might support themselves and their families. These are not within the provisions of the law.' ‡

And it was long before the legislature assented to any extension of the 43d Elizabeth. The 8th and 9th Will. III. cap. 30, passed nearly a century afterwards, "To the intent that the money raised *only* for the relief of *such as are impotent as well as poor*, may not be misapplied," requires all persons receiving relief, and their families, to wear a badge, containing a large Roman P, and the first letter of the name of the parish from which they received relief; the object being not, as has been supposed, to degrade the pauper, but to afford an easy means of detecting the overseer who had relieved an able-bodied person.

The oppressive legislation of the Plantagenets and Tudors was unsuccessful. The provisions on which its efficacy depended, namely, the regulation of wages by the justices, the punishment of those who refused to work for such wages, or who paid more than such wages, and the punishment of those who left their parishes without license, became gradually obsolete. Legally considered, they remained in force until the present century. Sir Frederic Eden has collected regulations of wages by the justices, from the 35th of Eliz. (1593) down to 1725. And the last which he gives, that regulating wages for the county of Lancaster in 1725, contains an exposition of the law by the justices, in the spirit of the times of Henry VIII. or Elizabeth: "That the transgressors may be inexcusable when punished, we, the said justices, publish these denunciations, penalties, punishments, and forfeitures which

‡ See Lord Hale's paper at length, in *Burn's History of the Poor Laws*, p. 144.

the statutes impose. No servant that hath been in service before, ought to be retained without a testimonial that he or she is legally licensed to depart, and at liberty to serve elsewhere, to be registered with the minister of the parish whence the servant departs. The master retaining a servant without such testimonial forfeits five pounds. The person wanting such testimonial shall be imprisoned till he procure it. If he do not produce one within twenty-one days, to be whipped as a vagabond. The person that gives more wages than is appointed by the justices shall forfeit five pounds, and be imprisoned ten days; the servant that takes more to be imprisoned twenty-one days. Every promise or gift whatever to the contrary shall be void. We, the said justices, shall make strict enquiries, and see the defaults against these ancient and useful statutes severely corrected and punished.

Free society is a recent and small experiment. The English Poor Laws and the English poor constitute its only history; for only in England has the experiment been made on a large scale for several centuries. If we have not proved its total and disastrous failure in England, in our *Sociology*, and in this chapter, we are resolved to prove it before we have done.

It is a favorite political maxim of Englishmen that taxation and representation should go hand in hand, and that none shall be taxed without their own consent. Yet in Great Britain, the working men, who pay every cent of tax, are not represented at all, have no vote in elections, and are taxed without and against their own consent; whilst the capitalist class, who pay no taxes, but, as Gerrit Smith truly says, are the mere conduits that pass them from the laborers to the government. This vampire capitalist class imposes all the taxes, and pays none. Alas! poor human nature! It is ever grasping at truth, and hugging itself.

# XII

# THE FRENCH LABORERS AND THE FRENCH REVOLUTION

Each of the many French revolutions was occasioned by destitution almost amounting to famine among the laboring classes. Each was the insurrection of labor against capital. But until the revolution of 1848, the revolutionists were unconscious alike of their motives and their objects. They believed, till then, that political changes would remedy the evils which oppressed them. After the revolution of 1830, philosophers and statesmen, seeing the inadequacy of change of dynasty or of political policy, to alleviate the distresses of the great working classes, began to search deeper for the causes of social embarrassment. Suddenly the discovery was made, not only in France, but throughout Western Europe, that the disease was social, not political. That it was owing to the too unequal distribution of capital, and to its exploitation of labor. The ablest minds saw, as well in England as in France, that in transferring the reins of government from the hands of hereditary royalty and nobility to those of the capitalist class that the people had exchanged a few masters for thousands of extortioners. Never did so vast a moral, intellectual, and social movement arise so suddenly, and spread so rapidly. The thing became the rage and fashion. Even in America, our Northern folks affected a disease, which they did not feel, just as Alexander's courtiers aped his wry neck; and anti-rentism and land monopoly became the constant theme of conversation, lectures, speeches, books, and essays. In France and in England, prior to 1830, there had been a few Socialists, such as Fourier and St. Simon, Owen and Fanny Wright — but they were little heeded, and generally considered about half crazy. Immediately thereafter, by far the greater portion of the literary mind of Europe imbibed, in whole or in part, the doctrines of these early Socialists. The infection soon reached the lower classes, and occasioned revolution, intended to be social as well as political, throughout Western Europe. The Provisional Government in France, which immediately succeeded to the expulsion of Louis Philippe, was composed entirely of Socialists, and its programme and attempted measures were thoroughly socialistic.

The subject of the condition of the laboring classes in Europe, and especially in France, was handled with an accuracy of detail and a breadth of scientific expression in a review of our own work in the *Literary Messenger* of March, 1855, of which we are incapable. The author, Professor Holmes of Virginia, is our corresponding acquaintance only. Informed by letter that he would review us, and that he concurred in the general truth of our theory, we suggested to him in reply that he should, from his vast stores of learning, strengthen our main positions. He thought the suggestion a good one, and fulfilled our request, with an ability and learning that no other man, on so short a notice, could have done. As we have prompted if not caused his toil, we make no apology for appropriating so much of his review as seems to be a reply to our suggestion:

From the principles as laid down in theory and exemplified in practice, we proceed to the effects. That religion has been undermined, morals contaminated, crime increased, misery extended, deepened, and multiplied, want and starvation augmented, society agitated, and orderly government endangered by the progress of the so-called prosperity of the free labor system, is evident, without further proof, to anyone who reads contemporary literature, who pays attention to the statements of newspapers, and of Poor Law Reports, who notes the cases brought before the police or criminal courts, or is cognizant from any source of information, of the actual condition of the multitude and of the poor in England, Scotland, Ireland, Germany, Prussia, and parts of Switzerland, and in New England and the Northern States. The connection of the results with the causes, is ably traced by Mr. Fitzhugh, but not with sufficient care, minuteness, and precision; and the actual character and enormity of the results is exhibited by him, and by an indefinite array of the most various and unexceptional testimony. The History of the Working Classes, by Robert du Var [*sic*],[1] which we have joined with the *Sociology for the South* as the text for the present observation, is full of evidence to this effect with regard to France; and for the other countries specified, ample testimony may be easily obtained. The Boston papers will suffice to illustrate the wretchedness of the laboring classes in New England: the *New York Herald* and *Tribune*, the works of Stephen Pearl Andrews, and of Greeley himself, will render the same service for the other Northern States; Alton Locke, Mary Barton, Mayhew's London Labor and the London Poor, the debates in Parliament, the Reports of the Poor Iaw Commissioners, and the English Reviews will amply illustrate the condition of Great Britain and Ireland; and for Germany, reference may be made to Hacklander's *Europarsches Sclavenleben*,[2] a work which has followed the example of *Uncle Tom's Cabin*, and portrayed the condition of the inferior classes in Europe as a much more legitimate object of European sympathy and consideration than American Slavery. Where the evidence is so abundant and voluminous, selection would be as unnecessary as it would be tedious. It is within the reach of everyone who desires to consult it; and we need not load our pages with extracts to prove what has been frequently and sufficiently proved before, and what is so notoriously true as to be undeniable. A few quotations to illustrate the condition of free labor societies we may indeed quote at a later period, in connection with a different division of the argument; but they are wholly unnecessary to confirm the allegation of the wretchedness and depravity which are consuming the vitals of the principal free societies of the Nineteenth Century. They are rendered still more unnecessary by the fact that the acceptability of Socialism in all of those communities, betrays the extent of both the misery and the social disease to be cured; and the confession of the multitude of recent writers on social topics, admits not merely the evils which we have specified, and their dependence on the theory and practice of free societies, but acknowledges also the truth of the general conclusion, that the free societies enumerated have unquestion-

[1] Du Var Robert, *Histoire de la Classe Ouvrière depuis l'esclave jusque au Prolétaire de nos Jour . . .*, 4 vols. (Paris, 1845–1846).

[2] F. W. Hackländer, *Europäisches Sclavenleben*, 4 vols. (Stuttgart, 1854).

ably failed, they have not produced the permanent or general blessings anticipated from them, they have produced overwhelming social disaster, multiplied indefinitely the woes and the vices of the poor, threatened all society and government and national existence in those communities, and announced a future so dark that little more than its gloom and spectral shapes can be distinctly recognized.

We regard Mr. Fitzhugh's employment of these admissions by European writers and Northern reformers, as constituting the most important position of his argument, and the most characteristic novelty in his defence of the South. The testimonies which he adduces are very strong and pointed, but they may be easily multiplied, and will gain an accession of strength from such multiplications. For years we have carefully collected similar acknowledgments from foreign writers, and cheerfully contribute them to the cause of the South, and the fortification of Mr. Fitzhugh's position. And let it be remembered, that neither in the *Sociology for the South*, nor in the quotations which will be shortly introduced here, is the sole or principal obligation due to Chartists, Socialists, Communists, or Agrarians of any sort. From such authors some admissions have been received, but the chief contributions are derived from those who have been the most strenuous supporters of past social arrangements, and who, notwithstanding a great diversity of views, abilities, studies, and opportunities of knowledge, still represent the sober conservative sense of their repsective communities. We regret that Mr. Fitzhugh should have extended so much countenance to the Socialists, and should have partially identified Socialism and Slavery, but the strongest part of his testimonies to the failure of free societies, is derived from other declarations than theirs, and we shall imitate his example.

We begin, however, with a Socialist, but almost the only one whom we shall summon to the stand:

"The French Revolution was an abortion. The trading classes (*la bourgeoisie*) organized themselves in the name of capital, and, instead of becoming a man, the serf became a prolétaire. What then was his situation? The most painful of all, the most intolerable which can be conceived. Like all the *prolétaires*, the trading classes had shouted: 'Liberty, Equality, Fraternity.' The result has been that every thing which was *prolétaire* — that is to say, all those who have no capital, groan under the most cruel usage (*exploitation*). They cannot be freemen, nor brothers, nor equals. Not free, because their daily bread depends on a thousand accidents produced and engendered by the competition of capitalists among themselves; not brothers, because, with hearts crushed and lacerated by the evils which overwhelm them, they cannot love those whose creed is so fatal to them; not equals, because capital being the supreme law, it is only through it that any participation or concurrence in social power is possible."*

An apology is due for not attempting to translate the term *prolétaires* in the above passage, but every one familiar with the condition of modern free societies, is aware that it is absolutely untranslatable. It is an indispensable word in modern times, and the impossibility of avoiding its use is a stronger proof of the failure of free societies, than the invention of the phrase Sociology, which Mr. Fitzhugh regards in this light. It ought to be unhesitatingly introduced into the English language; it can boast of a very respectable Latin descent; it occurs in the XII Tables, and originally signified a person of the lowest class, too poor to pay taxes, and unable to serve the State otherwise than by raising children and thus increasing the population † — a very doubtful service in modern Europe.

We return to Mr. Robert du Var [*sic*]:

"It must be remarked, that what is called pauperism, this sore, this ulcer, which infests, and more and more consumes the body social, could not exist in the same degree amongst the nations of antiquity. It is a phenomenon which could only arise as the consequence of the transformation of slavery into serfdom, and of serfdom into free labor (*prolétariat.*) * * * In antiquity, everyone, whether free or not, citizen or slave, was always connected with some center which ensured at least his material support.‡

"As a result of the individual liberty, independent of any central power, proclaimed by Christianity, favored and developed by the instincts of the Northern barbarians, legitimated and transformed into a social doctrine by the institution of Communes, was formed and agglomerated throughout Europe an innumerable population, having no material connection with the regular society, and having for itself nothing but the most naked liberty, that is to say, misery, poverty, isolation. Thence issued the poor, the beggars, the thieves — in one word, parias of every description, with whom society was compelled to compound, willingly or reluctantly, by the foundation of establishments intended to palliate the bleeding wound of the pauperism which had been engendered by liberty.§

"From whatever point the modern system is regarded, it seems impossible not to recognize that the Politico-economical rule of free

* Du Var Robert, "Dédicace aux Travailleurs," *Hist. de la Classe Ouvrière,* I, pp. x–xi.

† Aulus Gellius, *Noct. Alt.*, XVI, x.

‡ *Hist. de la Classe Ouvrière,* Book IX, chap. VII, III, 100.

§ *Ibid.*, p. 102.

competition is the negation, as its name indicates, of all ties and communion of interests between the members of society. Free competition is a free field open to every individual, provided or not with the elements necessary and indispensable to its manifestations; free competition, in a word, is liberty, but liberty without other rule than the material and moral force, of which each one may be able to dispose in the presence of the thousand causes which produce a difference in the position of individuals.*

"But, we say that a system which thus arms, morally, the poor against each other, is a barbarous system, and contrary to civilization; it is barbarous, inasmuch as it developes all the bad tendencies of the human heart; it is contrary to civilization, because, instead of facilitating harmonious relations among men, it inclines them to mutual repulsion and hostility." †

This is a sufficient sample of M. Robert du Var's [sic] testimony. The greater part of his work is to the same effect: and there is a singular accordance between his censures of Political Economy,‡ and those uttered by Mr. Fitzhugh. They merit especial attention.

We will cite another Socialist, M. Vidal:

"The ox, the horse, the hog eat according to their hunger; their desires are even anticipated; they have their subsistence assured. It is the same thing in the case of the slave. For the ox, the horse, the hog, the slave, belong to a master, and their loss is the loss of the owner: *res perit domino*,[3] says the Digest. But with the hired laborer it is different! He belongs to himself. His death is the loss of his family whom he maintained, and who will no longer find the means of living. What matter to an employer is the death of a hired laborer? Are there not every where millions of arms always ready to offer themselves at reduced wages?" §

Let us turn to evidence of a different character. Here is Sir Robert Peel's testimony to the condition of Ireland before 1844, previous to the potato-rot and the famine:

"It may be assured that the fourth class of houses, (according to the census,) are generally unfit for human habitation; and yet it would appear that in the best circumstanced county, in this respect, the county of Down, 24.7 per cent, or one-fourth of the population, live in houses of this class; while in Kerry, the population is 66.7 per cent, or about two-thirds of the whole; and, taking the average of the whole popula-

* *Ibid.*, Book XIV, chap. I, IV, 285–6.
† *Ibid.*, Book XIII, chap. II, IV, 247.
‡ *Ibid.*, Book XII, chap. III, IV, 50–105.
§ Vidal, *Repartition des Richesses*, Part II, chap. III.
[3] "The thing lost is lost to the master."

tion of Ireland, as given by the census commissioner, we find that in the rural districts about 43 per cent of the families, and in the civic districts, about 36 per cent inhabit houses of the fourth class. * * *

"The lowest, or fourth class, remember, comprises all mud cabins, having but one room."*

Mr. Kay, from whom the foregoing remarks of Sir Robert Peel are quoted, thus comments upon a murder committed in open day in Ireland. The two murderers had escaped:

"Why," he asks, "were not these men apprehended? Because of the rottenness that there is in the state of society in these districts; because of the sympathy which there is on the part of the great bulk of the population with those who, by these dreadful acts of vengeance, are supposed to be the conservators of the rights of the tenant, and supposed to give him that protection which imperial legislation has denied. The first thing that ever called my attention to the condition of Ireland, was the reading an account of one of these outrages. I thought of it for a moment, but the truth struck me at once: and all I have seen since confirms it. When law refuses its duty — when government denies the right of a people — when competition is so fierce for the little land, which the monopolists grant to cultivation in Ireland — when, in fact, for a bare potato, millions are scrambling, these people are driven back from law and from the usages of civilization to that which is termed the law of nature, and, if not of the strongest, the law of the vindictive; and in this case the people of Ireland believe, to my certain knowledge, that it is only by these acts of vengeance, periodically committed, that they can hold in suspense the arm of the proprietor and the agent, who, in too many cases, if he dared, would exterminate them." †

A pretty result, this, for free labor and free competition, and abolitionism, to have arrived at. But Ireland was always esteemed *un mauvais sujet*. Let us cross St. George's Channel:

"The English peasant is thus deprived of almost every motive to practice economy, and self-denial, beyond what suffices to provide his family with food and clothing. Once a peasant in England, and a man cannot hope that he himself, or his children, will ever be anything better, than a mere laborer for weekly hire.

"This unhappy feature of an English peasant's life was most powerfully, and only too justly depicted in those articles of the *Times*, to which I have referred above. It was there shown that during the last half century, everything has been done to deprive the peasant of any

* Joseph Kay, Esq., M. A., *The Social Condition and Education of the People of England and Europe*, I, chap. I, 314.

† *Ibid.*, pp. 317–318.

interest in the preservation of public order; of any wish to maintain the existing constitution of society; of all hope of raising himself in the world, or of improving his condition of life; of all attachment to his country; of all feelings of there really existing any community of interest between himself and the higher ranks of society; and of all consciousness that he has anything to lose by political changes; and that everything has been done to render him dissatisfied with his condition, envious of the richer classes, and discontented with the existing order of things." ‡

This, too, is a pretty picture, which is not relieved by the further information that,

"In the year 1770, there were, it is said, in England alone, 250,000 freehold estates in the hands of 250,000 different families. In the year 1815, at the close of the revolutionary war, the whole of the lands of England were concentrated in the hands of only 32,000 proprietors.§

"What is the result? The labor market in the manufacturing towns is constantly overstocked; the laborers and shopkeepers find new and eager competitors constantly added to the list; competition in the towns is rendered unnaturally intense; profits and wages are both unnaturally reduced; the town work-houses and the town gaols are crowded with inmates; the inhabitants are overburdened with rates; and the towns swarm with paupers and misery.

"I know not what others may think, but to me it is a sad and grievous spectacle, to see the enormous amount of vice and degraded misery which our towns exhibit, and then to think, that we are doing all we can to foster and stimulate the growth and extension of this state of things, by that system of laws, which drives so many of the peasants of both England and Ireland to the towns, and increases the already vast mass of misery by so doing.

"I speak with deliberation, when I say, that I know of no spectacle so degraded, and if I may be allowed to use a strong word, so horrible, as the back streets and suburbs of English and Irish towns, with their filthy inhabitants; with their crowds of half-clad, filthy, and degraded children, playing in the dirty kennels; with their numerous gin-palaces, filled with people, whose hands and faces show how their flesh is, so to speak, impregnated with spirituous liquors — the only solaces, poor creatures, that they have! — and with poor young girls, whom a want of religious training in their infancy, and misery, has driven to the most degraded and pitiful of all pursuits.*

‡ Kay, I, chap. II, 361.

§ Kay, II, chap. II, 370, citing Rev. H. Worsley's *Essay on Juvenile Depravity*, p. 53.

* Kay, I, chap. I, 372–3.

"Of 1600 [pauper children in London] who were examined, 162 confessed that they had been in prison, not merely once, nor even twice, but some of them several times; 116 had run away from their homes; 170 slept in the 'lodging-houses;' 253 had lived altogether by beggary; 216 had neither shoes nor stockings; 280 had no hat or cap, or covering for the head; 101 had no linen; 349 had never slept in a bed; many had no recollection of ever having been in a bed; 68 were the children of convicts.[†]

"The further we examine, the more painful, disgusting and incredible does the tale become.

"We see on every hand stately palaces, to which no country in the world offers any parallel. The houses of our rich are more gorgeous and more luxurious than those of any other land. Every clime is ransacked to adorn or furnish them. The soft carpets, the heavy rich curtains, the luxuriously easy couches, the beds of down, the services of plate, the numerous servants, the splendid equipages, and all the expensive objects of literature, science, and the arts, which crowd the palaces of England, form but items in an *ensemble* of refinement and magnificence, which was never imagined or approached, in all the splendor of the ancient empires.

"But look beneath all this display and luxury, and what do we see there? A pauperized and suffering people.

"To maintain a show, we have degraded the masses, until we have created an evil so vast, that we now despair of ever finding a remedy." [‡]

We may now dismiss Mr. Kay — this testimony is sufficiently direct and sufficiently ample; and yet it would have been easy to have introduced many more and stronger statements made by him, which have been omitted because they were too long to be quoted. Mr. Kay is neither Chartist nor Socialist. He is a graduate of Trinity College, Cambridge, a Barrister-at-law, and has traveled over Europe for eight years, under an appointment from the Senate of the University of Cambridge, as Traveling Bachelor of the University, commissioned "to travel through Western Europe in order to examine the social condition of the poorer classes of the different countries." [§] The evidence of such a man should be authoritative, but we will continue our quotations:

"It is undeniable that morality has declined in our days with the progress of knowledge." [*]

† *Ibid.*, p. 395.
‡ *Ibid.*, pp. 452–3.
§ *Ibid.*, p. 4.
* Saisset, *Sur la Philosophie et la Religion du XIX Siècle*, p. 222.

"One word more, and we have done. On many questions of practical duty, men are now affecting to be wiser and better than the Bible. Plans of social progress and improvement are rife, that have an air of transcendental refinement about them, unknown to the homely morality of the Word of God. We are becoming too sentimental to endure that even the murderer shall be put to death. And now we are for bettering God's ordinance of marriage itself; and we see a fine, romantic, tender charm in an alliance of brothers and sisters, on which God has stamped his curse. What may such things betoken? Are they ominous of such unbridled lawlessness and lust as marked the days before the Flood? Are they signs of the days not unlike these that are to precede the coming of the Son of Man?" †

"The task of restoring health and soundness to a society so fearfully diseased as ours unquestionably is, is on all hands acknowledged to be at once the noblest and the most imperative to which citizens or statesmen can now direct their energies." ‡

"Society, such as it now is in England, will not continue to endure, &c." §

"The last battle of civilization is the severest: the last problem the knottiest to solve. Out of all the multitudinous ingredients and influences of the past; out of the conquest of nature, and the victory of freedom; out of the blending and intermixture of all previous forms of polity and modifications of humanity, has arisen a complex order of society, of which the disorders and anomalies are as complex as its own structure. We are now summoned to the combat, not with material difficulties, nor yet with oppressors nor with priests, but with an imperfect and diseased condition of that social world of which we form a part; with pains and evils appalling in their magnitude, baffling in their subtlety, perplexing in their complication, and demanding far more clear insight and unerring judgment, than even purity of purpose, or commanding energy of will. This conflict may be said to date from the first French Revolution; and it has been increasing in intensity ever since, till it has reached to a vividness and solemnity of interest, which surpasses and overshadows the attractions of all other topics, &c. &c." *

"England's rapidly accelerating decline is a very remarkable and mournful phenomenon; it is a mortal sickness for which there is no

† *North British Review,* Am. Ed., No. XXIV (Feb. 1850), Art. IX, 299–300.

‡ *Edingb. Rev.*, Engl. ed. (Oct. 1849), Art. VI, 497–8.

§ Chateaubriand, *Essays on English Literature* (Paris 1838), cited by Kay.

* *Westminster Review,* No. CXI (Jan. 9, 1852), Art. III.

remedy. I liken the English of the present day to the Romans of the third century after Christ." †

The analogy might be extended to nearly all of modern civilization. "Tremendous catastrophes have come to pass, and there is no resistance; not a semblance of great men, no joy or enthusiasm, no hopes for the future, except that the time will one day come, when by means of mutual instruction every peasant boy shall be able to read. The truth of the thing is the unveiled destitution of the populace, who are resolved to bear it no longer, and this again paves the way for a revision of property; which is not, indeed, something new under the sun, but has been unheard of for centuries past, and even now seems quite inconceivable to our politicians, who have set property, in the place of God, in the Holiest of Holies, &c, &c." ‡

We cannot venture to extend our extracts, though we have the materials before us to increase them ten — nay, twenty-fold. We contribute these merely as a confirmation of Mr. Fitzhugh's position, that, really and confessedly, Free Society has proved a clamitous and irremediable failure in the principal communities of Christendom.

† Niebuhr, *Life and Letters,* p. 506.
‡ *Ibid.,* p. 528. *See also,* p. 525.

## XIII

# THE REFORMATION—THE RIGHT OF PRIVATE JUDGMENT

The Reformation, like the American Revolution, was originated and conducted to successful issue by wise, good, and practical men, whose intuitive judgments and sagacious instincts enabled them to feel their way through the difficulties that environed them. Wise men know that there is too much of complexity in the tangled web of human affairs to justify the attempt at once to practice and philosophise, to act and to reason. Fools and philosophers too often mar the good works of such men, by pretending to see clearly, and to define accurately, the principles of action which have led to those works. A Washington, a Peel, or a Wellington, never "writes himself down an ass" by appealing to abstract principles to justify measures which are rendered necessary by a thousand minute and peculiar circumstances of the hour, which common sense and experience instinctively appreciate, but which philosophy in vain attempts to detect or to generalize. Common sense never attempts "to expel nature," but suggests and carries through a thousand useful reforms by recurrence to and comparison with the past, and by cautious experimentation.

Common sense sometimes errs by excess of conservation; but it is better to err with Pope, who thought "Whatever is, is right," than with Jefferson, whose every act and word proves that he held that "Whatever is, is *wrong*.

The Reformation was not the thought and the act of Luther, Calvin, Cranmer, and Erasmus; but the thought and the act of society – the *vox Populi, vox Dei.* Popes and cardinals are not infallible, but society is. Its harmony is its health; and to differ with it is heresy or treason, because social discord inflicts individual misery; and what disturbs and disarranges society, impairs the happiness and well-being of its members.

This doctrine of the infallibility of society, is suggested, though not expressed, in the maxim – *Salus populi, est suprema lex.*[1] The Puritans, in the early days of New England, acted it out; and if they hung a few troublesome old women, the good that they achieved was more than compensated for by any errors they may have committed. Liberty of the press, liberty of speech, freedom of religion, or rather freedom from religion, and the unlimited right of private judgment have borne no good fruits, and many bad ones. Infidels, Skeptics, Millerites, Mormons, Agrarians, Spiritual Rappers, Wakemanites, Free Negroes, and Bloomers disturb the peace of society, threaten the security of property, offend the public sense of decency, assail religion, and invoke anarchy. Society has the right, and is in duty bound, to take care of itself; and when public opinion becomes powerless, law should intervene and punish all acts, words, or opinions which have become criminal by becoming dangerous or injurious.

We would rejoice to see intolerance of error revived in New England. Laxity of role and laxity of public opinion is sin of itself, and leads to thousands of sins. New England is culpable for permitting Parker and Beecher to stir up civil discord and domestic broils from the pulpit. These men deserve punishment, for they have instigated and occasioned a thousand murders in Kansas; yet they did nothing more than carry into practice the right of private judgment, liberty of speech, freedom of the press and of religion. These boasted privileges have become far more dangerous to the lives, the property, and the peace of the people of this

[1] "The welfare of the people is the supreme law."

Union than all the robbers and murderers and malefactors put together.

The Reformation was but an effort of Nature—the *vis medicatrix naturæ*[2]—throwing off what was false, vicious, or superfluous, and retaining what was good.

The great men of the day but show larger portions of the common thought. Men, and all other social and gregarious animals, have a community of thought, of motions, instincts, and intuitions. The social body is of itself a thinking, acting, sentient being. This is eminently observable with the lower animals. Bees and herds perform their evolutions with too much rapidity and precision to leave any doubt but that one mind and one feeling, either from within or without, directs their movements. The great error of modern philosophy is the ignorance or forgetfulness of this fact. The first departure from it was not the Reformation—for that was preëminently a social idea and a social movement—but the doctrine of the right of private judgment, which speculative philosophers and vain schismatics attempted to engraft upon it, or deduce from it. Human equality, the social contract, the let-alone and selfish doctrines of political economy, universal liberty, freedom of speech, of the press, and of religion, spring directly from this doctrine, or are only new modes of expressing it. Agrarianism, Free Love, and No Government, are its logical sequences: for the right to judge for ourself implies the right to act upon our judgments, and that can never be done in a world where the private appropriation of all capital and the interference of government restricts our free agency, and paralyzes our action on all sides.

We sometimes think the burning of the Alexandrian Library was a providential purification, just as the fictitious burning by Cervantes of Don Quixote's library ridded the world of the useless rubbish of the Middle Ages, by the ridicule so successfully attached to it. Sure we are that a fire that would consume all the theological and other philo-

[2] "The healing power of nature."

sophical speculations of the last two centuries would be a happy Godsend.

Our Revolution, so wise in its conception and so glorious in its execution, was the mere assertion by adults of the rights of adults, and had nothing more to do with philosophy than the weaning of a calf. It was the act of a people seeking national independence, not the Utopian scheme of speculative philosophers, seeking to establish human equality and social perfection.

But the philosophers seized upon it, as they had upon the Reformation, and made it the unwilling and unnatural parent of the largest and most hideous brood of ills that had ever appeared at one birth since the opening of the box of Pandora. Bills of Rights, Acts of Religious Freedom, and Constitutions, besprinkled with doctrines directly at war with all stable government, seem to be the basis on which our institutions rest. But only seem to be; for, in truth, our laws and government are either old Anglo-Saxon prescriptive arrangements, or else the gradual accretions of time, circumstance, and necessity. Throw our paper platforms, preambles and resolutions, guaranties and constitutions, into the fire, and we should be none the worse off, provided we retained our institutions — and the necessities that begot, and have, so far, continued them.

All government proceeds *ab extra.* Neither individuals nor societies can govern themselves, any more than the mouse can live in the exhausted receiver, or the clown lift himself by the lapel of his pantaloons. The South is governed by the necessity of keeping its negroes in order, which preserves a healthy conservative public opinion. Had the negroes votes, the necessity would be removed, because the interest of the governing class would cease to be conservative. The necessity, the governing power *ab extra,* would be removed. The little republics of ancient Greece were able to preserve the most artificial social arrangements, under the necessities which slavery and foreign hostile pressure from without begot. They were afraid of change, because insurrection was dangerous.

If government on paper were really useless and harmless, we should say nothing about it. But it is fraught with danger, first because we are apt to rely on it for safety and security of rights, and secondly because it rarely suits the occasion. Men and societies are endowed by Providence generally with sufficient knowledge and judgment to act correctly or prudently under circumstances as they arise; but they cannot foresee or provide for the future, nor lay down rules for other people's conduct. All platforms, resolutions, bills of rights, and constitutions, are true in the particular, false in the general. Hence all legislation should be repealable, and those instruments are but laws. Fundamental principles, or the higher law, are secrets of nature which God keeps to himself. The vain attempt of "frequent recurrence to them" is but the act of the child who builds card houses for the pleasure of knocking them down. Recurrence to fundamental principles and appeals to the higher law are but the tocsin of revolution that may upset everything but which will establish nothing, because no two men are agreed as to what the higher law, alias "fundamental principles," is.

Moses, and Lycurgus, and Solon, and Numa built their institutions to last, enjoined it on the people never to change them, and threw around them the sanctity of religion to ward off the sacrilegious hand of future innovation. "A frequent recurrence to fundamental principles" and the kicking down of card houses was not part of their science of government. We have often thought that of all the lost arts, the art of government was the only one whose loss we would deplore, or whose recovery is worth the pains of study and research.

To us it seems that "first causes," "fundamental principles," and the "higher law" mean one and the same thing: an *ignis fatuus* that it is dangerous to pursue, and hopeless to overtake.

We may be doing Mr. Jefferson injustice in assuming that his "fundamental principles" and Mr. Seward's "higher law" mean the same thing; but the injustice can be very little, as they both mean just nothing at all, unless it be a determination to inaugurate anarchy, and to do all sorts of mischief. We refer the reader to the chapter on the Declaration of Independence, &c., in our *Sociology* for a further dissertation on the fundamental powder-cask abstractions, on which our glorious institutions *affect* to repose. We say *affect*, because we are sure neither their repose nor their permanence would be disturbed by the removal of the counterfeit foundation.

The true greatness of Mr. Jefferson was his fitness for revolution. He was the genius of innovation, the architect of ruin, the inaugurator of anarchy. His mission was to pull down, not to build up. He thought everything false as well in the physical as in the moral world. He fed his horses on potatoes, and defended harbors with gunboats, because it was contrary to human experience and human opinion. He proposed to govern boys without the authority of masters or the control of religion, supplying their places with Laissez Faire philosophy, and morality from the pages of Lawrence Sterne. His character, like his philosophy, is exceptional—invaluable in urging on revolution, but useless, if not dangerous, in quiet times.

We would not restrict, control, or take away a single human right or liberty which experience showed was already sufficiently governed and restricted by public opinion. But we do believe that the slaveholding South is the only country on the globe that can safely tolerate the rights and liberties which we have discussed.

The annals of revolutionary Virginia were illustrated by three great and useful men. The mighty mind of Jefferson, fitted to pull down; the plastic hand of Madison to build up; and the powerful arm of Washington to defend, sustain, and conserve.

We are the friend of popular government, but only so long as conservatism is the interest of the governing class. At the South, the interests and feelings of many non-property holders, are identified with those of a comparatively few property holders. It is not necessary to the security of property, that a majority of voters should own property; but where the pauper majority becomes so large as to disconnect the mass of them in feeling and interest from the property holding class, revolution and agrarianism are inevitable. We will not undertake to say that events are tending this way at the North. The absence of laws of entail and primogeniture may prevent it; yet we fear the worst, for, despite the laws of equal inheritance and distribution, wealth is accumulating in few hands, and pauperism is increasing. We shall attempt hereafter to show that a system of very small entails might correct this tendency.

# XIV

# THE NOMADIC BEGGARS AND PAUPER BANDITTI OF ENGLAND

Under various names, such as Proletariat in France, Lazzaroni in Italy, Leperos in Mexico, and Gypsies throughout all Europe, free society is disturbed and rendered insecure by the class, a description of which we shall draw from the British writers. We do not hesitate to assign to the Gypsies the same origin with the rest. They are all the outgrowth of runaway and emancipated serfs. The time of the appearance of the Gypsies is coeval with the universal liberation and escape of the villeins.

If this *diluvies* [1] of society is by nature vicious, nomadic, and incapable of any self-control, it is obvious they should be enslaved. If emancipation of their ancestors and the throwing them upon the world without property or other means of support made them and their posterity, from necessity, beggars, Pariahs and Ishmaelites, they should be restored to slavery, unless some better disposition of them can be discovered.

*North British Review*, "Literature and Labor Question," February No., 1851. – the passage we quote is from a work of Mr. Mayhew:

That we, like the Hottentots, Kaffirs, and Fins, are surrounded by wandering hordes, the *sonquas* and *fingons* of this country, paupers, beggars and outcasts, possessing nothing but what they acquire by depredation from the industrious, provident, and civilized portion of the community; that the heads of these nomads are remarkable for a greater development of the jaws and cheek bones, than of the skull,

[1] "Diluve" or "deluvy" is an obsolete English word meaning deluge.

and that they have a secret language of their own — an English *cuzecat*, or "slang," as it is called, for the concealment of their designs; these are points of coincidence so striking, that, when placed before the mind, they make us marvel why the analogy has been so long unobserved. The resemblance once discovered, however, becomes of great service in enabling us to use the moral characteristics of the nomadic races of other countries, as a means of comprehending more readily those of the vagabonds and outcasts of our own. * * * The nomad there is distinguished from the civilized man by his repugnance to regular and continuous labor — by his want of providence in laying up a store for the future; by his inability to perceive consequences ever so slightly removed from immediate apprehension; by his passion for stultifying herbs and roots, and when possible, for intoxicating fermented liquors; for his extraordinary powers of enduring privation; by his comparative insensibility to pain; by an immoderate love of gaming; frequently risking his own personal liberty on a single cast; by his love of libidinous dances; by the pleasure which he experiences in witnessing the sufferings of sentient creatures; by his delight in warfare and all perilous sports; by his desire for vengeance; by the looseness of his notions as to property; by the absence of chastity among his women, and his disregard of female honor; and lastly by his vague sense of religion, his rude idea of a Creator, and utter absence of all appreciation of the mercy of the Divine Spirit.

The nomadic races of England are of many distinct kinds — from the habitual vagrant, half beggar, half thief, sleeping in barns, tents, and casual wards, to the mechanic on the tramp, obtaining his bed and supper from the trade societies in the different towns on his way to seek work. Between these two extremes, there are several mediate varieties, consisting of pedlars, showmen, harvest men, and all that large class who live by either selling, showing or doing something through the country. There are, so to speak, the rural nomads — not confining their wanderings to any one particular locality, but ranging often from one end of the land to the other. Besides these, there are urban and suburban travellers, or those who follow some itinerant occupation in and about the large towns. Such are in the metropolis, more particularly the pickpockets, the beggars, the prostitutes, the street sellers, the street performers, the cab-men, the coachmen, the watermen, the sailors, and such like. In each of these classes, according as they partake more or less of the family vagabond, doing nothing whatever for their living, but moving from place to place, preying upon the earnings of the more industrious part of the community — so will the attributes of the nomad tribe be found to be more or less marked.

To the same effect, read the following from July No., 1852, of [the] *Edinburgh Review*, in [an] article on "Mendicity: Its Causes and Statistics":

> There live, then, in the midst and about all the English population, a distinct population, fearful in numbers, constantly and rapidly increasing, having a language, manners, and customs of its own — living, in nine cases out of ten, in a course of life most immoral and profligate; and yet so living, and so increasing, in spite of the laws, in spite of the municipal arrangements of the last few years, so favorable to their detection and punishment; in spite of the new poor-law arrangements; and in spite of the general feeling that the poor-rates and the union ought to provide for all real cases of destitution and misery. This population has its signs, free-masonry, its terms of art, its correspondence, its halting-houses, its barns still kept open, and even well-strawed by farmers and country gentlemen; its public-houses, its well-known and even recognized lodging-houses; and its manifold plans to extract or extort, to win or to scold, out of its reluctant but deceived victims, sums amounting, we are inclined to believe, to not less than £1,375,000; being one-third of the total amount of poor-rates! This sum may at first appear utterly extravagant; but it will not be found to be so when it is remembered that on an average each begging family extorts £55 per annum from the public. The annual poor law expenditure for the year ending in March, 1840, in England, was, in round numbers, £4,300,000. In England, including the three ridings of Yorkshire, there are forty-two counties. The population of those counties is nearly fifteen millions. If we take at this moment a rough and general, though a tolerably correct estimate of that population, with its dense misery in towns and cities, and its diffused but not less individually intense misery in the agricultural districts, we may fairly calculate that one out of every one hundred is a beggar or lives in a state of practical vagrancy — looking in one form or other, to alms for support. The one-hundreth part of the population is 150,000; and if each begging family, raising £55 per annum from the public by alms, be estimated as consisting of six, we shall have 25,000 English begging families, raising £55 per annum each, or the total sum of £1,375,000. But we believe that we have underrated, instead of overstated the facts of the case in these calculations. In London alone and its vicinity, in spite of all the efforts of the police, a very large part of that sum is extorted; and we have not taken into consideration the wholesale mendicity which is now deplorably manifest in the larger English manufacturing towns. We have also omitted all Irish mendicants;

and yet they are nearly in the proportion of one to three in the English agricultural districts. Naturally anxious as we are to avoid even the appearance of exaggeration, we are still bound to state, that the estimate we have made is greatly deficient, and that we have understated the real statistics.

The begging population of England, existing and increasing in spite of municipal police, and notwithstanding the penalties of the vagrant act, is divided into several classes; and we now propose to draw upon a little pamphlet, mentioned at the head of this article, which has been recently published at Birmingham, and which contains very accurate details of the mendicant population — written by one who long frequented the haunts of the vagrant community. The portion of the community to which his details extend, belong principally to the hereditary and professional class of beggars.

The writer of this family thus proceeds with his descriptive details:

"In order fully to explain each individual character I shall begin with those vagrants who generally obtain the most and are considered of the *first class*, and are by some termed *Silver Beggars*, but by travelers *Lurkers*.

"*Lurkers* are persons who go about with briefs, containing false statements of losses by fire, shipwrecks, accidents, &c. The seals and signatures of two or more magistrates are affixed to those briefs, and they are so well written, that thousands of persons are daily imposed upon by them. As there are so many different ways used by these persons, it will be necessary to explain each of them separately."

The writer then enters into details as to the "*Fire-Lurkers*," or those "who go about begging for loss by fire." They have false briefs, pretended to be signed by two magistrates and the clergyman of the place where the fire is alleged to have taken place. The documents are accompanied by a sham subscription-book, and the brief is called, in the mendicant's parlance, "a sham," whilst the subscription-book they name a "delicate." With this "sham and delicate" the "lurkers," or beggars, proceed all over the country; and the author states that one man, with whom he was acquainted, "had been a fire-lurker for fourteen years, and had travelled through every county in England, and the greater part of Wales."

Then there is,

"*The Shipwrecked Sailor's Lurk.* — Persons who go on this lurk, generally represent themselves as captains or masters of merchant ships, which have been wrecked, and they have, of course, lost all their property; and their pretended loss always amounts to many hundred pounds, sometimes even to thousands. This class of imposters are very respectably dressed, having moustaches, gold chains, &c.; they have either a well-written brief, or one partly printed and filled up with writing and the seals and signatures of two or three magistrates are placed at the bottom. I have seen briefs of this description from almost every part of the kingdom."

He goes on to say, that one named Captain Johnstone had "followed the lurk of a shipwrecked captain for many years, had been over every county in England and Wales many times, and obtained not only hundreds, but thousands of pounds." He relates various anecdotes of the most successful "Lurkers" in this department.

"*The Foreigner's Lurk.* — Considerable numbers proceed on this lurk, representing themselves as foreigners in distress. . . . Of late years, by far the greatest number have represented themselves as *Polish* noblemen or gentlemen, who had been driven by the tyranny of Russia from their native country to seek a refuge. . . . Their briefs have the names and seals of two magistrates attached, and are always well written. Whenever they present their briefs, they affect not to be able to speak a word of English, and the few words they utter are spoken in broken accent. . . . One of these lurkers, known among mendicants by the nickname of 'Lord Dundas,' had often got several pounds in a day. . . . There are also many females who go on the foreigner's lurk. . . . I knew a female who went on the foreigner's lurk, who dressed very well; she had a boy with her, and often succeeded in getting two or three pounds in a day. When she called on any one, she *pattered* (spoke) in French, and affected not to be able to converse in the English language.

"4. *The Accident Lurk.* — Lurkers of this description have a sham and delicate (brief and book), and the sham states that by some dreadful accident the bearer has lost all, or at least the greater part of his property, sometimes by storm, and at other times by a flood, or in some other way; but, in whatever way the accident has happened, the bearer has always suffered a very considerable loss, and is deprived of the means of supporting himself and family. The sums raised vary from five shillings to a pound per day.

"5. *The Sick Lurk.* — This is worked in so many different ways that it will be necessary to say a little on each. It would seem, 1st, That a common method of imposing upon the public is, by applying blistering ointment to the arms, causing them to have the appearance of having been badly scalded. 2d, That others go about with hands and arms tied up, said to be injured by lightning, or by some other deplorable accident. 3d, Others affect fits. 4th, Others affect pregnancy and destitution. 5th, Others obtain alms by the husband remaining at home and affecting indisposition, in case any one should visit his lodgings to examine the merits of the case, whilst the wife goes out begging for wine, rags, clothes, &c., for the sham invalid. 6th, Others pretend to have bad wounds, and beg for linen rags and small bottles to contain medicine necessary for their cure. I saw a man who got, in one day, by this means, thirteen pounds' weight of white rags, and more than five dozen of phial bottles. Rags and bottles sell well. 7th, Others affect to have children confined with scarlet fever, &c. &c., and beg for *them.* They state that they have obtained a note to take their children to an infirmary or to an hospital, and want a few clothes and a little money.

"6. *The Deaf and Dumb Lurk.* — I have known many persons of both sexes, who have acted as if deaf and dumb, and by this means succeeded very well in obtaining money, food, &c. Many of them pretend to tell fortunes, and frequently get something considerable by such practices. They carry a slate and pencil with them, to write questions and answers."

It would appear from the pamphlet before us, that sometimes these deaf and dumb lurkers affect even in the lodging-houses to be thus afflicted; but in such cases they are generally found out by their fellow vagrants.

"7. *The Servants' Lurk.* — There are considerable numbers who go on the servants' lurk, or as servants out of place; and both males and females frequently succeed well in imposing on servants and others by false statements and tales of distress. . . . The greater part of those who go on this lurk are neatly dressed, and have exactly the appearance of servants in gentlemen's families. . . . Many of them have the *Court Guide,* which, as it contains a list of the nobility and gentry, enables them to do the thing completely.

"8. *Collier's Lurk.* — This is followed by thousands who were never in a coal-pit, and numbers of such are daily imposing up on the public as colliers out of employ. They generally say they have been thrown out of work by some accident, such as the flooding of the works or the falling in of the pit. . . . They often go in parties from two to seven or eight. . . . Others have printed papers, which are left at each house, and called for again in a few hours. . . . Others have written statements of the pretended masters of the accidents, and the supposed signatures of the works are affixed to them. . . . Some of these obtain as much as fourteen or fifteen shilling per diem.

"9. *The Weaver's Lurk.* — There are at the present time great numbers who go on this lurk, many of them having printed papers or small handbills, and leave one at each house, and then call again for them, and to receive what persons are disposed to give. . . . I have seen men who represented themselves as weavers of every kind, and from all the manufacturing parts of the kingdom — men who I well knew had never been near a loom, but had been born and bred vagrants.

"10. "*The Cotton Spinner's Lurk.* — There are many going on this lurk with printed papers or small handbills also. . . . Some who go on this lurk carry sewing cotton for sale, alleged to be their own spinning. . . . One man I know, who travels on this lurk, has been doing so for twelve years. He sometimes obtains as much as from twelve to fifteen shillings in one day.

"11. *The Calenderer's Lurk.* — Those who go on this lurk represent themselves as calenderer's out of employ, through the depression of trade and improvement in machinery. They, like sham weavers and colliers, have false papers, which are printed, some in poetry."

The sums raised by these descriptions of "lurks" must be immense, especially where the individuals have a good address, and can explain and enforce the written and printed appeals they take with them.

"*High-Fliers*, or begging letter writers, are, it would seem, the next in order of importance, after the Lurkers. "These begging letter-writers scribble false statements of their having been unfortunate in business, or suffered great losses, which have reduced them to a state of extreme distress. In London, but especially in the watering and sea-bathing places, these letters procure as much as from five to one pound per day.

"*Shallow Coves* are impostors begging through the country as shipwrecked sailors. They generally choose winter, and always go nearly naked. Their object in doing so is to obtain left-off clothes. . . . They have a long, pitiful got-up tale of pretended distress, which they shout through the streets, of having been shipwrecked, &c. . . . Shallow Coves generally go in *companies*, (or, technically speaking, in *school*) of from two to ten. There is generally one selected to be the spokesman. . . . As Shallow Coves only call at respectable houses, they often obtain a great deal of money.

"*Shallow Motts* are females who, like the Shallow Coves, go nearly naked. They also adopt that mode of begging in order to obtain wearing apparel. . . . They plead long and severe sickness, but only ask for *clothes*. The clothes are disposed of as soon as possible, none being ever kept for their own use. . . . I knew one of these who in ten days obtained at Kingston-upon-Thames between seven and eight pounds' worth of clothes.

"*Cadgers* are those who make begging their trade, and depend upon it for their support. *Cadgers on the downright* are those who beg from door to door, and *Cadgers on the fly* are those who beg as they pass along the *tober* (road). Cadging on the fly is a profitable occupation in the vicinity of bathing-places and large towns. A person of this description generally gets many shillings in the course of the day. Cadging on the downright (from door to door) is like all other trades, getting worse; but still thousands do very well at it, and frequently get more food than they can consume. . . . I have often seen food, which many working people would gladly have eaten, shamefully and wantonly wasted.

"*Cadgers Children* (kiddies) are so well instructed in the arts of imposition by their parents, that they frequently obtain more in money and food than grown-up cadgers.

"*Cadgers' Screeving.* — There are many cadgers who write short sentences with chalk on the flags, and some of them can do it remarkably well; these are called *screevers.* I have seen the following sentences frequently written by them in places where there were numbers passing by, and where they thought it would be likely to get plenty of half-pence (*browns*) and now and then a *tanner* or a *bob* (sixpence or a shilling):

Hunger is a sharp thorn, and biteth keen.
I cannot get work, and to beg I am ashamed.

I have known them by this means obtain seven shillings a day.

"*Cadgers' Sitting Pad.* — Whenever cadgers *stand* or *sit*, either in towns or by the road side, to beg, they call it *sitting* or *standing pad;* and this often proves a very profitable method. Some of them affect blindness; whilst others represent themselves as unable to follow any employment, in consequence of being subject to fits. Some cadgers save very considerable sums of money; but these are very few, compared with the great number who live by this trade of beggary.

"*Match-sellers* never entirely depend upon selling matches, for they cadge as well; in fact, they only carry matches as a cloak for begging, and never offer them at any house where they expect to get more without them. . . . Match-sellers, as well as all other cadgers, often get what they call *a back-door cant;* that is, anything they can carry off where they beg, or offer their matches for sale.

"*Cross Coves*, though they beg their bread, can tell a long story about being out of employ through the badness of trade, &c., yet get what they call *on the cross* (by theft). . . . One of their chief modes of getting things *on the cross* is by shoplifting (called *grabbing*). . . . Another method is to *star the glaze* (i. e. break or cut the window).

"*Prigs* (or pickpockets) are another class of vagrants, and they frequent races, fairs, and prize-fights. . . . Like cross coves, they are generally young men who have been trained to vagrancy, and have been taught the arts of their profession in their childhood.

"*Palmers* are another description of beggars, who visit shops under pretence of collecting *harp* half-pence; and to induce shopkeepers to search for them, they offer thirteen-pence for a shilling's worth, when many persons are silly enough to empty a large quantity of copper on their counters to search for the half-pence wanted. The *palmer* is sure to have his hand amongst it; and while he pretends to search for the harps, he contrives to conceal as many as possible in the palm of his hand, and whenever he removes his hand from the coppers on the counter, always holds his fingers out straight, so that the shopkeeper has not the least suspicion that he is being robbed. Sums varying from five to fifteen shillings per diem are frequently got in this way, by characters of that description."

## Extract from *Edinburgh Review*, Jan. No. 1844:

### IRISH PEASANTRY

It is obvious that the insecurity of a community in which the bulk of the population form a conspiracy against the law, must prevent the importation of capital; must occasion much of what is accumulated there to be exported; and must diminish the motives and the means of accumulation. Who will send his property to a place where he cannot rely on its being protected? Who will voluntarily establish himself in a country which to-morrow may be in a state of disturbance? A state in which, to use the words of Chief Justice Bushe, 'houses, and barns, and granaries are leveled, crops are laid waste, pasture lands are ploughed, plantations are torn up, meadows are thrown open to cattle, cattle are maimed, tortured, killed; persons are visited by parties of banditti, who inflict cruel torture, mutilate their limbs, or beat them almost to death; men who have in any way become obnoxious to the insurgents, or opposed their system, or refused to participate in their outrages, are deliberately assassinated in the open day; and sometimes the unoffending members of a family are indiscriminately murdered by burning the habitation." A state in which even those best able to protect themselves, the gentry, are forced to build up all their lower windows with stone and mortar; to admit light only into one sitting-room, and not into all the windows of that room, to fortify every other inlet by bullet proof barricadoes; to station sentinels around during all the night, and the greater part of the day; and to keep fire-arms in all the bedrooms, and even on the side-table at breakfast and dinner time. Well might even Bishop Doyle exclaim — "I do not blame the absentees; I would be an absentee myself if I could."

# XV

## *RURAL LIFE OF ENGLAND*

From *Rural Life of England*, by WM. H. HOWITT,[1] we take the following extract:

The wildness into which some of these children in the more solitary parts of the country grow (recollect this is in Lancashire, near the great city of Manchester) is, I imagine, not to be surpassed in any of the back settlements of America. On the 5th July, 1836, the day of that remarkable thunder-storm which visited a great part of the kingdom with much fury, being driven into a cottage at the foot of Pendle by the coming on of this storm, and while standing at the door watching its progress, I observed the head of some human creature, carefully protruded from the doorway of an adjacent shed, and as suddenly withdrawn on being observed. To ascertain what sort of a person it belonged to, I went into the shed, but at first found it too dark to enable me to discover anything. Presently, however, as objects became visible, I saw a little creature, apparently a girl about ten years old, reared very erectly against the opposite wall. On accosting her in a kind tone, and telling her to come forward and not be afraid, she advanced from the wall, and behold! there stood another little creature, about the head shorter, whom she had been concealing. I asked the elder child whether this younger one were a girl. She answered, "Ne'a." Was it a boy? "Ne'a." What! neither boy nor girl? Was she a girl herself "Ne'a." What! was it a boy I was speaking to? "Ne'a." What in the name of wonder were they then? "We are childer." Childer! and was the woman in the house their mother? "Ne'a." Who was she, then? "Ar mam." O! your mam! and do you keep cows in this shed? "Ne'a — bee-as." In short, common English was quite unintelligible to these poor little creatures, and their appearance was as wild as their speech. They were two fine young creatures, nevertheless — especially the elder, whose form and face were full of that symmetry and fine grace that are sometimes the growth of unrestrained Nature, and would have delighted the sculptor or painter. Their only clothing was a sort of little boddice

[1] William H. Howitt, *The Rural Life of England*, 2nd ed. (London, 1840).

with skirts, made of a reddish stuff, and rendered more picturesque by sundry patches of scarlet cloth, no doubt from their mother's old cloak. Their hands, bosoms, and legs to the knees, were bare to all the influences of earth and heaven; and on giving each of them a penny, they bounded off with the fleetness and elasticity of young roes. No doubt the hills and the heaths, the wild flowers of summer, and the swift waters of the glens, were the only live long day companions of these children, who came home only to their oatmeal dinner, and a bed as simple as their garments. Imagine the violent change of life by *the sudden capture and confinement of these little English savages in the night-and-day noise, labor, and foul atmosphere of the cotton purgatories!*

In the immediate neighborhood of towns, many of the swelling ranges of hills present a much more cultivated aspect, and delight the eye with their smooth, green, and flowering outlines; and the valleys, almost everywhere, are woody, watered with clear, rapid streams, and in short, are beautiful. But along the rise of the tall chimneys of vast and innumerable factories, and even while looking on the places of the master manufactories, with their woods, and gardens, and shrubbery lawns around them, *one cannot help thinking of the horrors detailed before the committee of the House of Commons, respecting the Factory System;* of the parentless and friendless wretches, sent by wagon loads from distant work-houses to these prisons of labor and despair; of the young frames crushed to the dust by incessant labor; of the beds into which one set of children got, as another set got out, so that they were said never to be cold the whole year round, till contagious fires burnt out and swept away by hundreds these little victims of Mammon's ever-urging never-ceasing wheel. Beautiful as are many of these wild recesses, where, before the introduction of steam, the dashing rivulet invited the cotton-spinners to erect their mills; and curious as the remains of those simple original factories are, with their one great water-wheel, which turned their spindles while there was water, but during the drought of summer quite as often stood still; yet one is haunted even there, among the shadows of the fine old trees that throw their arms athwart streams dashing down their beds of solid rock, by the memory of little tender children, that never knew pity or kindness, but labored on and on, through noon and through midnight, till they slept and yet mechanically worked, and were often awaked only by the horrid machinery rending off their limbs. In places like these, where now the old factories and large houses of the proprietors stand deserted, or are inhabited by troops of poor creatures, whose poverty only makes them appear the more desolate. We are told by such men as Mr. Fielden, of Oldham, once a factory child himself, and now a great manufacturer, who dares to reveal the secrets of the prison-house, that little children have even committed suicide to escape from a life worse than ten deaths. And what a mighty system is this now become? What a perpetual and vast supply of human energy and human life it requires, with all the facilities of improved machinery, with all the developed power of steam, and with all the glowing thirst of wealth to urge it on! We are told that the state of the factories is improved, and I trust they are; but if there be any truth in the evidence given before the Parliamentary committees, there is need of great amelioration yet; and it is when we recollect these things, how completely the laboring class has, in these districts, been regarded as mere machinery for the accumulation of enormous capitals, that we cease to wonder at their uncouth and degraded aspect, and at the neglect in which they are suffered to swarm over these hills, like the very weeds of humanity, cast out into disregarded places, and left to spread and increase in rank and deleterious luxuriance.

What is so poetically and graphically described by Mr. Howitt, is verified in its minutest details in *The Glory and Shame of England*, a very interesting work by C. Edwards Lester, an abolitionist of New York.

# XVI

# THE DISTRESSED NEEDLE-WOMEN AND HOOD'S "SONG OF THE SHIRT"

We take what follows from the January No., 1849, of the *Westminster Review* — we having nothing to remark, except as to the line from the French song, which has taken the place of the Marseillaise as the great National Song, we should rather say, National Dirge. It is the maddening cry of hunger for employment and bread, and more resembles the howl of the wolves of the Pyrennes, as they start in quest of prey, than the Anthem of Liberty. It truly represents, embodies, and personifies the great Socialistic movement of the day. Whilst statesmen and philosophers speculate, the mass agitate, organize and threaten. Winter before last, they took possession of the streets of New York, and levied enforced charity. This spring, they meet in the Park and resolve "that there were fifty thousand men and women in vain seeking employment during the last inclement winter." America echoes to France, "Vivre en travaillant, ou mourir en combatant!"[1] 'Tis the tocsin and the watchword of free society. 'Tis the grumbling noise of the heaving volcano that threatens and precedes a social eruption greater than the world has yet witnessed. But let us give the language of the Reviewer:

The question of human misery — its causes and their removal, is at the bottom of the movement which is now convulsing Europe, and which threatens to agitate it for some time to come. Could some practicable scheme of relief, generally acceptable to all classes and adequate to cope with the magnitude of the evil, be but suggested, what a load

[1] "Live in labor or die in battle."

of anxiety would be taken from the mind of many a Minister of State! —what comfort would be offered to many a desponding philanthropist!

Human misery has at last found tongues and pens to make itself heard and felt. It appeals to our feelings and our understandings, to our sympathies and fears. Its wails melt us to pity, its ravings terrify us, its woes sicken us. It will no longer hide itself. We must either remove it, or submit to have it constantly exposed to our gaze in all its horrid deformity.

Hitherto the comfortable classes have virtually answered the bitter complaints of the uncomfortable classes in some such terms as these: "Poor people! we are very sorry for your suffering — we really feel for you — take this trifle — it will be some relief. We wish we could do more; — and now pray be quiet — don't distress us with your writhings and agonies — resign yourselves to the will of Providence, and bear hunger and cold in peace and seclusion; — above all, attempt no violence, or we must use violence to keep you quiet." The answer of the uncomfortable classes to such admonitions, day by day becoming more unmistakable, is: "Relieve us, relieve us! Make us comfortable, or show us how we may make ourselves comfortable: otherwise we must make you uncomfortable. We will be comfortable or uncomfortable together."

"Vivre en travaillant, ou mourir en combatant." In our last number, we ventured to offer a few indications as to what we considered a part, an important part, of the remedial measures to be resorted to for the prevention of human misery. We were then dealing with that question as a whole. We now propose to address ourselves to miseries of a class.

The sufferings of the distressed needle-woman have obtained an infamous notoriety — they are a scandal to our age and a reproach to our boasted civilization. They have been clothed in language at once truthful and impressive, full of pathos and yet free from exaggeration. Well known as Hood's immortal lines may be, we reproduce them here, because no narrative, no statistics of ours, could be more true nor half so much to the purpose.

THE SONG OF THE SHIRT.

With fingers weary and worn,
    With eyelids heavy and red,
A woman sat, in unwomanly rags,
    Plying her needle and thread.

Stitch — stitch — stitch!
In poverty, hunger, and dirt;
And still, with a voice of dolorous pitch,
She sang the "Song of the Shirt!"

Work — work — work!
While the cock is crowing aloof!
And work — work — work!
Till the stars shine through the roof!
It's O! to be a slave,
Along with the barbarous Turk,
Where woman has never a soul to save,
If this is Christian work!

Work — work — work!
Till the brain begins to swim;
Work — work — work!
Till the eyes are heavy and dim!
Seam and gusset and band,
Band and gusset and seam,
Till o'er the buttons I fall asleep,
And sew them on in a dream!

O! men, with sisters dear!
O! men, with mothers and wives,
It is not linen you're wearing out!
But human creatures' lives!
Stitch — stitch — stitch!
In poverty, hunger, and dirt;
Sewing at once, with a double thread,
A shroud as well as a shirt!

But why do I talk of death?
That phantom of grisly bone?
I hardly fear his terrible shape,
It seems so like my own!
It seems so like my own,
Because of the fasts I keep —
Oh, God! that bread should be so dear,
And flesh and blood so cheap!

Work — work — work!
My labor never flags;
And what are its wages? A bed of straw,
A crust of bread, and — rags.

That shatter'd roof, and this naked floor,
  A table — a broken chair;
And a wall so blank, my shadow I thank
  For sometimes falling there!

Work — work — work!
  From weary chime to chime,
Work — work — work,
  As prisoners work for crime!
Band and gusset and seam,
  Seam and gusset and band,
Till the heart is sick and the brain benumb'd,
  As well as weary hand.

Work — work — work!
  In dull December light,
And work — work — work,
  When the weather is warm and bright —
While underneath the eaves
  The brooding swallows cling,
As if to show me their sunny backs
  And twit me with the Spring.

Oh! but to breathe the breath
  Of the cowslip and primrose sweet —
With the sky above my head,
  And the grass beneath my feet,
For only one short hour —
  To feel as I used to feel,
Before I knew the woes of want
  And the walk that costs a meal!

Oh, but for one short hour!
  A respite however brief!
No blessed leisure for Love or Hope,
  But only time for Grief!
A little weeping would ease my heart —
  But in their briny bed
My tears must stop, for every drop
  Hinders needle and thread!

With fingers weary and worn,
  With eyelids heavy and red,
A woman sat, in unwomanly rags,
  Plying her needle and thread —

Stitch — stitch — stitch!
In poverty, hunger, and dirt,
Would that its tone could reach the rich!
She sang this "Song of the Shirt!"

We annex part of an article from *Jerrold's Magazine*, which draws quite as clear a picture of the condition of the English poor, and points out the only feasible remedy for the evils of that condition:

## SLAVERY

### THE ONLY REMEDY FOR THE MISERIES OF THE ENGLISH POOR.

BY A PHILANTHROPIST.

Whoever is unprepared to cast aside not only his prejudices, but many of what may be considered well-formed opinions, had better not attempt to peruse the following few pages. I must demand of my reader that he come to the perusal, the *beau ideal* of a juryman. No information that he has gained elsewhere, no feelings that he has cherished as virtues, no sentiments that he has cultivated as noble, and no opinions that he may have formed as infallible, must interfere with his purely and simply receiving the following arguments on their own cogency and truth alone.

The writer considers he has made a great discovery in moral and political science; and elevated by his subject above all personal influences, he commits it to be worked out by others, without the ostentation of recording his name, or deeming that the applause of present or of future generations can add to his sublime delight, in discovering and applying a "panacea" to the varied and bitter ills that beset three-fourth of the poor inhabitants of the "*United* Kingdom."

As some account of the means by which a great discovery has been arrived at is necessary, in order to prepare the mind for its reception with due respect, I shall give a brief outline of the process by which this all-important truth was elicited.

Born with natural sensibilities, I early learnt to shrink from pain endured by others, as if felt actually and bodily by myself. Thus constituted, what a scene was displayed to me when I came into the great and moving society of mankind! What mighty heaps of misery did I discern! What details did the records of the various courts of justice disclose! What regions of squalor, misery, and degradation did my travels reveal to me in every city, and every hamlet, I visited! The bent of my future avocation was soon fixed, and I became a philanthropist by profession. Not to make a trade of it at monster meetings, or fancy fairs, but as a pursuit to which I felt myself called by a spiritual voice, as distinct, I should say, as that which ever called a theologian from a curacy of fifty pounds a year to a bishopric of twenty thousand.

It is not necessary to recapitulate the horrors I have witnessed in the regions of poverty. It is said that the eras of pestilence and famine are passed, but so will not those say who have visited the dwellings of the operatives of our great manufacturing towns, when the markets are glutted, and the mills and manufactories are closed. Pestilence still rages fiercely as ever, in the form of typhus, engendered by want. In the mission I have called myself to, I have stood upon the mud floor, over the corpse of the mother and the new-born child — both the victims of want. I have seen a man (God's image) stretched on straw, wrapped only in a mat, resign his breath, from starvation, in the prime of age. I have entered, on a sultry summer's night, a small house, situate on the banks of a common sewer, wherein one hundred and twenty-seven human beings, of both sexes and all ages, were indiscriminately crowded. I have been in the pestilential hovels of our great manufacturing cities, where life was corrupted in every possible mode, from the malaria of the sewer to the poison of the gin-bottle. I have been in sheds of the peasant, worse than the hovel of the Russian, where eight squalid, dirty, boorish creatures were to be kept alive by eight shillings per week, irregularly paid. I have seen the humanities of life desecrated in every way. I have seen the father snatch the bread from his child, and the mother offer the gin-bottle for the breast. I have seen, too, generous sacrifices and tender considerations, to which the boasted chivalries of Sydney and Edward were childish ostentation. I have found wrong so exalted, and right so debased — I have seen and known of so much misery that the faith in good has shivered within me.

For a time, when I urged these things in the circles of the comfortable, I received many various replies. By some it was said that it was the lot of humanity — that it had always been so, and, therefore, always must. That to enlarge on the evil was only to create discontent, and so injure "the better classes." It was in vain I urged to these reasoners that for hundreds, and, perhaps, thousands of years, creatures little better than Calibans infested the morasses and forests of Europe. That civilization had an onward progress, and that the history of the world proved the one great truth — that man is the creature of circumstances. By some, the evils were denied; by some few, deplored. By all, the discussion was avoided; though the destruction that menaced the Roman empire from the invasion of the barbarian world was never so imminent, nor could the consequence be so dreadful, as that which the wealthy, and civilization itself, would sustain from the insurrection of outraged poverty.

I next tried the politicians. I devoted some years to history and political economy. I even entered the senate. In politics, I found no means of relief. The struggle there was for the preponderance in power, and the reply, "Help us to get into power, and then we will see what we can do." The utmost was to institute inquiries; and from the information thus gathered has been collected a record of misery such as never was before displayed.

It is true, some steps have at last been taken in the right direction; some few noble spirits have spoken out to the "comfortable" the dreadful truths. That something must be done is now acknowledged by all who think. The foolish, the careless, and the truculent can no longer avowedly declare the cries and groans of the miserable multitude to be seditious discontent; nor ascribe their sufferings to the results of retributive justice.

Baffled in every search for a remedy at home, I determined to search foreign nations, and having carefully journeyed through Europe, I sought successively the East and West, until I had traversed the civilized countries of the world. It was in the remote regions of the East and West that I found a clue to my discovery. I here found mankind as multitudinous as at home, but much more happy. Starvation, except in cases of general famine, was unknown; and, on the contrary, I heard the sounds of revelry and dancing, of mirth and leisure, amongst the lowest classes. How different to the everlasting toil of the superior Englishman! "These, then," I said, "are the concomitants of bondage!" Having thus struck out the idea, I followed it up with logical severity, and enunciated the truth that *slavery and content, and liberty and discontent, are natural results of each other.* Applying this, then, to the toil-worn, half-fed, pauperized population of England, I found that the only way to permanently and efficiently remedy the complicated evils, would be to ENSLAVE *the whole of the people of England who have not property.*

Of course, I expect a shout of execration and contempt at such a bold proposition; but, as I have already said, I seek only to gain the hearing, at first, of the impartial and the original thinker. That I am disinterested, will at once be allowed, when I declare I do not seek to be one of the enslaved. But let us proceed to examine how this mighty benefit would manifest itself. The first great advantage would be that the lower classes of society would be placed on an equality with the domestic animals; and by becoming property, become valuable and valued. At present there can be no doubt that a horse that is worth fifty pounds is much more cared for than a man who is worth nothing. We have lately seen a case where a woman was allowed to expire in parturition, because no more than eight shillings was allowed for the midwife's fee; whereas, when a famous racing mare foaled, ten guineas were not thought too great a sum to secure the attendance of a first-rate veterinary surgeon. Now, had the woman been a slave, her offspring would have been worth something, and, of course, her safety secured.

Like all great discoveries, the ramifications of the advantages are found to be endless, and, if once fully entertained, would be irresistible. Entire and complete slavery of the poor would put an end to all the discussions of their rights, and clearly and definitely work out the relative duties of all classes. We should have no more occasion for vague special pleading, such as we find in Paley and other moral philosophers, who endeavor to reconcile dependence and independence, and liberty and obedience. Sedition would be at once annihilated; for where there was no hope nor recognition of equality, there would be no attempt to raise claims which were stifled before born. All vain ambition, such as that now subsisting, between the potboy and the peer, as manifested in Chesterfield's mosaic gold and cigars, would be prevented. The potboy would be a contented slave, and the peer left to his superiority in clothes, trinkets, and sensualities.

It will of course be asserted that the people would not be contented as slaves, but it is only to make a state inevitable, and humanity is soon reconciled to it, as we are to death, governments, and the income-tax. Besides, what is liberty? a word now almost forgotten; a battle sound used to juggle men in every age and country; in Greece, Rome, and America, the war-cry of slaves to fight for the liberty of slavery. Must we, then, ever remain the tools of words; reject all the true advantages of slavery because we cannot bear the name, and take all its evils, and more, because we wish to renounce the sound? What are soldiers and sailors but bondsmen? Indeed, they are a happy specimen of slavery; well fed, clad, and tended; with plenty of leisure and repose. Why, then, should they be happier than the peasant, who pines away his dreary existence on bread and potatoes and water? What is the convict but a slave, who by his crimes has earned his right to be kept well and safe from the elements and want? We reward the criminal with slavery and competence, and leave the honest man to liberty and want.

If, indeed, the old noble cry of "Liberty *and Beer*" could be realized, then it were vain to urge my discovery; but as Englishmen, in proportion as they have gained their liberty, have lost their beer, it behooves us to see whether they had not better hasten back to that state when inventoried with their masters' swine they shared also their superfluities.

# XVII

## THE *EDINBURGH REVIEW* ON SOUTHERN SLAVERY

The *Edinburgh Review* well knows that the white laborers of England receive more blows than are inflicted on Southern slaves. In the Navy, the Army, and the Merchant Service of England, there is more cruelty, more physical discomfort than on all the farms of the South. This *Review*, for twenty years, has been a grand repository of the ignorance, the crimes, and sufferings of the workers in mines and factories, of the agricultural laborers, of the apprentices, and, in fine, of the whole laboring class of England. We might appeal to its pages almost *passim* to establish these facts. Half the time of Parliament is consumed in vain efforts to alleviate the condition of the cruelly treated and starving poor; and much of this *Review* is taken up in chronicling the humane but fruitless action of Parliament. No man in the South, we are sure, ever bred slaves for sale. They are always sold reluctantly, and generally from necessity, or as a punishment for misconduct. The Southwest has been settled in great part by farmers from the older slave States, removing to them with their negroes. The breaking up of families of whites and of blacks keeps equal pace. But we have no law of impressment in the South to sever the family ties of either blacks or whites. Nor have we any slavery half so cruel as that to which the impressed English seaman is subjected. The soldiers torn from their wives and children, to suffer and to perish in every clime and on every sea, excite not the sympathies of the Reviewer; they are all reserved for imaginary cases of distress occasioned by the breaking up of families of Southern negroes. The so-called slave trade of the South is no evil, because the instances of the improper severing of family ties are rare. Will some Yankee or Englishman, ere the charge is repeated that slaves are bred to be sold like horses, when they are old enough for market, point out a single instance in the present, or the past, of a Southerner's pursuing such a business? Yankees and Englishmen kill their wives annually, yet it has not occurred to Englishmen at all, and not to the Yankee till very lately, to abolish the marriage relation. When Englishmen correct the thousand real and pressing evils in their society, it will be time enough to call on us to do away with the imaginary abuses of slavery. These remarks have been elicited from us by an article on Southern slavery, in the April number of the *Edinburgh Review*, which is equally distinguished for the falsity of its charges and the ill nature of its comments. As a full justification for the indefinite continuance of negro slavery, we give below an extract from an able article from the same *Review*, in its January number, 1846, entitled "Legislation for the Working Classes." In showing the many evils arising from emancipating the whites, the Reviewer demonstrates, though not intending it, the absurdity of emancipating negroes. If Irishmen, who are as intellectual a race of men as any in all Europe, have lost infinitely in physical comfort, and gained nothing in morals or in mind by liberty, what will it avail negroes? Let Haiti and Jamaica answer. But Frenchmen, Scotchmen and Englishmen, we mean the masses, the proletariat, have lost as much by emancipation as Irishmen. History and statistics, the jails, the gallows, and the poorhouse tell the same sad tale everywhere. We would be willing, if necessary, to rest the complete justification of negro slavery on this single extract:

From the *Edinburgh Review*, 1846.

The moral and domestic feelings of the slave are sacrificed, and his intellect is stunted; but in respect of his physical condition he may be a gainer. "It is necessary," says Aristotle, in his celebrated justification of slavery, "that those who cannot exist separately should live together. He who is capable of foreseeing by his intellect, is naturally a master; he who is able to execute with his body what another contrives, is naturally a slave: wherefore the interest of the master and slave is one." There is a certain degree of force in this argument, if it is limited to the economical relations of the two parties. It is the interest of the master to maintain his slave in good working order. In general, therefore, he is comparatively well fed, clothed, and lodged; his physical wants are provided for; his food descends into his mouth like the manna in the wilderness; he is clothed like the lilies of the field; he has no thought or care for the morrow. Although complaints were made of insufficient food and overwork, the arguments against negro slavery in our West India colonies were founded, mainly, on the necessity of constant punishment — on the *driving system,* as it was called — and the cruelty of the inflictions. The Report of the French Commission, framed by the Duc de Broglie, which recommended the gradual abolition of slavery, likewise bears testimony to the excellent physical condition of the slaves in the French colonies. It is on account of the advantages which may belong to dependence upon a wealthy lord, as compared with a needy independence, that the slave in Menander exclaims that "it is better to obtain a good master, than to live meanly and wretchedly as a freeman." So the Rhetorician Libanus, who lived in the fourth century, in a declamation entitled a *Vituperation of Poverty,* after having enumerated the privations and sufferings which fall to the lot of the poor freeman, proceeds thus: "None of these evils belong to slavery. The slave sleeps at his ease, being fed by the cares of his master, and supplied with all the other things needful for his body. But the poor freeman is constantly awake, seeking the means of subsistence, and subjected to the severe dominion of want which compels him to hunger." The well-informed author of *Haji Baba* describes the astonishment of the vizier of the Shah of Persia on hearing from the British ambassador that there is no slavery in England, and that the king is using his influence to put it down in other States. "Indeed!" said the vizier, "you surely cannot be so cruel! What would become of the poor slaves if they were free? Nothing can be happier than the lot of ours; but if they were abandoned to their fate, they would starve and die. They are our children, and form a part of our family."

A similar feeling is described by Mr. Kohl as existing among the serfs in the Baltic provinces of Russia, with respect to their recent emancipation. The serf is now no longer *abscriptus* [*sic*] *glebæ;* [1] but it

[1] "Bound to the soil."

is not difficult for his lord to find the means of detaining him on the estate if he wishes so to do. Mr. Kohl continues thus: — "Though the right which the peasant has thus obtained is so frequently useless to him, the counter right of his master, of banishing him from his native place, is very often turned against him. Formerly, a noble could not, by any means, get rid of his serfs; and, whenever they were in want, he was forced to support and maintain them. At present, the moment a peasant becomes useless and burdensome, it is easy to dismiss him; on account of which the serfs, in some parts of the provinces, would not accept of the emancipation offered, and bitterly lamented the freedom, as it was called, which was forced upon them. The serf often mournfully complains that he has lost a father and kept a master, and his lord now often refuses the little requests of his peasants, saying, 'You know you are not my children now.'" A similar state of feeling is likewise reported to exist among the serfs of Russia Proper, who, in many cases, prefer the certainty of slavery to the risks of emancipation. Mr. Featherstonhaugh, in his Travels in the Slave States of North America,[2] relates that Mr. Madison, the ex-President, informed him that he had once assembled all his numerous slaves, and offered to manumit them immediately; "but they instantly declined it, alleging that they had been born on his estate, had always been provided for by him with raiment and food, in sickness and in health, and, if they were made free, they would have no home to go to, and no friend to protect and care for them. They preferred, therefore, to live and die as his slaves, who had always been a kind master to them."

Slavery excludes the principle of competition, which reduces the wages of the free laborer, increases his hours of work, and sometimes deprives him of all means of subsistence. The maintenance of slaves as one household, or *familia*, likewise conduces to thrift; their supply on a large scale is, or ought to be, less expensive than when each laborer, as in a state of freedom, has a separate cottage and a family of his own. With slaves thus supported, there is no more waste than with horses or cattle. There is none of the loss or damage which arises from the drunkenness and improvidence of the free laborer expending his own wages. Again, the slave-master can regulate the number of his workmen, and can in this manner control the amount of population. The means may doubtless be harsh and cruel, but they are effective for their end. In general, indeed, slave classes show a disposition to diminish rather than increase in number; and, where

[2] George William Featherstonhaugh, *Excursion Through the Slave States* (New York, 1844).

the slave trade has not been prohibited, the number is kept up rather by new importation than by births. Hence the evils of an abundant population never manifested themselves while the mass of the people was in a servile and semi-servile state. Moreover, it can scarcely be doubted, that under certain circumstances industry may be promoted, and the produce of the land increased, by the existence of a slave class. Mr. M'Culloch, indeed, thinks that the tropical countries can never be effectually cultivated by free labor. "Were the slaves completely emancipated in the United States, Cuba, and Brazil," says he, "it is all but certain that the culture of sugar and cotton would be as completely abandoned in them as in Haiti. And if the change were accompanied by a considerable improvement in the condition of the black population, the sacrifice might not, perhaps, be deemed too great. But where is the ground for supposing that such would be the case? Indeed, the fair presumption seems to be the other way. Little, at all events, would be gained by turning a laborious, well-fed slave, into an idle, improvident, and perhaps beggarly freeman." If we look merely to the present, and confine our views to *economical* results, Mr. M'Culloch's arguments certainly appear strong. And although it is true that all hope of *future* improvement, in respect of his physical condition, is denied to the slave, yet it must be admitted, that practically, and looking to the actual generation, the absence of a power of rising in the world is no severe privation to a peasant class. Neither in England among the agricultural laborers, nor in the Continental States among the small proprietors, are there many instances of a person quitting the condition in which he is born. Nor is any slavery so indelible (where the slaves have the same colored skin as their masters) as to prevent frequent emancipations of individual slaves from personal affection and other causes. The freedmen formed a numerous class among the Romans; and it is known to what important posts slaves have risen in the Turkish empire.

After these remarks (the intention of which cannot be misunderstood by any reader of this Journal) we can better estimate the effects of the change from slavery to personal freedom upon the emancipated slave. He is relieved from the liabilities and burdens, but he at the same time forfeits the advantages of slavery. While the slave is exonerated from his legal obligations to his master, the master is exonerated from his legal and moral obligations towards his slave, and his interest in the conservation and protection of his slave is at an end. The slave (to use the common phrase) becomes his own master. With the acquisition of this power, he incurs the obligations of self-support. He becomes independent; and, being so, he must provide for his self-defence. Self-dominion is not an unmixed good to the work. It imports onerous duties. It implies the necessity of providing for a man's own wants, and those of his family. The freedman is no longer forced, by the fear of corporal punishment, to do a prescribed task of work. But he must work in order to earn wages; and, what is more, he must find work for himself. He is no longer incapable of acquiring property, or of reaping the fruits of his own industry. But he is, in consideration of this power, bound to provide for his own support. He is no longer incapable of contracting a lawful marriage, or begetting free legitimate children. But he is bound to maintain his wife and children by his own exertions; and if he deserts them, or allows them to starve, he is subject to legal punishment. He is no longer fed and maintained merely according to his physical wants, without reference to the value of his services; but, on the other hand, he is delivered over to the unchecked operation of the principle of competition; and he must content himself with the scanty pittance which the rivalry of the labor market may assign him. He is no longer treated as a mere animal or implement of production, without feeling, mind, or moral character; he does not follow the religion of his master, and he may voluntarily choose his own creed. But, in becoming a free moral agent, he accepts the responsibilities of that condition; his path is open to virtue, but he is answerable for his acts and their consequences if he deviates into other ways; he can, by foresight, determine his own lot, but he must, in compensation, suffer the penalties of his own improvidence.

When we contemplate the actual results of the change in question, and compare the state of the working classes in countries where they are free, with the state of a slave class, we find that the only benefits of freedom, which have been fully enjoyed by the laboring classes, are the *negative* ones, (such as exemption from bodily inflictions, and other ill treatment;) but that the *positive* benefits which they have hitherto derived from the social independence, have been less prominent. The *positive* benefits — which are economical and domestic — which consist in the acquisition, enjoyment and transmission of wealth, and in the development of the family affections — are more remote, and depend on numerous preliminary conditions which hitherto have rarely co-existed in any community. The entire harvest of the change will not be reaped until civilization has made further progress — until the providence, industry, intelligence, and peaceableness of the working man are such as to render him altogether fit for self-support, and to protect society against the shocks arising from his delusions and violence.

But, in proportion as the positive advantages are distant, the disadvantages of the change make themselves sensibly felt. As soon as slavery has ceased to exist, the freedom of action for the working classes is complete; they are masters of their own conduct, and their conduct determines the condition of the great mass of the community. If, then, their moral state is low, and they are exempt from all legal compulsion, they are likely to make a bad use of their liberty. Whenever the moral restraints are weak, and the rights of the freeman are exercised without limitation, and with an inward consciousness of power, political or social dangers cannot be far off. A slave-class, emancipated at once, affords the strongest example of the evils arising under this influence. Their moral condition is, at the best, like that of children; they have had no experience of self-management; and the rights of freedom are, from their novelty, prized more highly. Some countries, however, from which slavery has long been banished, exhibit a nearly similar state of things. Thus, in Ireland, the freedom of the working classes has produced the smallest amount of positive advantages, combined with the largest amount of disadvantages. The peasantry are in the lowest physical degradation; they derive the smallest possible quantum of happiness from their power of disposing of themselves and their families, and of acquiring property; while their rights of citizenship are too frequently perverted to purposes detrimental to themselves, and dangerous to the public peace.

When the slavery of the working classes had been gradually extinguished in Western Europe, it began to be seen that the theory of personal freedom could not be carried consistently into practical effect for the entire community. A man might, in the eye of the law, be presumed able and bound to maintain himself and his family; but want of industry, or intelligence, or providence, or the rapine of the strong, might reduce him to destitution and helplessness. Accordingly, unless many of the laboring class were to be permitted to die of hunger and neglect, it was necessary to find some means of alleviating their sufferings.

In further reply to the Edinburgh Reviewer, and to illustrate by examples our theory of *Cannibals All; or, Slaves without Masters*, read the following from the *North British Review* for November, 1855, on the Rural Population of England:

Have we not come upon a very paradise of rural seclusion? Is it not a spot to be chosen by those who are intending to while away existence among the never tiring sweets of a country life? But let us step on a little way, and overtake the group of children that is just now crossing the common. Alas! yet should we not refrain from expressing the sad feelings which the first sight of these infant shadows has awakened? feelings heightened by contrast; for lately we were making our way through a fourth class street, where the prime necessities of life are amply provided for. Besides, if we look a second time at these shrunken forms — such is the beneficence of the Creator — we see that childhood will have its smiles, its laughs, its gambols, under conditions even the most forlorn. Moreover, there is, notwithstanding that famished, watery look — there is, taking the group altogether — there is an air of pure rusticity — there is an innocence, comparatively, and a modest propriety — there is a respectfulness in their style and deportment which is greatly in their favor when thought of in comparison with the bold, unreverential sauciness of the infant Hercules of manufacturing towns.

But look at these unfortunates — the infant serfs of a neglected rural district! Look at them physiologically — observe their lank, colorless hair, screening the sunken eye, and trailing upon the bony neck; look at the hollow cheeks, the candle-like arms, and the unmuscular shanks which serve the young urchins for legs! But are not these children breathing a pure atmosphere? Are they not Nature's own? Yes; but there is one thing wanting to them — one ominous word clears up the mystery. Starvation! Not, indeed, such starvation as brings the sorrows of a sad lot to a speedy end; but such as drags its pining sufferings out through the overshadowed years of childhood and youth; through those spasmodic years of manhood during which the struggle to exist wears an aspect of rugged vigor; and then through that residue of early decrepitude, haggard, bent, idiot-like, which is indeed an unblessed end of an unblessed existence. This rural population does pretty well if the father be ablebodied and sober, and the mother managing, through the summer season, of wheat-hoeing, haymaking, and wheat harvest; that is to say, when the labor of the mother and her children comes in to swell a little the weekly wages. During these weeks something of needed clothing is obtained, rent is paid up, and a pittance of animal food, weekly, is added to the bread, and the tea, and the potato of the seven months' diet.

It would be doing a wrong to our worthy farmer friends, and to the rural sporting gentry, to affirm that these miserables are actually dying of want. No, they are not dying, so as inquests must be held before they may be buried — would to God they were — they are the living — they are living to show what extremities men, women, and children may endure, and yet not die; or what they hold to be worse, not to betake themselves to "the union"! But how do these same men, women, and children pass five months of the year? Gladly would one find them curled round like hedgehogs, and hibernating in hollow trees, in rabbit burrows, lost to consciousness. We should, indeed, count it a miracle if, on a May morning, we were to see a group of human beings start up alive from the award, along with the paiglus and the cowslips. But it is much less than a miracle to see the people of a depressed rural district stepping alive out of the winter months! * * * *

The instances are extremely rare in which those who were born to the soil, and destined to the plow, rise above their native level. Such instances — two, three, or five — might be hunted up, if an agricultural county were ransacked for the purpose; but the agricultural laborer, even if he had the brain and the ambition requisite, and if otherwise he could effect it, would seldom bring with him that which the social mass, into which he might rise, especially needs, namely, a fully developed and robust body. Meantime, what is it that is taking place in hundreds of instances and every day, throughout the entire area of the manufacturing region? Men, well put together, and with plenty of bone, and nerve, and brain, using with intense ardor those opportunities of advancement which abound in these spheres of enterprise and prosperous achievement — such men are found to be making themselves heard of among their betters, are seen well-dressed before they reconcile themselves to the wearing of gloves; by rapid advances they are winning for themselves a place in society — a place which, indeed, they well deserve; and there they are doing what they had not thought of —they are regenerating the mass within which they have been received.

We extract the following from an article in the *Edinburgh Review* on Juvenile and Female Labor in its January No., 1844. It is of the highest authority, being part of a report of commissioners appointed by Parliament, and stands endorsed as well by the action of Parliament as by the authority of the Reviewer.

Our limits will not allow us to go through all the employments reported upon in these volumes; but, as specimens, we will give a short account of the condition of the people engaged in Coal mines, Calico-printing, Metal wares, Lace-making, and Millinery.

*Coal Mines.* — The number of children and young persons employed in these mines is enormous; and they appear to commence working, even underground, at an earlier age than is recorded of any other occupation except lace-making. The Commissioners report—

"That instances occur in which children are taken into these mines to work as early as *four* years of age, sometimes at five, not unfrequently between six and seven, and often from seven to eight, while from eight to nine is the ordinary age at which their employment commences. . . . That a very large proportion of the persons employed in these mines is under thirteen years of age; and a still larger proportion between thirteen and eighteen. That in several districts female children begin to work in the mines as early as males.

"That the nature of the employment which is assigned to the youngest children, generally that of 'trapping,' requires that they should be in the pit as soon as the work of the day commences, and, according to the present system, that they should not leave the pit before the work of the day is at an end.

"That although this employment scarcely deserves the name of labor, yet, as the children engaged in it are commonly excluded from light, and are always without companions, it would, were it not for the passing and repassing of the coal carriages, amount to solitary confinement of the worst order.

"That in some districts they remain in solitude and darkness during the whole time they are in the pit, and, according to their own account, many of them never see the light of day for weeks together during the greater part of the winter season, excepting on those days in the week when work is not going on, and on the Sundays.

"That at different ages, from six years old and upwards, the hard work of pushing and dragging the carriages of coal from the workings to the main ways or to the foot of the shaft, begins: a labor which all classes of witnesses concur in stating requires the unremitting exertion of all the physical power which the young workers possess.

"That, in the districts in which females are taken down into the coal mines, both sexes are employed together in precisely the same kind of labor, and work for the same number of hours; that the girls and boys, and the young men and the young women, and even married women and women with child, commonly work almost naked, and the men, in many mines, quite naked; and that all classes of witnesses bear testimony to the demoralizing influence of the employment of females underground.*

* It is, however, but fair to state, that many competent and most respectable observers declare, that though the *facts* stated by the Commissioners may be perfectly true, yet that the tone and spirit of the *Report* bears token of material exaggeration.

"That, in the east of Scotland, a much larger proportion of children and young persons are employed in these mines than in other districts, many of whom are girls; and that the chief part of their labor consists in carrying the coals on their backs up steep ladders.

"That when the work-people are in full employment, the regular hours of work for children and younger persons are rarely less than eleven; more often they are *twelve*; in some districts they are *thirteen*; and in one district they are generally *fourteen* and upwards.

"That in the great majority of these mines night-work is a part of the ordinary system of labor, more or less regularly carried on according to the demand for coals, and one which the whole body of evidence shows to act most injuriously both on the physical and moral condition of the work-people, and more especially on that of the children and young persons.

"That in many cases the children and young persons have little cause of complaint in regard to the treatment they receive, while in many mines the conduct of the adult colliers to them is harsh and cruel; the persons in authority who must be cognizant of this ill usage never interfering to prevent it, and some of them distinctly stating that they do not conceive they have a right to do so. That with some exceptions little interest is taken by the coal-owners in the children employed in their works after the daily labor is over. . . . That in all the coal-fields accidents of a fearful nature are extremely frequent, and of the work-people who perish by such accidents, the proportion of children and young persons sometimes equals, and rarely falls much below that of adults." — (*First Report*, p. 255–7.)

With respect to the general healthiness of the employment, there is considerable discrepancy in the evidence adduced; many witnesses stating that the colliers generally, especially the adults, are a remarkably healthy race, showing a very small average of sickness,† and recovering with unusual rapidity from the severest accidents; — a peculiarity which the medical men reasonably enough attribute to the uniform temperature of the mines, and still more to the abundance of nutritious food which the high wages of the work-people enable them to procure. The great majority of the witnesses, however, give a very different impression. Upwards of two hundred, whose testimony is quoted, or referred to in the *Report of the Central Commissioners*, testify to the extreme fatigue of the children when they return home at night, and to the injurious effect which this ultimately produces on their constitution.

While the effect of such early and severe labor is, to cause a peculiar

† The colliers in the east of Scotland, however, are excepted.

and extraordinary degree of muscular development in collier children, it also stunts their growth, and produces a proportionate diminution of stature, as is shown by the following comparison.— (*Physical and Moral Condition of Children*, p. 55.‡

| | *Inches in Height* |
|---|---|
| 10 Farmers' boys, between 12 and 14 years, measured, each . . . . . . . | 56.4 |
| 10 Colliers' boys . . . . . . . . . | 53.4 |
| Difference . . . . . . | 3. |
| 10 Farmers' girls, between 14 and 17 years, measured, each . . . . . . . | 60.5 |
| 10 Colliers' girls . . . . . . . . . | 55.6 |
| Difference . . . . . . | 4.9 |
| 51 Farmers' children, 10 years old, measured, each . . . . . . . . . | 51. |
| 60 Colliers' children . . . . . . . | 48. |
| Difference . . . . . . | 3. |
| 49 Farmers' children, 15½ years old, measured, each . . . . . . . . . | 59. |
| 50 Colliers' children . . . . . . . | 53. |
| Difference . . . . . . | 6. |

Labor in coal mines is also stated, by a great number of most respectable witnesses, to produce a crippled gait, and a curvature of the spinal column, as well as a variety of disorders — among which may be enumerated, affections of the heart, rupture, asthma, rheumatism, and loss of appetite; — and this not merely in a few cases, but as an habitual, and almost inevitable result of their occupation.

"Of the effect of employment in the coal mines of the East of Scotland in producing an early and irreparable deterioration of the physical condition, the Sub-commissioner thus reports: — 'In a state of society, such as has been described, the condition of the children may be easily imagined, and its baneful influence on the health cannot well

‡ It is curious to contrast this with a similar comparison instituted by the Factory Commissioners, and embracing upwards of 1000 children. — (*Analysis of the Evidence Taken Before the Factory Commissioners*, p. 9.)

| | |
|---|---|
| Boys *not* in factories averaged | 55.56 inches. |
| Boys in factories | 55.28 |
| Difference | .28! |
| Girls *not* in factories | 54.979 |
| Girls in factories | 54.951 |
| Difference | .028!! |

be exaggerated; and I am informed by very competent authorities, that six months' labor in the mines is sufficient to effect a very visible change in the physical condition of the children: and indeed it is scarcely possible to conceive of circumstances more calculated to sow the seeds of future disease, and, to borrow the language of the instructions, to prevent the organs from being developed, to enfeeble and disorder their functions, and to subject the whole system to injury, which cannot be repaired at any subsequent stage of life.'—(*Frank's Report*, s. 68: App. Pt. I, p. 396.) In the West of Scotland, Dr. Thomson, Ayr, says:—'A collier at fifty generally has the appearance of a man ten years older than he is.'"—(*Evidence*, No. 34; App. Pt. I, p. 371, l. 58.)

If we turn to the testimony as to the moral, intellectual, and spiritual state of the great mass of the collier population, the picture is even darker and more appalling than that which has been drawn of their physical condition. The means of instruction to which they have access are scanty in the extreme;—their readiness to avail themselves of such means, if possible still scantier; and the real results of the instruction they do obtain, scantiest of all—as the following extracts will show:—

"As an example of the mental culture of the collier children in the neighborhood of Halifax, the Sub-commissioner states, that an examination of 219 children and young persons at the bottom of one of the coal-pits, he found only 31 that could read an easy book, not more than 15 that could write their names, these latter having received instruction at some day-school before they commenced colliery labor, and that the whole of the remaining number were incapable of connecting two syllables together.—(Scriven, *Report, Mines*: App. Pt. II, 73, s. 91.)

"Of the state of education in the coalfields of Lancashire, the Sub-commissioner gives the following account:—'It was my intention to have laid before the Central Board evidence of the effects of education, as shown by the comparative value of educated and uneducated colliers and children employed in coal mines, as workmen, and to have traced its effects, as shown by the superior moral habits and generally more exalted condition of those who had received the benefits of education over those who had not, which I had observed and proved to exist in other branches of industry. I found, however that the case was hopeless; there were so few, either of colliers or their children, who had even received the first rudiments of education, that it was impossible to institute a comparison.'—(Kennedy, *Report, Mines*: App. Pt. II, p. 183, s. 268.)

"In the coalfields of North Lancashire examined by Mr. Austin, it is stated that the education of the working-people has been almost wholly neglected; that they have received scarcely any instruction at all, either religious or secular; that they cannot therefore be supposed to have any correct conception of their moral duties, and that in fact their intellects are as little enlightened as their places of work — 'darkness reigns throughout.' — (*Report, Mines*: App. Pt. II, p. 805, s. 26.)

"In the East of Scotland a marked inferiority in the collier children to those of the town and manufacturing population. Upwards of 100 heads of collier families, most of whom leave their children to themselves — to ignorance and irreligion." — (*Ibid.*, p. 426, l. 42.) 'Many of the children are not educated at all.' " — (*Ibid.* p. 248, l. 30.)

It appears that, in the principal mining districts, few of the colliers attend any place of worship; and of their entire ignorance of the most elementary truths, either of secular or religious knowledge, the following extracts will give some idea: —

"Yorkshire. — 'With respect even to the common truths of Christianity and facts of Scripture,' says Mr. Symons, 'I am confident that a majority are in a state of heathen ignorance. I unhesitatingly affirm that the mining children, as a body, are growing up in a state of absolute and appalling ignorance; and I am sure that the evidence I herewith transmit, alike from all classes — clergymen, magistrates, masters, men, and children — will fully substantiate and justify the strength of the expressions which I have alone felt to be adequate to characterize the mental condition of this benighted community.'

" 'Throughout the whole district of the coal-field,' says Mr. Scriven, 'the youthful population is in a state of profaneness, and almost of mental imbecility.'

" 'The ignorance and the degraded state of the colliers and their children,' says Mr. Kennedy, 'are proverbial throughout this district. They are uneducated, ignorant, and brutal; deteriorated as workmen and dangerous as subjects.' "

But nothing can show their mental state in so striking a manner, as the evidence derived from the examination of the children themselves, by the Sub-commissioner: —

"A girl eighteen years old — 'I never learnt nought. I never go to church or chapel. I have never heard that a good man came into the world, who was God's Son, to save sinners. I never heard of Christ at all. Nobody has ever told me about him, nor have my father and mother ever taught me to pray. I know no prayer: I never pray. I have been taught nothing about such things.' — (*Evidence, Mines*,

p. 252, ll. 35, 39.) 'The Lord sent Adam and Eve on earth to save sinners.'— (*Ibid.* p. 245, l. 66.) 'I don't know who made the world; I never heard about God.'— (*Ibid.* p. 228, l. 17.) 'Jesus Christ was a shepherd; he came a hundred years ago to receive sin. I don't know who the Apostles were.'— (*Ibid.* p. 232, l. 11.) 'Jesus Christ was born in heaven, but I don't know what happened to him; he came on earth to commit sin. Yes; to commit sin. Scotland is a country, but I don't know where it is. I never heard of France.'— (*Ibid.* p. 265, l. 17.) 'I don't know who Jesus Christ was; I never saw him, but I've seen Foster, who prays about him.'— (*Ibid.* p. 291, l. 63.) 'I have been three years at a Sunday-school. I don't know who the Apostles were. Jesus Christ died for his son to be saved.'— (*Ibid.* 245, l. 10.) Employer (to the Commissioner), 'You have expressed surprise at Thomas Mitchell (the preceding witness) not having heard of God. I judge there are are few colliers hereabouts that have.'"— (*Second Report*, p. 156.)

The moral state of the collier population is represented by the Sub-commissioners as deplorable in the extreme: —

"Lancashire. —'All that I have seen myself,' says the Sub-commissioner, 'tends to the same conclusion as the preceding evidence; namely, that the moral condition of the colliers and their children in this district, is decidedly amongst the lowest of any portion of the working-classes.'— (*Ibid., Report*, s. 278, *et seq.*)

"Durham and Northumberland. — The religious and moral condition of the children, and more particularly of the young persons employed in the collieries of North Durham and Northumberland, is stated by clergymen and others, witnesses, to be 'deplorable.' 'Their morals,' they say, 'are bad, their education worse, their intellect very much debased, and their carelessness, irreligion, and immorality' exceeding any thing to be found in an agricultural district."— (Leifchild, *Report*, *Mines*: Evidence, Nos. 795, 530, 500, 493, 668.)

*Calico-Printing.* — This employs a vast number of children of both sexes, who have to mix and grind the colors for the adult work-people, and are commonly called *teerers.* They begin to work, according to the Report, sometimes before five years of age, often between five and six, and generally before nine. The usual hours of labor are twelve, including meal-time; but as the children generally work the same time as the adults, "it is by no means uncommon in all the districts for *children of five or six years old to be kept at work fourteen and even sixteen hours consecutively.*"— (*Second Report*, p. 59.) In many instances, however, it will be seen that even these hours are shamefully exceeded, during a press of work.

"352. Thomas Sidbread, block-printer, after taking a child who had already been at work all day to assist him as a teerer through the night, says — 'We began to work between eight and nine o'clock on the Wednesday night; but the boy had been sweeping the shop from Wednesday morning. You will scarcely believe it, but it is true — I never left the shop till six o'clock on the Saturday morning; and I had never stopped working all that time, excepting for an hour or two, and that boy with me all the time. I was knocked up, and the boy was almost insensible.'

"353. Henry Richardson, block-printer, states — 'At four o'clock I began to work, and worked all that day, all the next night, and until ten the following day. I had only one teerer during that time, and I dare say he would be about twelve years old. I had to shout to him towards the second night, as he got sleepy. I had one of my own children, about ten years old, who was a teerer. He worked with me at Messrs. Wilson & Crichton's, at Blakely. We began to work together about two or three in the morning, and left off at four or five in the afternoon.' "

Night-work, too, with all its evil consequences, is very common in this trade; — and of the general state of education among the block-printers in Lancashire, the Commissioners thus speak (p. 172):

"The evidence collected by Mr. Kennedy in the Lancashire district tends to show that the children employed in this occupation are excluded from the opportunities of education; that this necessarily contributes to the growth of an ignorant and vicious population; that the facility of obtaining early employment for children in print-fields empties the day-schools; that parents without hesitation sacrifice the future welfare of their children through life for the immediate advantage or gratification obtained by the additional pittance derived from the child's earnings, and that they imagine, or pretend, that they do not neglect their children's education if they send them to Sunday-schools."

*Metal Wares.* — The chief seats of manufactures in metal are Birmingham, Wolverhampton, and Sheffield; but many of the minor branches are carried on in different parts of Scotland, and in Worcestershire and Lancashire. In the various departments of this species of manufacture many thousands of children of both sexes are employed. They begin to work generally about their *eighth* year, as in Birmingham and Sheffield, but often earlier; while in *pin-making,* as carried on at Warrington, both boys and girls commence when *five* years old, and work *twelve hours* a-day, and sometimes, though rarely, even more. The hours of work in most of the metal manufactures are very irregular, generally from ten to thirteen a day; but, especially in the neighborhood of Wolverhampton, it is by no means unfrequent to extend them to fifteen or sixteen for weeks together. The places in which the occupations are carried on are occasionally large, clean, and well ventilated; but in the great majority of cases, a very different description of them is given.

"In general the buildings are very old, and many of them are in a dilapidated, ruinous, and even dangerous condition. Nothing is more common than to find many of the windows broken; in some cases I observed more broken than whole panes; great and just complaint is made upon this point by those employed. The shops are often dark and narrow; many of them, especially those used for stamping, are from four to seven feet below the level of the ground; these latter, which are cold and damp, are justly complained of by the workers. From defective construction all these old shops are liable to become 'suffocatingly hot in summer (and also at night when the gas is lighted) and very cold in winter. Efficient ventilation is a thing unknown in these places. The great majority of the shops are never whitewashed, but there are many creditable exceptions to this statement.'

"It has been already stated, that although the whole population of the town of Wolverhampton and the neighborhood, of all ranks, are engaged in the different manufactures of the place, yet that there are few manufactories of large size, the work being commonly carried on in small workshops. These workshops are usually situated at the backs of the houses, there being very few in the front of a street; so that the places where the children and the great body of the operatives are employed are completely out of sight, in narrow courts, unpaved yards, and blind alleys. In the smaller and dirtier streets of the town, in which the poorest of the working classes reside, 'there are narrow passages, at intervals of every eight or ten houses, and sometimes at every third or fourth house. These narrow passages are also the general gutter, which is by no means always confined to one side, but often streaming all over the passage. Having made your way through the passage, you find yourself in a space varying in size with the number of houses, hutches, or hovels it contains. They are nearly all proportionately crowded. Out of this space there are other narrow passages, sometimes leading to other similar hovels. The workshops and houses are mostly built on a little elevation sloping towards the passage.'" — (*Second Report*, p. 33.)

The most painful portions, however, of the *Report* on the metal manufactures, are those which relate to the treatment of the children and apprentices at Willenhall, near Wolverhampton, and to the noxious influences of those departments which are carried on at Sheffield.—(P. 83).

"455. The district which requires special notice on account of the general and almost incredible abuse of the children, is that of Wolverhampton and the neighborhood. In the town of Wolverhampton itself, among the large masters children are not punished with severity, and in some of the trades, as among the japanners, they are not beaten at all; but, on the other hand, in the nail and tip manufactories, in some of the founderies, and among the very numerous class of small masters generally, the punishments are harsh and cruel; and in some cases they can only be designated as ferocious.

"456. In Willenhall the children are shamefully and most cruelly beaten with a horsewhip, strap, stick, hammer handle, file, or whatever tool is nearest at hand, or are struck with the clenched fist or kicked.

"457. In Sedgley they are sometimes struck with a red-hot iron, and burnt and bruised simultaneously; sometimes they have 'a flash of lightning' sent at them. 'When a bar of iron is drawn white-hot from the forge it emits fiery particles, which the man commonly flings in a shower upon the ground by a swing of his arm before placing the bar upon the anvil. This shower is sometimes directed at the boy. It may come over his hands and face, his naked arms, or on his breast. If his shirt be open in front, which is usually the case, the red-hot particles are lodged therein, and he has to shake them out as fast as he can.' . . . 'His master's name is ———, of Little London. There is another apprentice besides him, who is treated just as bad.' ———, aged fifteen, 'works at Knoblocks with ———. Is a fellow-apprentice with ———. Lives in the house of his master. Is beaten by his master, who hits him sometimes with his fists, and sometimes with the file haft, and sometimes with a stick—it's no matter what when he's a bit cross; sometimes hits him with the locks; has cut his head open four or five times; so he has his fellow-apprentice's head.'

"466. The Rev. Isaac Clarkson, magistrate, vicar of Wednesbury: 'In his capacity of magistrate complaints often come before him, made by boys against masters, from different places round about, such as Willenhall and Darlaston, but he did not encourage them, as they should more properly apply to the magistrates of Wolverhampton. More complaints came before him from the mines than from the manufactories; but sometimes there was very bad usage in the latter. A boy from Darlaston has recently been beaten most unmercifully with a red-hot piece of iron. The boy was burnt — fairly burnt. Wished to cancel the indentures; but the master had been to the board of guardians, or to the clerk of the Stafford union, and promised to behave better in future. Has had various similar cases brought before him.' "

The following statements of the Commissioners demand serious consideration. — (*Second Report*, p. 105.)

"581. But the chief disease is that produced by the occupation of the grinder, which is the most pernicious of any branch of manufacture in England. The inhalation of the dust of the grindstone and of the steel of the knife, or whatever he may be grinding, is so pernicious, that the life of a dry grinder scarcely averages thirty-five years, whilst that of a wet grinder is seldom prolonged to more than forty-five years. The bent posture and pressure on the stomach aggravate the evil. Fork-grinding is the most pernicious, because it is done dry, and a great deal more of the steel has to be ground off. Dr. Knight states that he cannot better express how injurious grinding is to the health than by stating, that 'they who are the greatest drinkers among the grinders are sometimes the longest lived, owing to their more frequent absence from their work.'

"582. Dust flues, in the state of perfection to which they have now been brought, appear to be capable of greatly diminishing if not of entirely obviating the evil. The Sheffield grinders cannot, however, be induced to avail themselves of this security; they know that they are doomed to an early death, yet they are absolutely unwilling that the evil to which they are exposed should in any degree be lessened; they regard every precaution to prolong life with jealousy, as a means of increasing the supply of labor and lowering wages; they are for 'a short life and a merry one,' and hence, even when the masters are at the expense of erecting the apparatus, these men refuse to use it, and even frequently kick it down and break it under their feet.' " — (*Ibid., Evidence.*)

As to the moral state of this class of work-people, the Report speaks thus. — (*Second Report*, p. 176–178.)

"933. The moral and religious state of the children and young persons employed in the trades and manufactures of Birmingham, is described by the Sub-commissioner as very unfavorable. The social and domestic duties and affections are but little cultivated and practiced; great numbers never attend any place of religious worship; and of the state of juvenile crime some conception may be formed from the statement that of the total number of known or suspected offenders in this town, during the last twelve months, namely 1223, at least one-half were under fifteen years of age.

"934. As to illicit sexual intercourse, it seems to prevail almost universally, and from a very early period of life: to this conclusion witnesses of every rank give testimony.

"936. Wolverhampton. — Of the moral condition of the youthful population in the Wolverhampton district, Mr. Horne says — 'Putting together all I elicited from various witnesses and conversations with working people, abroad and at home, and all that fell under my observation, I am obliged to come to the conclusion, that the moral virtues of the great majority of the children are as few in number and as feeble in practice as can well be conceived of those who are born in a civilized country, surrounded by religious and educational institutions, and by individuals anxious for the improvement of the condition of the working classes.' He adds of Willenhall — 'A lower condition of morals, in the fullest sense of the term, could not, I think, be found. I do not mean by this that there are many more prominent vices among them, but that moral feelings and sentiments do not exist among them. They have no morals.'

"940. Sheffield. — In all the Sheffield trades employing large numbers of children, it is stated that there is a much closer intermixture of the younger children with the elder youths, and with the men, than is usual in the cotton, woollen, and flax factories; and that the conversations to which the children are compelled to listen, would debase their minds and blunt their moral feelings even if they had been carefully and virtuously educated, but that of course this result takes place more rapidly and completely in the case of those who have had little or no religious culture, and little but bad example before their eyes from their cradle upwards.

"943. Habits of drinking are formed at a very early age, malt liquor being generally introduced into the workshops, of which the youngest children are encouraged to partake. 'Very many,' say the police officers, 'frequent beer-shops, where they play at dominoes, bagatelle, &c., for money or drink.' Early intemperance is assigned by the medical men as one cause of the great mortality of Sheffield. 'There are beer-houses,' says the Rev. Mr. Farish, 'attended by youths exclusively, for the men will not have them in the same houses with themselves. In these beer-houses the youth of both sexes are encouraged to meet, and scenes destructive of every vestige of virtue or morality ensue.'

"945. But it is stated by all classes of witnesses, that 'the most revolting feature of juvenile depravity in this town is early contamination from the association of the sexes;' that 'juvenile prostitution is exceedingly common.' 'The evidence,' says the Sub-commissioner, 'might have been doubled which attests the early commencement of sexual and promiscuous intercourse among boys and girls.'

"953. SEDGLEY. — At Sedgley and the neighboring villages, the number of girls employed in nail-making considerably exceeds that of the boys. Of these girls Mr. Horne reports — 'Their appearance, manners, habits, and moral natures (so far as the word *moral* can be applied to them) are in accordance with their half-civilized condition. Constantly associating with ignorant and depraved adults and young persons of the opposite sex, they naturally fall into all their ways; and drink, smoke, swear, throw off all restraint in word and act, and become as bad as a man. The heat of the forge and the hardness of the work render few clothes needful in winter; and in summer, the six or seven individuals who are crowded into these little dens find the heat almost suffocating. The men and boys are usually naked, except a pair of trousers and an open shirt, though very often they have no shirt; and the women and girls have only a thin, ragged petticoat, and an open shirt without sleeves.' "

*Lace-Making.* — In this occupation it is proved, by unquestionable evidence, that it is *customary* for children to begin to work at the age of four, five, and six years; and instances were found in which a child only *two* years old was set to work by the side of its mother. The work is of course very slight, but is trying to the eyes. The Sub-commissioner, after detailing a case, says —

"58. In this case, if the statement of the mother be correct, one of her children, four years of age, works twelve hours a-day with only an interval of a quarter of an hour for each meal, at breakfast, dinner, and tea, an never going out to play: and two more of her children, one six and the other eight years of age, work in summer from 6 a. m. till dusk, and in winter from seven in the morning till ten at night, fifteen hours.

"59. This family is singular only in the children being set to work at the ages of two or three. It is common in this district for children to commence work at four, five, and six; the evidence renders this fact undubitable." — (*Second Report*, p. 10.)

The following extracts relate to the hours of work in the lace trade: —

"336. In the Nottingham, Leicester, and Derby districts, partly from the causes just assigned, and partly from the dissipated habits of the workmen, 'the hours of labor are so extremely irregular that it is impossible to speak of them with exact precision.' The hand-machines, especially the wide machines, are usually double-handed;

some very large ones have three men each; the men work such machines by 'spells for shifts.' The most common time is sixteen, eighteen, and occasionally twenty hours. 'However long,' adds the Sub-commissioner, 'may be the hours during which the machines are propelled, even for the whole twenty-four, either by hand or power, there are scarcely ever two complete sets of threaders.'

"341. Mr. William Hinde, aged twenty-nine, operative — 'Among the small masters, who have each one or two machines, it is the custom for one set of children to work for two or three masters. The masters often live a long way from each other; children have often to go one or two miles. They are always wanted when the machine comes off, whatever may be the hour of the day or night; they are required just as much by night as by day, unless the men will accommodate the children, which is very rarely done, especially when trade is good. When there has been a good pattern, and the machine in constant use, the children 'have scarcely a bit of peace,' they have no regular time for meals, 'no time for nothing'; when one machine is off, another is on. Was himself formerly a threader, and then a winder. Has often gone at six in the morning, and has had no time to get any thing to eat, except a mouthful now and then, till three or four in the afternoon. It is the same now, when trade is good. The children have no regular time for meals; they have their food sent to them, and they eat when they can; some have nothing but a bit of bread. There is no more regular time for sleeping than for eating; the children often lie down 'in the middle of the shop floor, when it is warm.' Thinks hundreds have been sent to the grave by this work. It is enough to kill the children, going half fed and clothed to work in the night, at this time of the year. (The thermometer last night was 102.)" — (*Second Report*, p. 56–9.)

Of course, work of this nature, for such hours, and at such an early age, cannot but be followed by deplorable consequences to health in after life, as well as to moral character. Accordingly the Commissioners report. — (II, p. 109, 110, 181.)

"598. From the nature of their occupation, the long and irregular hours of work, the frequency of night-work, and the insufficient time allowed for meals — an evil of the greatest magnitude in the case of growing children — the constitution is frequently seriously impaired. 'The majority of the children whom I saw,' says the Sub-commissioner, 'were pale and unhealthy-looking, and several were of diminutive stature. The health and sight are often greatly impaired, especially among the runners, who occasionally faint while at work; indeed, there cannot be an occupation which more seriously deteriorates the constitution. Short-sightedness, amaurosis, distortion of the spine, excessive constitutional debility, indigestion, and derangement of the uterine functions may be said to be almost universal: all the evidence points to this conclusion.'

"'In the town of Nottingham,' says Mr. Grainger, 'all parties, clergy, police, manufacturers, work-people, and parents agree that the present mode of employing children and young persons as threaders and winders is a most fertile source of immorality. There can, in fact, be but few states more immediately leading to vice and profligacy. Children of both sexes are called out of their parents' houses at all hours of the night, and, as it is quite uncertain how long they may be required, whether for two hours or the whole night, a ready and unanswerable excuse for staying out is furnished.' — (No. 138.)

"The moral condition of the lace-makers in Northamptonshire, Oxfordshire, Beds and Bucks, is stated by Major Burns to be extremely low, and prostitution is rife among them, from their scanty earnings, their love of finery, and the almost total absence of early moral culture." — (*Report*: App. Pt. I, p. A, 12, s. 104.)

*Millinery and Dressmaking.* — The portion of these instructive volumes which describes the condition of the young women employed as milliners and mantua-makers in our great cities, and especially in London, is, however, that which has left the most painful impression upon our minds — not only because the work of these unfortunate girls is of all the most severe and unremitting — nor because it is inflicted exclusively upon the weaker sex, and at a period of life the most susceptible of injury from overstrained exertion — nor yet because the actual consequences which are shown to ensue in thousands of cases are so peculiarly deplorable — but because the excess of labor (with all its pernicious and fatal results) is endured in the service, and inflicted in execution of the orders, of a class whose own exemption from toil and privation should make them scrupulously careful not to increase, causelessly or selfishly, the toils and privations of their less favored fellow-creatures — a class, too, many of whom have been conspicuously loud in denouncing the cruelties of far more venial offenders, and in expressing a somewhat clamorous and overacted sympathy with sufferings which cannot for a moment be compared in severity with those which are every day inflicted on the helpless of their own sex, in ministering to their own factitious and capricious wants. The remark may appear harsh, but the evidence before us fully warrants it — that probably in no occupation whatever — not in the printing fields of Lancashire — not in the lace trade of Nottingham — not in the collieries of Scotland — scarcely in the workshops of Willenhall

— most assuredly not in the cotton factories of Manchester (which a few years ago the fashionable fair of London were so pathetic in lamenting) — can any instances of cruelty be met with which do not "whiten in the shade" of those which every spring and autumn season sees practiced — unreprobated, and till now nearly unknown — in the *millinery establishments* of the metropolis.

The following extracts will show that we are guilty of no exaggeration. — (II, p. 114–122.)

"622. It is estimated that there are in London, in the millinery and dressmaking business, at least 1500 employers, and that the number of young people engaged by each employer varies from two or three to twenty-five or thirty-five — the average in each establishment being about ten, making in the whole 15,000; but this does not include journeywomen who work at their own houses, of whom also there are great numbers.

"623. In some of what are considered the best regulated establishments, during the fashionable season, occupying about four months in the year, the regular hours of work are fifteen, but on emergencies, which frequently recur, these hours extend to eighteen. In many establishments the hours of work, during the season, are unlimited, the young women never getting more than six, often not more than four, sometimes only three, and occasionally not more than two hours for rest and sleep out of the twenty-four; and very frequently they work all night.

"625. Miss O'Neil, Welbeck street, an employer, says — 'In the spring season the hours of work are unlimited.' The common hours are from six a. m. till twelve at night — sometimes from four a. m. till twelve. Has herself often worked from six a. m. till twelve at night for two or three months together. It is not at all uncommon, especially in the dressmaking, to work all night; just in the 'drive of the season,' the work is occasionally continued all night three times a week. Has worked herself twice in the week all night. In some houses which profess to study the health of their young people, they begin at four a. m. and leave off at eleven p. m., never earlier. Has heard there are houses in London which work on Sundays.

"628. Miss ——— ———, manager — 'has been ten years a "first hand," which signifies the party who takes the superintendence of the business, as overlooker of the young persons, cutter-out of the work, &c. The common hours of business are from eight a. m. till eleven p. m. in the winter; in the summer from six or half-past six a. m. till twelve at night. During the fashionable season, that is from April to the end of July, it frequently happens that the ordinary hours are greatly exceeded: if there is a drawing-room, or grand fete, or mourning to be made, it often happens that the work goes on for twenty hours out of the twenty-four, occasionally all night. Every season in at least half the houses of business, it happens that the young persons occasionally work twenty hours out of the twenty-four, twice or thrice a week. On special occasions, such as drawing-rooms, general mournings, and very frequently wedding orders, it is not uncommon to work all night; has herself worked twenty hours out of the twenty-four for three months together; at that time she was suffering from illness, and the medical attendant remonstrated against the treatment she received. He wished witness to remain in bed at least one day longer, which the employer objected to, required her to get up, and dismissed the surgeon. It frequently happened that the work was carried on till seven o'clock on Sunday morning. If any particular order was to be executed, as mournings or weddings, and they left off on Saturday night at eleven, they worked the whole of Sunday; thinks this happened fifteen times in the two years. In consequence of working so late on Sunday morning, or all that day occasionally, could very rarely go to church; indeed it could not be thought of, because they generally rested in bed.'

"639. The correctness of these representations is confirmed, among others, by the following medical witnesses: — Sir James Clark, Bart., Physician to the Queen — 'I have found the mode of life of these poor girls such as no constitution could long bear. Worked from six in the morning till twelve at night, with the exception of the short intervals allowed for their meals, in close rooms, and passing the few hours allowed for rest in still more close and crowded apartments — a mode of life more completely calculated to destroy human health could scarcely be contrived, and this at a period of life when exercise in the open air, and a due proportion of rest, are essential to the development of the system. Judging from what I have observed and heard, I scarcely believed that the system adopted in our worst-regulated manufactories can be so destructive of health as the life of the young dressmaker.'

"647. 'The protracted labor described above,' says the Sub-commissioner, 'is, I believe, quite unparalleled in the history of manufacturing processes. I have looked over a considerable portion of the Report of the Factory Commission, and there is nothing in the accounts of the worst-conducted factories to be compared with the facts elicited in the present enquiry. Gentlemen who, from their official situation, were well qualified to judge, have also stated, in answer to my questions, that they knew of no instance in which the hours of work were so long as those above stated.'

"663. Of the general treatment and condition of these young people, the Sub-commissioner reports: — 'The evidence of all parties establishes the fact that there is no class of persons in this country, living by their labor, whose happiness, health, and lives, are so unscrupulously sacrificed as those of the young dressmakers. It may without exaggeration, be stated, that, in proportion to the numbers employed, there are no occupations, with one or two questionable exceptions, such as needle-grinding, in which so much disease is produced as in dressmaking or which present so fearful a catalogue of distressing and frequently fatal maladies. It is a serious aggravation of all this evil, that the unkindness of the employer very frequently causes these young persons, when they become unwell, to conceal their illness from the fear of being sent out of the house; and in this manner, the disease often becomes increased in severity, or is even rendered incurable. Some of the principals are so cruel as to object to the young women obtaining medical assistance.'" — (No. 626.)

# XVIII

# THE *LONDON GLOBE* ON WEST INDIA EMANCIPATION

We find the following frank and explicit admission in the *Globe* of 10th July, 1856:

> Our own West India Islands are fast relapsing into primitive savageness. When the rich lands of Jamaica are being yearly abandonded, and when in Trinidad and Guiana cultivation has almost ceased, it is not likely that England will care to extend her sovereignty further over tropical territory, which can only be brought into use by a system which has been solemnly condemned.

Now, let us rigidly examine and ascertain what is the condemned system, what the approved system that has been generally adopted in its stead, and why this system is approved, and the free negro system condemned as a failure.

There is no doubt the writer alludes to the system of domestic slavery, in the general, as the condemned system, and especially, to that serfdom or villeinage which lately prevailed, but is now abolished throughout Western Europe. In asserting that the system of slavery has been condemned, and yet admitting West India emancipation to be a failure, he in effect maintains that the liberation of the villeins has been no failure. He means that it has been no failure, because the liberated villeins do work; aye, just twice as hard and as long as their ancestors, the serfs. He means it is no failure, because they not only work harder and longer, but work for half the pay or allowance of their servile ancestors. He means it is no failure, because the once masters, now employers, get their labor for half what it cost to support them as slaves. He means it is no failure, because free labor in England is more plentiful and far cheaper than slave labor in America. He means it is no failure, because the employers, besides getting cheaper and more abundant labor, are relieved of all the cares and anxieties of governing and providing for their laborers, in health and in sickness, in old age and in infancy. In fine, he means it is no failure, because the laborers of England are not half so free now as before their pretended emancipation. They have lost all their rights, half their liberty (for they work harder than before), and their former masters have been relieved of all their legal obligations and responsibilities. No – British emancipation has not failed, if we look solely to the selfish interests of the property class. And British liberty, we shall show in another chapter, means the unlimited right of the property class to oppress the laboring class, uncoupled with the obligation to provide for them. But this writer well knew that looking to the effect of emancipation on the condition of the laboring class in England, it has been a cruel and monstrous failure, from first to last. They are almost as savage and ignorant as West India negroes, know nothing of the Bible, and live in a state of continued destitution, hunger, and excessive labor, from generation to generation – from infancy to old age.

West India emancipation was a blunder of swindling philanthropy. People were told that the negroes, after emancipation, would work harder, work for less, and be more of slaves than before, just as had happened with emancipated English. But philanthropy "hath bad luck." It overlooked, or forgot, the few wants and indolent habits of the negro, the abundance of mountain lands, the fertile soil, the volunteer fruits and mild climate of Jamaica. The negro *is really* free, and luxuriates in sloth, ignorance, and liberty, as none but a negro can. The mistake and the failure consisted in setting him really free, instead of nominally so. *Hinc illæ lachrymæ*! [1]

[1] "Hence these tears."

What vile hypocrisy to shed crocodile tears over the happy negro, and boast of British Liberty, which is daily and hourly consuming, by poverty, and cold, and foul air and water, and downright starvation, the lives of ten millions of your white brethren and neighbors!

But this system, which carried to untimely graves three hundred thousand Irishmen in a single season, has not been *condemned.* No; it is profitable to the oppressors, and will not be condemned.

In all countries where a few own the property and the population is tolerably dense, laborers relieved from domestic slavery are remitted to the exploitation of skill and capital, which renders them less free and worse situated in all respects after emancipation than before. To prove this great truth, is the chief object of our present work. We know that the philosophy of the subject is intricate and complex, and that we have the prejudices, fanaticism, and prepossessions of a world to oppose and conquer. We therefore indulge in frequent iteration, and adduce numerous proofs, examples, and illustrations.

# XIX

# PROTECTION AND CHARITY TO THE WEAK

A mere verbal formula often distinguishes a truism from a paradox. "It is the duty of society to protect the weak"; but protection cannot be efficient without the power of control; therefore, "It is the duty of society to enslave the weak." And it is a duty which no organized and civilized society ever failed to perform. Parents, husbands, guardians, teachers, committees, &c., are but masters under another name, whose duty it is to protect the weak, and whose right it is to control them. The blacks in America are both positively and relatively weak. Positively so, because they are too improvident to lay up for the exigencies of sickness, of the seasons, or of old age. Relatively so, because they are wholly unequal to the whites among whom they live, in the war of the wits and free competition, which universal liberty begets, and political economy encourages.

In old countries the white laborers are relatively weak, because all property is closely appropriated, and the capitalist class possess the means of unlimited oppression. Everybody admits that in such countries the poor need protection. But there can be no efficient protection without enslavement of some sort. In England, it has often been remarked, that all the legislation for the poor is borrowed from the system of domestic slavery.

Public and private charity is a fund created by the labor of the industrious poor, and too often bestowed on the idle or improvident. It is apt to aggravate the evils which it intends to cure.

Those who give should have the power to control, to some extent, the conduct and expenditure of the objects of their charity. Not till then can they be sure that their gifts will be promotive of good. But such power of control would be slavery.

Can abolitionists solve these social problems?

Ambition has ever been considered the most noble of human failings. It is, however, no failing, or crime, at all. Ambition desires power, and without power there can be no safe, prudent, and active benevolence. The selfish, the indolent, and the timid are without ambition, and eschew power, because of the trouble, the expenses, and the responsibilities which it imposes. The actively good are always ambitious, and desire to possess power, in order that they may control, in some measure, the conduct of those whom they desire to benefit.

The best thing a philanthropist can do is to buy slaves, because then his power of control is greatest – his ability to do practical good most perfect.

We take this occasion to correct an error into which we had fallen as to Northern character. Benevolence, affection, generosity, and philanthropy are equally common North and South; and only differ in their modes of manifestation. We are one people.

The daily and hourly exercise of these qualities is elicited at the South, because it is safe, prudent and expedient so to exercise them. The reverse is true at the North: yet, "expel Nature and she will return again." Man is social and philanthropic, and his affections, dammed out in one direction, find vent and gush out in another. The people of the North are far more generous and munificent in the endowment of public charities, and other public institutions, than we. This correction of our error does not affect our theories – if it be true, that you can only safely be charitable to dependents whom you can control. But if it did or does affect, neutralize, and subvert them, it is due to truth – and if we advance the cause of truth, we are ready for the sacrifice of all else.

"Our Trip to the North" excited doubts as to our estimate of Northern character; and subsequent observation, reading, and reflection have brought us to the conclusion, which we now with pleasure avow. We would rather be right than consistent.

# XX

# THE FAMILY

All modern philosophy converges to a single point — the overthrow of all government, the substitution of the untrammelled "Sovereignty of the Individual" for the Sovereignty of Society, and the inauguration of anarchy. First domestic slavery, next religious institutions, then separate property, then political government, and, finally, family government and family relations, are to be swept away. This is the distinctly avowed programme of all able abolitionists and socialists; and towards this end the doctrines and the practices of the weakest and most timid among them tend. Proudhon, and the French socialists generally, avow this purpose in France, and Stephen Pearl Andrews re-echoes it from America. The more numerous and timid class are represented by Mr. Greeley and the *Tribune*, who would not "at once rush," like French revolutionists, "with the explosive force of escapement, point blank to the bull's eye of its final destiny," but would inaugurate social conditions that would gradually bring about that result. Mr. Greeley does not propose to do away at once with marriage, religion, private property, political government and parental authority, but adopts the philosophy and the practices of Fourier, which promise gradually to purify human nature, and fit it, in a few generations, for that social millennium into which the bolder and more consistent Andrews urges society at once to plunge.

The Christian socialists are beautifully and energetically collaborating with the infidel socialists and abolitionists to bring about this millennium. They also are divided into two parties. The one would wait upon Providence—only help it a little, like Mr. Greeley—and permit our poor old effete world to pass out of existence by gentle euthanasia. The other and bolder party feel themselves "called" as special instruments to give at once the coup de grâce to the old world, and to usher in the new golden age of free love and free lands, of free women and free negroes, of free children and free men.

We like the Northern socialist theoretical abolitionists—read their speeches, essays, lectures, and books, because they agree with us that their own form of society is a humbug and a failure; and in their efforts, speculation and schemes to reorganize it, afford the most beautiful, perfect and complete specimen of the *reductio ad absurdum.* A lecture from Mr. Andrews on No-government, an Oneida den of incest, a Greeley phalanstery, or a New York free love saloon afford equally good instances of this mode of demonstration by the absurdities which they exhibit, and equally good proofs of the naturalness and necessity of slavery, since such horrid abuses are everywhere the approved and practiced outgrowth of free society. As all our thoughts, arguments, proofs and demonstrations are suggested by or borrowed from the abolitionists, it seems to us we ought to dedicate to them. The *Tribune* very properly remarked that our *Sociology* was the first attempt of the kind at the South. It ridiculed our ignorance, too, severely. It should have recollected that were there no sickness there would be no physicians. We assure the *Tribune* we are quite a prodigy in these matters for a Southern man. We have no social diseases, and therefore no social doctors to write about them or cure them. Such diseases have been rare; for Aristotle complains that there are no terms to express the relations of husband and wife, or parent and child. These relations have worked so smoothly in slave society to this day that we in writing have felt the same want of language of which Aristotle, more than two thousand years ago, complained. You should invent such terms at the North, if it be true, as Mr. Andrews states in italics, that there are ten fugitives from Northern matrimony to one from Southern slavery — from which he seems to infer very logically that the necessity of abolishing the family at the North is ten times as great as that for abolishing slavery at the South. He and you are experts, and we know it is presumptuous in us to dispute what you say about your own society. Still we are dead against your phalansteries and his love saloons. Gentlemen and scholars, generally at the South, would as soon be caught studying or practicing the black art, as in reading Owen or Fourier, or in building phalansteries. For ourselves, like the Bastard in *King John*, we learn these things, "not to deceive, but to avoid deceit." We have whole files of infidel and abolition papers, like the *Tribune*, the *Liberator* and *Investigator*. Fanny Wright, the Devil's Pulpit and the Devil's Parson, Tom Paine, Owen, Voltaire, et *id genus omne*, are our daily companions. Good people give our office a wide berth as they pass it, and even the hens who loiter about it, have caught the infection of Woman's Rights, for we saw but a few days ago a Shanghai cock under its eaves hovering a brood of twenty chickens, whilst madam hen was strutting about in as large a liberty as any Bloomer or wise woman of the North.

Love and veneration for the family is with us not only a principle, but probably a prejudice and a weakness. We were never two weeks at a time from under the family roof, until we had passed middle life, and now that our years almost number half a century, we have never been from home for an interval of two months. And our historical reading, as well as our habits of life, may have unfitted us to appreciate the communist and fusion theories of Fanny Wright, Owen and Mr. Greeley. In attempting to vindicate and justify the ways of God and Nature, against the progressiveness of Black Republicanism in America, and Red Republicanism in Europe, we would forewarn the reader that we are a prejudiced witness. We are the enthusiastic admirer of the social relations exhibited in the histories of Abraham, Isaac and Jacob. The social relations established in Deuteronomy, and 25th chapter Leviticus, and as practiced by the Jews to this day, elicit our unfeigned admiration and approval. Moses is with us the Prince of Legislators, and the twenty-fifth Leviticus the best of political platforms. The purity of the family seems to be his paramount object.

Homer, too, especially in his *Odyssey*, charms and enchains us with his beautiful descriptions of family felicity and family purity. As conquest and commerce introduced wealth and corrupted morals and manners, the family was corrupted and disrupted, as it is now, at the most commercial points in the North. But we have only to pass over to Italy, and there, from the earliest days of tradition until the extinction of liberty, begun by Sylla and Marius, and ended by Augustus, we find the family a pure, a holy and sacred thing. From that era till slavery arose in the South, the family never resumed its dignity and importance. Feudalism did something to correct the loose morality of the Augustan Age, but it adopted its colonial slavery, relaxed family ties, and never drew together in sufficiently close connection and subordination, the materials which nature dictates should form the human hive or social circle.

Aristotle understood this subject thoroughly; and it seems to have been generally so well comprehended in his day, that he takes little trouble to cxplain and expound it. He commences his treatise on Politics and Economics with the family, and discourses first of the slaves as a part of the family. He assumes that social life is as natural to man as to bees and herds; and that the family, including husband, wife, children, and slaves, is the first and most natural development of that social nature. As States are composed of families, and as a sound and healthy whole cannot be formed of rotten parts, he devotes much of his treatise to family education and government. Would that modern statesmen, philosophers and politicians, would become practical like Aristotle, and not attempt to build social and political edifices, until they were sure of the soundness of the materials of which they would construct them. As all human beings live for the greatest part of their lives in families, it is all important that they should look to the wise arrangement of this old and universal institution.

We wish to prove that the great movement in society, known under various names, as Communism, Socialism, Abolitionism, Red Republicanism and Black Republicanism, has one common object: the breaking up of all law and government, and the inauguration of anarchy, and that the destruction of the family is one of the means in which they all concur to attain a common end. We shall quote only from Stephen Pearl Andrews, because he is by far the ablest and best informed of American Socialists and Reformers, and because he cites facts and authorities to show that he presents truly the current thought and the general intention. Mr. Andrews is a Massachusetts gentleman, who has lived at the South. He has been an Abolition Lecturer. He is the disciple of Warren, who is the disciple of Owen of Lanark and New Harmony. Owen and Warren are Socrates and Plato, and he is the Great Stygarite, as far surpassing them, as Aristotle surpassed Socrates and Plato. But it is not merely his theories on which we rely; he cites historical facts that show that the tendency and terminus of all abolition is to the sovereignty of the individual, the breaking up of families, and no-government. He delivered a series of lectures to the elite of New York on this subject, which met with approbation, and from which we shall quote. He established, or aided to establish, Free Love Villages, and headed a Free Love Saloon in the city of New York, patronized and approved by the "Higher Classes." He is indubitably the philosopher and true exponent of Northern Abolitionism. With this assertion, which none who read his *Science of Society* we think will deny, we proceed to quote from his able and beautiful lectures, embodied in a publication entitled *Science of Society*. Our first quotation is from his first lecture and the first chapter of his work:

Every age is a remarkable one, no doubt, for those who live in it. When immobility reigns most in human affairs, there is still enough of movement to fix the attention, and even to excite the wonder of those who are immediately in proximity with it. This natural bias in favor of the period with which we have most to do is by no means sufficient, however, to account for the growing conviction, on all minds, that the present epoch is a marked transition from an old to a new order of things. The scattered rays of the gray dawn of the new era date back, indeed, beyond the lifetime of the present generation. The first streak of light that streamed through the dense darkness of the old *regime* was the declaration by Martin Luther of the right of private judgment in matters of conscience. The next, which shed terror upon the old world, as a new portent of impending revolutions, was the denial, by Hampden, Sidney, Cromwell, and others, of the divine right of kings, and the assertion of inherent political rights in the people themselves. This was followed by the American Declaration of Independence, the establishment of a powerful Democratic Republic in the western world upon the basis of that principle, followed by the French Revolution, the Reign of Terror, the Reaction, and the apparent death in Europe of the Democratic idea. Finally, in our day, comes the red glare of French Socialism, at which the world is still gazing with uncertainty whether it be some lurid and meteoric omen of fearful events, or whether it be not the actual rising of the Sun of Righteousness, with healing in His wings; for there are those who profoundly and religiously believe that the solution of the social problem will be the virtual descent of the New Jerusalem — the installation of the Kingdom of Heaven upon earth.

First in the religious, then in the political, and finally in the social relations of men, new doctrines have thus been broached, which are full of promise to the hopeful, and full of alarm and dismay to the timid and conservative. This distinction marks the broadest division in the ranks of mankind. In church, and state, and social life, the real parties are the Progressionists and the Retrogressionists — those whose most brilliant imaginings are linked with the future, and those whose sweetest remembrances bind them in tender associations to the past. Catholic and Protestant, Whig and Democrat, Anti-Socialist and Socialist, are terms which, in their origin, correspond to this generic division; but no sooner does a new classification take place than the parties thus formed are again subdivided, on either hand, by the ever-permeating tendency, on the one side toward freedom, emancipation, and progress, and toward law, and order, and immobility on the other.

Hitherto the struggle between conservatism and progress has seemed doubtful. Victory has kissed the banner, alternately, of either host. At length the serried ranks of conservatism falter. Reform, so called, is becoming confessedly more potent than its antagonist. The admission is reluctantly forced from pallid lips that revolutions — political, social, and religious — constitute the programme of the coming age. Reform, so called, for weal or woe, but yet Reform, must rule the hour. The older constitutions of society have outlived their day. No truth commends itself more universally to the minds of men now, than that thus set forth by Carlyle: "There must be a new world if there is to be any world at all. That human things in our Europe can ever return to the old sorry routine, and proceed with any steadiness or continuance there — this small hope is not now a tenable one. These days of universal death must be days of universal new birth, if the ruin is not to be total and final! It is a time to make the dullest man consider, and ask himself, Whence he came? Whither he is bound? A veritable 'New Era,' to the foolish as well as to the wise." Nor is this state of things confined to Europe. The agitations in America may be more peaceful, but they are not less profound. The foundations of old beliefs and habits of thought are breaking up. The old guarantees of order are fast falling away. A veritable "new era" with us, too, is alike impending and inevitable.

So much to show the width and scope of the social revolution that is contemplated as well by destructives as conservatives; for Mr. Carlyle is like ourselves, and thinks society needs more government, screwing up, instead of relaxing. He, too, is a socialist, but a conservative socialist. He asserts, like Mr. Andrews, that society has failed, but proposes a different mode of reconstruction. At the very moment we in America were announcing the Failure of Free Society, he in Europe proclaimed the "Latter Day" of that Society. It was but a different mode of expressing the same thought. Now we will show from this same lecture of Mr. Andrews, that the annihilation of the Family is part of the programme of Abolition. He says, page 31, in this same lecture:

Every variety of conscience, and every variety of deportment in reference to this precise subject of love is already tolerated among us. At one extreme of the scale stand the Shakers, who abjure the connection of the sexes altogether. At the other extremity stands the association of Perfectionists, at Oneida, who hold and practice, and justify by the Scriptures, as a religious dogma, what they denominate complex marriage, or the freedom of love. We have, in this State, stringent laws against adultery and fornication; but laws of that sort fall powerless, in America, before the all-pervading sentiment of Protestantism, which vindicates the freedom of conscience to all persons and in all things, provided the consequences fall upon the parties themselves. Hence the Oneida Perfectionists live undisturbed and respected, in the heart of the State of New York, and in the face of the world; and the civil government, true to the Democratic principle, which is only the same principle in another application, is little anxious to interfere with this breach of his own ordinances, so long as they cast none of the consequences of their conduct upon those who do not consent to bear them.

And, page 33, he says:

In general, however, Government still interferes with the marriage and parental relations. Democracy in America has always proceeded with due reference to the prudential motto, *festina lente*.[1] In France, at the time of the first Revolution, Democracy rushed with the explosive force of escapement from centuries of compression, point blank to the bull's eye of its final destiny, from which it recoiled with such force that the stupid world has dreamed, for half a century, that the vital principle of Democracy was dead. As a logical sequence from Democratic principle, the legal obligation of marriage was sundered, and the Sovereignty of the Individual above the institution was vindicated.

Page 42:

I must apologize as well for the incompleteness as for the apparent dogmatism of any brief exposition of this subject. I assert that it is not only possible and rationally probable, but that it is rigidly consequential upon the right understanding of the constitution of man that all government, in the sense of involuntary restraint upon the Individual, or substantially all, must finally cease, and along with it the whole complicated paraphernalia and trumpery of Kings, Emperors,

[1] "Make haste slowly."

Presidents, Legislatures, and Judiciary. I assert that the indicia of this result abound in existing society, and that it is the instinctive or intelligent perception of that fact by those who have not bargained for so much, which gives origin and vital energy to the reaction in church and state and social life. I assert that the distance is less today forward from the theory and practice of Government as it is in these United States, to the total abrogation of all Government above that of the Individual, than it is backward to the theory and practice of Government as Government now is in the despotic countries of the old world.

The reader will thus see that Abolition contemplates the total overthrow of the Family and all other existing social, moral, religious and governmental institutions. We quote Mr. Andrews because he is *longo intervallo*,[2] the ablest Abolition Philosopher. Many volumes would be needed to display and expose the opinions of all the votaries of the New Philosophy. But every man who sets to work honestly to discover truth, will find at every step, that we have neither distorted nor exaggerated. The Family is threatened, and all men North or South who love and revere it, should be up and a-doing.

[2] "By all odds."

# XXI

# NEGRO SLAVERY

Until the lands of America are appropriated by a few, population becomes dense, competition among laborers active, employment uncertain, and wages low, the personal liberty of all the whites will continue to be a blessing. We have vast unsettled territories; population may cease to increase slowly, as in most countries, and many centuries may elapse before the question will be practically suggested, whether slavery to capital be preferable to slavery to human masters. But the negro has neither energy nor enterprise, and, even in our sparser population, finds, with his improvident habits, that his liberty is a curse to himself, and a greater curse to the society around him. These considerations, and others equally obvious, have induced the South to attempt to defend negro slavery as an exceptional institution, admitting, nay asserting, that slavery, in the general or in the abstract, is morally wrong, and against common right. With singular inconsistency, after making this admission, which admits away the authority of the Bible, of profane history, and of the almost universal practice of mankind – they turn round and attempt to bolster up the cause of negro slavery by these very exploded authorities. If we mean not to repudiate all divine, and almost all human authority in favor of slavery, we must vindicate that institution in the abstract.

To insist that a status of society, which has been almost universal, and which is expressly and continually justified by Holy Writ, is its natural, normal, and necessary status, under the ordinary circumstances, is on its face a plausible and probable proposition. To insist on less, is to yield our cause, and to give up our religion; for if white slavery be morally wrong, be a violation of natural rights, the Bible cannot be true. Human and divine authority do seem in the general to concur, in establishing the expediency of having masters and slaves of different races. The nominal servitude of the Jews to each other, in its temporary character, and no doubt in its mild character, more nearly resembled our wardship and apprenticeship, than ordinary domestic slavery. In very many nations of antiquity, and in some of modern times, the law has permitted the native citizens to become slaves to each other. But few take advantage of such laws; and the infrequency of the practice, establishes the general truth that master and slave should be of different national descent. In some respects, the wider the difference the better, as the slave will feel less mortified by his position. In other respects, it may be that too wide a difference hardens the hearts and brutalizes the feelings of both master and slave. The civilized man hates the savage, and the savage returns the hatred with interest. Hence, West India slavery of newly caught negroes is not a very humane, affectionate, or civilizing institution. Virginia negroes have become moral and intelligent. They love their master and his family, and the attachment is reciprocated. Still, we like the idle, but intelligent house-servants, better than the hard-used, but stupid outhands; and we like the mulatto better than the negro; yet the negro is generally more affectionate, contented and faithful.

The world at large looks on negro slavery as much the worst form of slavery; because it is only acquainted with West India slavery. Abolition never arose till negro slavery was instituted; and now abolition is only directed against negro slavery. There is no philanthropic crusade attempting to set free the white slaves of Eastern Europe and of Asia. The world, then, is prepared for the defence of slavery in the abstract—it is prejudiced only against negro slavery.

These prejudices were in their origin well founded. The Slave Trade, the horrors of the Middle Passage, and West India slavery were enough to rouse the most torpid philanthropy.

But our Southern slavery has become a benign and protective institution, and our negroes are confessedly better off than any free laboring population in the world.

How can we contend that white slavery is wrong, whilst all the great body of free laborers are starving; and slaves, white or black, throughout the world, are enjoying comfort?

We write in the cause of Truth and Humanity, and will not play the advocate for master or for slave.

The aversion to negroes, the antipathy of race, is much greater at the North than at the South; and it is very probable that this antipathy to the person of the negro, is confounded with or generates hatred of the institution with which he is usually connected. Hatred to slavery is very generally little more than hatred of negroes.

There is one strong argument in favor of negro slavery over all other slavery: that he, being unfitted for the mechanic arts, for trade, and all skillful pursuits, leaves those pursuits to be carried on by the whites; and does not bring all industry into disrepute, as in Greece and Rome, where the slaves were not only the artists and mechanics, but also the merchants.

Whilst, as a general and abstract question, negro slavery has no other claims over other forms of slavery, except that from inferiority, or rather peculiarity, of race, almost all negroes require masters, whilst only the children, the women, the very weak, poor, and ignorant, &c., among the whites, need some protective and governing relation of this kind; yet as a subject of temporary, but worldwide importance, negro slavery has become the most necessary of all human institutions.

The African slave trade to America commenced three centuries and a half since. By the time of the American Revolution, the supply of slaves had exceeded the demand for slave labor, and the slaveholders, to get rid of a burden, and to prevent the increase of a nuisance, became violent opponents of the slave trade, and many of them abolitionists. New England, Bristol, and Liverpool, who reaped the profits of the trade, without suffering from the nuisance, stood out for a long time against its abolition. Finally, laws and treaties were made, and fleets fitted out to abolish it; and after a while, the slaves of most of South America, of the West Indies, and of Mexico were liberated. In the meantime, cotton, rice, sugar, coffee, tobacco, and other products of slave labor, came into universal use as necessaries of life. The population of Western Europe, sustained and stimulated by those products, was trebled, and that of the North increased tenfold. The products of slave labor became scarce and dear, and famines frequent. Now, it is obvious, that to emancipate all the negroes would be to starve Western Europe and our North. Not to extend and increase negro slavery, *pari passu*, with the extension and multiplication of free society, will produce much suffering. If all South America, Mexico, the West Indies, and our Union south of Mason and Dixon's line, of the Ohio and Missouri, were slaveholding, slave products would be abundant and cheap in free society; and their market for their merchandise, manufactures, commerce, &c., illimitable. Free white laborers might live in comfort and luxury on light work, but for the exacting and greedy landlords, bosses and other capitalists.

We must confess, that overstock the world as you will with comforts and with luxuries, we do not see how to make capital relax its monopoly — how to do aught but tantalize the hireling. Capital, irresponsible capital, begets, and ever will beget, the *immedicabile vulnus*[1] of so-called Free Society. It invades every recess of domestic life, infects its food, its clothing, its drink, its very atmosphere, and pursues the hireling, from the hovel to the poor-house, the prison

[1] "Irreparable injury."

and the grave. Do what he will, go where he will, capital pursues and persecutes him. "Hæret lateri lethalis arundo!" [2]

Capital supports and protects the domestic slave; taxes, oppresses and persecutes the free laborer.

[2] "The lethal arrow clings to her side." Virgil, *Aeneid*, IV, 73

# XXII

## THE STRENGTH OF WEAKNESS

An unexplored moral world stretches out before us, and invites our investigation; but neither our time, our abilities, nor the character of our work, will permit us to do more than glance at its loveliness.

It is pleasing, however, to turn from the world of political economy, in which "might makes right," and strength of mind and of body are employed to oppress and exact from the weak, to that other and better, and far more numerous world, in which weakness rules, clad in the armor of affection and benevolence. It is delightful to retire from the outer world, with its competitions, rivalries, envyings, jealousies, and selfish war of the wits, to the bosom of the family, where the only tyrant is the infant—the greatest slave the master of the household. You feel at once that you have exchanged the keen air of selfishness, for the mild atmosphere of benevolence. Each one prefers the good of others to his own, and finds most happiness in sacrificing selfish pleasures, and ministering to others' enjoyments. The wife, the husband, the parent, the child, the son, the brother and the sister, usually act towards each other on scriptural principles. The infant, in its capricious dominion over mother, father, brothers and sisters, exhibits, in strongest colors, the "strength of weakness," the power of affection. The wife and daughters are more carefully attended by the father, than the sons, because they are weaker and elicit more of his affection.

The dependent exercise, because of their dependence, as

much control over their superiors, in most things, as those superiors exercise over them. Thus, and thus only, can conditions be equalized. This constitutes practical equality of rights, enforced not by human, but by divine law. Our hearts bleed at the robbing of a bird's nest; and the little birds, because they are weak, subdue our strength and command our care. We love and cherish the rose, and sympathize with the lily which some wanton boy has bruised and broken. Our faithful dog shares our affections, and we will risk our lives to redress injustice done him.

Man is not all selfish. "Might does not always make right." Within the family circle, the law of love prevails, not that of selfishness.

But, besides wife and children, brothers and sister, dogs, horses, birds and flowers – slaves, also, belong to the family circle. Does their common humanity, their abject weakness and dependence, their great value, their ministering to our wants in childhood, manhood, sickness and old age, cut them off from that affection which everything else in the family elicits? No; the interests of master and slave are bound up together, and each in his appropriate sphere naturally endeavors to promote the happiness of the other.

The humble and obedient slave exercises more or less control over the most brutal and hard-hearted master. It is an invariable law of nature, that weakness and dependence are elements of strength, and generally sufficiently limit that universal despotism, observable throughout human and animal nature. The moral and physical world is but a series of subordinations, and the more perfect the subordination, the greater the harmony and the happiness. Inferior and superior act and re-act on each other through agencies and media too delicate and subtle for human apprehensions; yet, looking to usual results, man should be willing to leave to God what God only can regulate. Human law cannot beget benevolence, affection, maternal and paternal love; nor can it supply their places; but it may, by breaking up the ordinary relations of human beings, stop and disturb the current of these finer feelings of our nature. It may abolish slavery; but it can never create between the capitalist and the laborer, between the employer and employed, the kind and affectionate relations that usually exist between master and slave.

## XXIII

## MONEY

From the days of Plato and Lycurgus to the present times, Social Reformers have sought to restrict or banish the use of money. We do not doubt that its moderate use is essential to civilization and promotive of human happiness and well-being — and we entertain as little doubt, that its excessive use is the most potent of all causes of human inequality of condition, of excessive wealth and luxury with the few, and of great destitution and suffering with the many, and of general effeminacy and corruption of morals. Money is the great weapon in free, equal, and competitive society, which skill and capital employ in the war of the wits, to exploitate and oppress the poor, the improvident, and weak-minded. Its evil effects are greatly aggravated by the credit and banking systems, and by the facilities of intercommunication and locomation which the world now possesses. Every bargain or exchange is more or less a hostile encounter of wits. Money vastly increases the number of bargains and exchanges, and thus keeps society involved, if not in war, at least in unfriendly collision. Within the family, money is not employed between its members. Where the family includes slaves, the aggregate use of money is greatly restricted. This furnishes us with another argument to prove that Christian morality is practicable, to a great extent, in slave society — impracticable in free society.

The Socialists derive this idea of dispensing with or restricting the use of money, from Sparta and other ancient States; and to the same sources may be traced almost all their schemes of social improvement. Plato, in his philosophy, borrowed from those sources, and subsequent Socialists have borrowed from him. We annex an interesting article on this subject of money from Sir Thomas More's *Utopia*:

UTOPIA; OR, THE HAPPY REPUBLIC

Therefore, I must say that, as I hope for mercy, I can have no other notion of all the governments that I see or know, than that they are a conspiracy of the richer sort, who, on pretence of managing the public, do only pursue their private ends, and devise all the ways and arts that they can find out; first, that they may, without danger, preserve all they have so ill acquired, and then, that they may engage the former sort to toil and labor for them at as low rates as possible, and oppress them as much as they please; and if they can but prevail to get these contrivances established by public authority, which is considered as the representative of the whole people, then they are accounted laws; and yet these wicked men, after they have, by a most insatiable covetousness, divided that among themselves, with which all the rest might have been well supplied, are far from that happiness that is enjoyed by the Utopians; *for the use as well as the desire of money being extinguished*, there is much anxiety and great occasion of mischief cut off with it. And who does not see that frauds, thefts, robberies, quarrels, tumults, contentions, seditions, murders, treacheries and witchcrafts, that are indeed rather punished than restricted by the severities of the law, would fall off, if money were not any more valued by the world. Their fears, solicitudes, cares, labors and watchings would all perish in the same moment that the value of money did sink.

# XXIV

# GERRIT SMITH ON LAND REFORM, AND WILLIAM LLOYD GARRISON ON NO-GOVERNMENT

Within the last week, we have received the *Land Reformer*, an agrarian paper, just started in New York, in which we are sure we recognize the pen of Gerrit Smith, the leader of the New York abolitionists; and also a No. of the *Liberator*, in which Mr. Garrison, the leader of the New England abolitionists, defines his No-Government doctrines.

In calling attention, North and South, to opinions openly and actively promulgated by such distinguished men, which opinions are at war with all existing institutions, we are rendering equal service to all sections of our common country.

Mr. Smith says:

Why should not this monopoly be broken up? Because, says the objector, vested rights forbid it. But there can be no vested rights against original and natural rights. No claim of a part of the human family to the whole earth can be valid against the claim of the whole human family to it. No passing of papers or parchments in former generations can foreclose the rights of the present generation. No bargains and no conventional titles can avail in justice against the great title-deeds, by which Nature grants and conveys herself to each generation, as it comes upon the earth; and by which she makes the living (simply because they are the living, and not at all because of their relation to the dead) the equal owners of her soil and seas, her light and air. No arrangements, by which the six thousand, who have monopolized the lands of Ireland, should be allowed to overcome the title of the six millions to it. If the natural and inherent right of the whole is not paramount to that, which the fractions claim to have acquired, then are *the six millions born into the world trespassers;* and then is the Creator chargeable with a lack of wisdom and goodness. If it is right that the mass of men should hold their standing-place on the earth by mere sufferance, or upon terms dictated by their fellows, then is it not true that God is an Impartial Father — for then it is not true that he has given the earth to all his children, but only to a select.

We, too, think Free Society a very bad thing, and a decided failure, but not half so bad as Mr. Smith paints it. There is a poor-house system in Ireland, which, to some extent, recognizes the doctrine that all men are entitled to live on the earth, and be supported from it. In practice, the system does not always work well; yet we are confident it works much better for all parties, than would Mr. Smith's plan of agrarianism.

But slavery does, in practice as well as in theory, acknowledge and enforce the right of all to be comfortably supported from the soil. There was, we repeat, no pauperism in Europe till feudal slavery was abolished.

It will be strange, indeed, if the voters in New York, a majority of whom own no land, do not take Mr. Smith at his word, and assert their superior claim, under his Higher Law and "Fundamental Principles," to all the land. 'Tis a concise and ingenious syllogism, to this effect: "The earth belongs equally to all mankind, under the Higher Law, or Law of God, which is superior to all human laws; therefore, the lackland majority have a better right to the soil than the present proprietors, whose title is derived from mere human law."

It never did occur to us, that the paupers had the best right to all the farms, until we saw this new application of the Higher Law. But 'tis clear as noonday, if you grant the Higher Law, as expounded by Mr. Seward; and we expect soon to hear that they are bringing their titles into court. Anti-rentism looked this way, and anti-rentism chose its own Governor and Judges.

But Mr. Garrison outbids Mr. Smith all hollow for the

pauper vote. He promises not only to everyone his "vine and fig-tree," but a vine and fig-tree that will bear fruit without culture. He is going to get up a terrestrial paradise, in which there will be no jails, no taxes, no labor, no want, no sickness, no pain, no government – in fact, no anything. But he shall speak for himself. We find the following in the *Liberator* of 1st August:

> Indeed, properly speaking, there is but one government, and that is not human, but divine; there is but one law, and that is "the Higher Law"; there is but one ruler, and that one is God, "in whom we live and move, and have our being." What is called human government is usurpation, imposture, demagoguism, peculation, swindling, and tyranny, more or less, according to circumstances, and to the intellectual and moral condition of the people. Unquestionably, every existing government on earth is to be overthrown by the growth of mind and moral regeneration of the masses. Absolutism, limited monarchy, democracy — all are sustained by the sword; all are based upon the doctrine, that "Might makes right"; all are intrinsically inhuman, selfish, clanish, and opposed to a recognition of the brotherhood of man. They are to liberty, what whiskey, brandy and gin are to temperance. They belong to the "Kingdoms of this World," and in due time are to be destroyed by the Brightness of the coming of Him, "whose right it is to reign"; and by the erection of a Kingdom which cannot be shaken. They are not for the people, but make the people their prey; they are hostile to all progress; they resist to the utmost all radical changes. All history shows that Liberty, Humanity, Justice, and Right have ever been in conflict with existing governments, no matter what their theory or form."

Mr. Greeley's Phalansteries, Mr. Andrews' Free Love, Mr. Goodell's Millennium, and Mr. Smith's Agrarianism, all pale before this Kingdom of Mr. Garrison's. He is King of the Abolitionists, Great Anarch of the North.

We cannot reconcile this millennial doctrine of Mr. Garrison's with another doctrine, which we have seen imputed to him in the *Richmond Examiner*, to wit, that there is no God, because no beneficent Creator would have so constituted mankind as to have made slavery almost universal. Now, assume, as he does, that slavery is a cruel, sinful, and wicked institution, destructive alike of human happiness and well-being, and his conclusion is irresistible. To be consistent, all anti-slavery men should be atheists. Ere long, we suspect, their consistency will equal their folly and profanity.

With us, who think slavery a benevolent institution, equally necessary to protect the weak, and to govern the wicked and the ignorant, its prevalence is part of that order and adaptation of the universe that "lifts the soul from Nature up to Nature's God."

# XXV

# IN WHAT ANTI-SLAVERY ENDS

Mr. Carlyle very properly contends that abolition and all the other social movements of the day, propose little or no government as the moral panacea that is to heal and save a suffering world. Proudhon expressly advocates anarchy; and Stephen Pearl Andrews, the ablest of American socialistic and abolition philosophers, elaborately attacks all existing social relations, and all legal and governmental restraints, and proposes No-Government as their substitute. He is the author of the Free Love experiment in New York, and a co-laborer and eulogist of similar experiments in villages or settlements in Ohio, Long Island and other places in the North and Northwest. He is a follower of Josiah Warren, who was associated with Owen of Lanark at New Harmony. We do not know that there is any essential difference between his system and that which has been for many years past practically carried out in Oneida County, New York, by the Perfectionists, who construe the Bible into authority for the unrestrained indulgence of every sensual appetite. The doctrines of Fourier, of Owen and Fanny Wright, and the other early Socialists, all lead to No-Government and Free Love. 'Tis probable they foresaw and intended this result, but did not suggest or propose it to a world then too wicked and unenlightened to appreciate its beatific purity and loveliness. The materials, as well as the proceedings of the infidel, woman's rights, negro's rights, free-everything and anti-every school, headed and conducted in Boston, by Garrison, Parker, Phillips, and their associate women and negroes, show that they too are busy with "assiduous wedges" in loosening the whole frame of society, and preparing for the glorious advent of Free Love and No-Government. All the Infidel and Abolition papers in the North betray a similar tendency. The Abolitionists of New York, headed by Gerrit Smith and Wm. Goodell, are engaged in precisely the same projects, but being Christians, would dignify Free Love and No-Government with the appellation of a Millennium. Probably half the Abolitionists at the North expect a great social revolution soon to occur by the advent of the Millennium. If they would patiently await that event, instead of attempting to get it up themselves, their delusions, however ridiculous, might at least be innocuous. But these progressive Christian Socialists differ not at all from the Infidel Socialists of Boston. They are equally intent and busy in pulling down the priesthood, and abolishing or dividing all property — seeing that whether the denouement be Free Love or a Millennium, the destruction of all existing human relations and human institutions is prerequisite to their full fruition.

Many thousand as have been of late years the social experiments attempting to practice community of property, of wives, children, &c., and numerous as the books inculcating and approving such practices, yet the existence and growth of Mormonism is of itself stronger evidence than all other of the tendency of modern free society towards No-Government and Free Love. In the name of polygamy, it has practically removed all restraints to the intercourse of sexes, and broken up the Family. It promises, too, a qualified community of property and a fraternal association of labor. It beats up monthly thousands of recruits from free society in Europe and America, but makes not one convert in the slaveholding South. Slavery is satisfied and conservative. Abolition, finding that all existing legal, religious, social and governmental institutions restrict liberty and occasion a quasi-slavery, is resolved not to stop short of the subversion of all those institutions, and the inauguration of Free Love and No-Government. The only cure for all this is for free society sternly to recognize slavery as right in principle, and necessary in practice, with more or less of modification, to the very existence of government, of property, of religion, and of social existence.

We shall not attempt to reconcile the doctrines of the Socialists, which propose to remove all legal restraints, with their denunciations of Political Economy. Let Alone is the essence of Political Economy and the whole creed of most of the Socialists. The Political Economists, Let Alone, for a fair fight, for universal rivalry, antagonism, competition, and cannibalism. They say the eating up the weaker members of society, the killing them out by capital and competition, will improve the breed of men and benefit society. They foresee the consequences of their doctrine, and are consistent. Hobbes saw men devouring one another, under their system, two hundred years ago, and we all see them similarly engaged now. The Socialists promise that when society is wholly disintegrated and dissolved, by inculcating good principles and "singing fraternity over it," all men will cooperate, love, and help one another.

They place men in positions of equality, rivalry, and antagonism, which must result in extreme selfishness of conduct, and yet propose this system as a cure for selfishness. To us their reasonings seem absurd.

Yet the doctrines so prevalent with Abolitionists and Socialists, of Free Love and Free Lands, Free Churches, Free Women and Free Negroes – of No-Marriage, No-Religion, No-Private Property, No-Law and No-Government, are legitimate deductions, if not obvious corollaries from the leading and distinctive axiom of political economy – Laissez Faire, or Let Alone.

All the leading Socialists and Abolitionists of the North, we think, agree with Fanny Wright, that the gradual changes which have taken place in social organization from domestic slavery to prædial serfdom and thence to the present system of free and competitive society, have been mere transitive states, each placing the laborer in a worse condition than that of absolute slavery, yet valuable as preparing the way for a new and more perfect social state. They value the present state of society the more highly because it is intolerable, and must the sooner usher in a Millennium or Utopia.

# XXVI

# CHRISTIAN MORALITY IMPRACTICABLE IN FREE SOCIETY—BUT THE NATURAL MORALITY OF SLAVE SOCIETY

It is strange that theories, self-evidently true so soon as suggested, remain undiscovered for centuries. What more evident, obvious, and axiomatic, than that equals must from necessity be rivals, antagonists, competitors, and enemies. Self-preservation, the first law of human and animal nature, makes this selfish course of action essential to preserve existence. It is almost equally obvious that in the natural, social, or family state, unselfishness, or the preference of others' good and happiness, is the dictate of nature and policy. Nature impels the father and husband to self-abnegation and self-denial to promote the happiness of wife and children, because his reflected enjoyments will be a thousand times greater than any direct pleasure he can derive by stinting or maltreating them. Their misery and their complaints do much more to render him wretched than what he has denied them can compensate for. Wife and children, too, see and feel that in denying themselves and promoting the happiness of the head of the family, they pursue true policy, and are most sensibly selfish when they seem most unselfish. Especially, however, is it true with slaves and masters that to "do as they would be done by" is mutually beneficial. Good treatment and proper discipline renders the slave happier, healthier, more valuable, grateful, and contented. Obedience, industry and loyalty on the part of the slave, increases the master's ability and disposition to protect and take care of him. The interests of all the members of a natural family, slaves included, are identical. Selfishness finds no place, because nature, common feelings and self-interest dictate to all that it is their true interest "to love their neighbor as themselves," and "to do as they would be done by," – at least, within the precincts of the family. To throw off into the world wife, children, and slaves, would injure, not benefit them. To neglect to punish children or slaves when they deserved it, would not be to do as we would be done by. Such punishment is generally the highest reach of self-abnegation and self-control. 'Tis easy and agreeable to be indulgent and remiss – hard to exact and enforce duty. Severe disciplinarians are the best officers, teachers, parents, and masters, and most revered and loved by their subordinates. They sacrifice their time and their feelings to duty, and for the ultimate good of others. Easy, lax, indulgent men are generally selfish and sensual, and justly forfeit the respect and affection of those whom they neglect to punish, because to do so would disturb their Epicurean repose. Christian morality is neither difficult nor unnatural where dependent, family, and slave relations exist, and Christian morality was preached and only intended for such.

The whole morale of free society is, "Every man, woman and child for himself and herself." Slavery in every form must be abolished. Wives must have distinct, separate, and therefore antagonistic and conflicting interests from their husbands, and children must as soon as possible be remitted to the rights of manhood. Is it not passing strange, wonderful, that such men as Channing and Wayland did not see that their world of universal liberty was a world of universal selfishness, discord, competition, rivalry, and war of the wits. Hobbes did see it, and supposing there was no other world, said "a state of nature was a state of war." But the family, including slaves, which the Abolitionists would destroy, has been almost universal, and is therefore natural. Christian morality is the natural morality in slave society, and slave society is the only natural society. Such society as that of the early Patriarchs of Judea, under Moses and Joshua, and as that of the South, would never beget a sceptic, a Hobbes, a Wayland, nor a Channing. In such society it is natural for men to love one another. The ordinary relations of men are not competitive and antagonistic as in free society; and selfishness is not general, but exceptionable. Duty to self is the first of duties: free society makes it the only duty. Man is not naturally selfish or bad, for he is naturally social. Free society dissociates him, and makes him bad and selfish from necessity.

It is said in Scripture, that it is harder for a rich man to enter the kingdom of heaven than for a camel to pass through the eye of a needle. We are no theologian; but do know from history and observation that wealthy men who are sincere and devout Christians in free society, feel at a loss what to do with their wealth, so as not to make it an instrument of oppression and wrong. Capital and skill are powers exercised almost always to oppress labor. If you endow colleges, you rear up cunning, voracious exploitators to devour the poor. If you give it to tradesmen or land owners, 'tis still an additional instrument, always employed to oppress laborers. If you give it to the really needy, you too often encourage idleness, and increase the burdens of the working poor who support everybody. We cannot possibly see but one safe way to invest wealth, and that is to buy slaves with it, whose conduct you can control, and be sure that your charity is not misapplied, and mischievous.

Is there any other safe way of investing wealth, or bestowing charity? We regret that delicacy restrains us from putting the question to a celebrated wealthy philanthropist of the North, who is candid, bold, experienced, and an Abolitionist to boot.

# XXVII

## SLAVERY — ITS EFFECT ON THE FREE

Beaten at every other quarter, we learn that a distinguished writer at the North, is about to be put forward by the Abolitionists, to prove that the influence of slavery is deleterious on the whites who own no slaves.

Now, at first view it elevates those whites; for it makes them not the bottom of society, as at the North — not the menials, the hired day laborer, the work scavengers and scullions — but privileged citizens, like Greek and Roman citizens, with a numerous class far beneath them. In slave society, one white man does not lord it over another; for all are equal in privilege, if not in wealth; and the poorest would not become a menial — hold your horse, and then extend his hand or his hat for a gratuity, were you to proffer him the wealth of the Indies. The menial, the exposed and laborious, and the disgraceful occupations are all filled by slaves. But filled they must be by someone, and in free society, half of its members are employed in occupations that are not considered or treated as respectable. Our slaves till the land, do the coarse and hard labor on our roads and canals, sweep our streets, cook our food, brush our boots, wait on our tables, hold our horses, do all hard work, and fill all menial offices. Your freemen at the North do the same work and fill the same offices. The only difference is, we love our slaves, and we are ready to defend, assist and protect them; you hate and fear your white servants, and never fail, as a moral duty, to screw down their wages to the lowest, and to starve their families, if possible, as evidence of your thrift, economy and management — the only English and Yankee virtues.

In free society, miscalled freemen fulfill all the offices of slaves for less wages than slaves, and are infinitely less liked and cared for by their superiors than slaves. Does this elevate them and render them happy?

The trades, the professions, the occupations that pay well, and whose work is light, is reserved for freemen in slave society. Does this depress them?

The doctor, the lawyer, the mechanic, the dentist, the merchant, the overseer, every trade and profession, in fact, live from the proceeds of slave labor at the South. They divide the profits with the owner of the slaves. He has nothing to pay them except what his slaves make. But you Yankees and Englishmen more than divide the profits—you take the lion's share. You make more money from our cotton, and tobacco, and sugar, and indigo, and wheat, and corn, and rice, than we make ourselves. You live by slave labor—would perish without it—yet you abuse it. Cut off England and New England from the South American, East and West India and our markets, from which to buy their food, and in which to sell their manufactures, and they would starve at once. You live by our slave labor. It elevates your whites as well as ours, by confining them, in a great degree, to skillful, well-paying, light, and intellectual employments—and it feeds and clothes them. Abolish slavery, and you will suffer vastly more than we, because we have all the lands of the South, and can *command* labor as you do, and a genial soil and climate, that require less labor. But while in the absence of slavery, we could support ourselves, we should cease to support you. We would neither send you food and clothing, nor buy your worse than useless notions.

# XXVIII

## PRIVATE PROPERTY DESTROYS LIBERTY AND EQUALITY

The Abolitionists and Socialists, who, alone, have explored the recesses of social science, well understand that they can never establish their Utopia until private property is abolished or equalized. The man without property is theoretically, and, too often, practically, without a single right. Air and water, 'tis generally believed, are the common property of mankind; but nothing is falser in fact as well as theory. The ownership of land gives to the proprietor the exclusive right to everything above and beneath the soil. The lands are all appropriated, and with them the air above them, the waters on them, and the mines beneath them. The pauper, to breathe the air or drink the waters, must first find a place where he may rightfully enjoy them. He can find, at all times, no such place, and is compelled, by his necessities, to inhale the close and putrid air of small rooms, damp cellars and crowded factories, and to drink insufficient quantities of impure water, furnished to him at a price he can ill afford. He pays for the water which he drinks, because it has ceased to be common property. He is not free, because he has no where that he may rightfully lay his head. Private property has monopolized the earth, and destroyed both his liberty and equality. He has no security for his life, for he cannot live without employment and adequate wages, and none are bound to employ him. If the earth were in common, he could always enjoy not only air and water, but by his industry might earn the means of subsistence. His situation is theoretically and practically desperate and intolerable. Were he a slave, he would enjoy in fact as well as in legal fiction, all necessary and essential rights. Pure air and water, a house, sufficient food, fire, and clothing, would be his at all times. Slavery is a form of communism, and as the Abolitionists and Socialists have resolved to adopt a new social system, we recommend it to their consideration. The manner in which the change shall be made from the present form of society to that system of communism which we propose is very simple. Negro slaves are now worth seven hundred dollars a head. As whites work harder, they are worth about a thousand. Make the man who owns a thousand dollars of capital the guardian (the term master is objectionable) of one white pauper of average value; give the man who is worth ten thousand dollars ten paupers, and the millionaire a thousand. This would be an act of simple mercy and justice; for the capitalists now live entirely by the proceeds of poor men's labor, which capital enables them to command; and they command and enjoy it in almost the exact proportions which we have designated. Thus, a family of poor laborers, men, women and children, ten in number, can support themselves, and make about six hundred dollars, for their employer, which is the interest on ten thousand. They would work no harder than they do now, would be under no greater necessity to work, would be relieved of most of the cares of life, and let into the enjoyment of all valuable and necessary rights. What would they lose in liberty and equality? Just nothing. Having more rights, they would have more liberty than now, and approach nearer to equality. It might be, that their security and exemption from care would render their situation preferable to that of their employers. We suspect it would be easier to find wards or slaves than guardians or masters — for the gain would be all on the laborer's side, and the loss all on that of the capitalist.

Set your miscalled free laborers actually free, by giving them enough property or capital to live on, and then call on us at the South to free our negroes. At present, you Abolitionists know our negro slaves are much the freer of the two; and it would be a great advance towards freeing your laborers, to give them guardians, bound, like our masters, to take care of them, and entitled, in consideration thereof, to the proceeds of their labor.

# XXIX

# THE *NATIONAL ERA* AN EXCELLENT WITNESS

In an article in the *Era* of August 16, 1855, criticising and denying our theory of the Failure of Free Society, the writer begins by asserting, "We demonstrated, last week, from history, that the condition of the poor of England has greatly improved in modern times, as they have become free from the restraints of feudal bondage." He then goes on to criticise us, but, before concluding, contradicts and refutes his work of the week before, and adopts our theory in its fullest extent. He admits the intolerable exploitation and oppression of capital over labor, but looks forward to the day when it will be corrected. He is, like all Abolitionists, agrarian. He holds our doctrine, too, that the serfs were set free to starve, not because liberty was a good or a boon. He further holds, that the poor laborers could not get masters if they wanted them, because the rich can get their labor on better terms. Thus he distinctly shows that Free Society has failed, and why it has failed. We know very well the rich of Western Europe would not willingly take the poor as slaves, but the law should compel them to do so; for that is the only feasible system of agrarianism, the only practicable way of letting in all men to a sufficient, if not equal, enjoyment of *terra matre*. Here is his refutation of himself, and confirmation of our theory, which he thinks he is upsetting. We never take up an abolition paper without finding doctrines like those of the *Era*, and only adduce it as a specimen:

Under despotic and corrupt governments, which oppress the people with taxes to support extravagant misrule and unnecessary war — which debauch them by evil example of those in high places, and discourage education or render it impossible — the condition of the poor and nominally free becomes truly deplorable. But it is not Freedom which is their undoing — it is rather the lack of it. It is their subjection, through ignorance, to bad rulers, which keeps them in poverty. We know that the claim laid by capital to the lion's share of profits is itself, under any circumstances, a great obstruction to the progress of the masses; but we believe that even that obstacle will one day be removed — that problem in political science be solved by civilization and Christianity. We believe that the human intellect will never, with the light of the Gospel to guide and inspire its efforts, surrender to the cold and heartless reign of capital over labor. But, at any rate, one thing is certain, under the worst form of government, or the best, namely: when Freedom becomes a burden and a curse to the poor, Slavery — that is to say, the enslavement of the mass of laborers, with responsibility on the part of the master for their support — is no longer possible. When freemen are unable to support themselves, among all the diversified employments of free societies, it would be impossible for them to find masters willing to take the responsibility. The masses in Europe, in fact, owe their liberty to the excessive supply of slave labor, which, when it becomes a burden to the land, was cast aside as worthless. Who believes that Irish landlords would take the responsibility of supporting the peasantry, on the condition of their becoming slaves? In fact, is it not notorious that they help them to emigrate to America, and often pull down their cabins and huts, in order to drive them off?

In further proof of the agrarian doctrines of the Abolitionists, we add an article from the *Northern Christian Advocate*, a clever Methodist paper, edited in the State of New York:

FACTORY OPERATIVES. — There is a class of laborers, consisting of men, women and children, whom we never contemplate but with regret — we see them, at least, in imagination, subsiding, in spite of all their care, into utter dependence and poverty. Hence, we never look upon a factory or large manufacturing establishment with unmingled pleasure. The men and women, who ply its machinery, are too apt to become identified with such establishments in an improper degree. This process of assimilation and identification goes on slowly, but surely, till at last the individual and the factory are so blended into one, that a separate existence is impossible. One or two generations are required to bring about this state of things. Pecuniary dependence, ignorance of other employments, physical malformation, and the general helplessness of a mere factory population are not the work of a day. Individuals cannot be detached from other pursuits at once — cannot have manufacturing knowledge and no other knowledge until they have had time to drift away from other occupations. But however retarded the effect, it is sure to follow, and consequently every large mechanical establishment must be considered as having certain malign tendencies, which are to be carefully guarded against.

The causes of the evil under consideration are very obvious, as is also their appropriate remedy. We must set down as the first and principal cause of injury, the fact that the capital which sustains mechanical business is not under the control of the operatives. The mills or machines may stop at any hour in spite of the wants or wishes of the employees. Wages may be put down, little or much, with or without notice. Operatives are not consulted in such cases. The motive may be good or bad — it may be to guard against bankruptcy, or to amass wealth from the sinews of a toiling, dependent race. But, whatever the motive and the decision, the operative is helpless — he can control neither the one nor the other. It is his to labor; others are charged with the regulation of prices, and the only check in his power is the precarious one of a *strike*. Strikes in business are like insurrections in civil governments — a last, desperate remedy, and as often fatal to the sufferer as protective of his interests. The same is true of the farmer who does not own the soil on which he labors, but is compelled to make terms with a landlord. Hence, the well known insurmountable evils of agricultural tenantry. In Europe it has produced serfdom and feudalism, besides a good deal of servitude and degradation concealed under the mild name of peasant. It matters not what the occupation may be, as soon as the laborer becomes thoroughly dependent, and feels that dependence, the system does him an incalculable injury. It is for this reason that large landholders always deteriorate the population, and society becomes worthless just in proportion as the means of independent existence pass from the hands of the many to the few. This difficulty is, and must be forever in the way of conducting manufacturing establishments on the present plan. Perhaps some means of diffusing capital among operatives, or, what is the same, of giving the laborer reasonable securities, may yet be discovered; but the change would require to be radical. The monopoly of capital is so nearly like the monopoly of land that we may readily see no partial measures can ever effect a cure.

# XXX

# THE PHILOSOPHY OF THE ISMS—SHOWING WHY THEY ABOUND AT THE NORTH, AND ARE UNKNOWN AT THE SOUTH

The exploitation, or unjust exactions of skill and capital in free society, excite the learned and philanthropic to devise schemes of escape, and impel the laborers to adopt those schemes, however chimerical, because they feel that their situation cannot be worsted. They are already slaves without masters, and that is the bathos of human misery. Besides, universal liberty has disintegrated and dissolved society, and placed men in isolated, selfish, and antagonistic positions—in which each man is compelled to wrong others, in order to be just to himself. But man's nature is social, not selfish, and he longs and yearns to return to parental, fraternal, and associative relations. All the Isms concur in promising closer and more associative relations, in establishing at least a qualified community of property, and in insuring the weak and unfortunate the necessaries and comforts of life. Indeed, they all promise to establish slavery—minus, the master and the overseer. As the evils which we have described are little felt at the South, men here would as soon think of entering the lion's cage, as going into one of their incestuous establishments. Mormonism is only a monster development of the Isms. They are all essentially alike, and that the most successful, because, so far, it has been Socialism—plus the overseer. The mantle of Joe Smith descended on Brigham Young, and if he transmit to a true prophet, there is no telling how long the thing may work. Mormonism had its birth in Western New York, that land fertile of Isms – where also arose Spiritual Rappings and Oneida Perfectionism – where Shakers, and Millennarians, and Millerites abound, and all heresies do most flourish. Mormonism now is daily gathering thousands of recruits from free society in Europe, Asia, Africa, and our North, and not one from the South. It has no religion, but in place of it, a sensual moral code, that shocks the common sense of propriety. But it holds property somewhat in common, draws men together in closer and more fraternal relations, and promises (probably falsely) a safe retreat and refuge from the isolated and inimical relations, the killing competition and exploitation, of free society. All the other Isms do the same – but mal-administration, or the want of a master, soon explodes them. We saw last year an advertisement, under the hammer, of the last of fourteen phalansteries, established at the North on the Greeley-Fourierite plan. The Shakers do better; but Mr. S. P. Andrews, who is an expert, informs us that they, like the Mormons, have a despotic head. Socialism, with such despotic head, approaches very near to Southern slavery, and gets along very well so long as the despot lives. Mr. S. P. Andrews should enlighten the public as to the progress of the Free Love villages of Trialville, in Ohio, Modern Zion, on Long Island, &c. "Self-elected despotism" is his theory of the perfection of society. Has any Cromwell, or Napoleon, or Joe Smith, seized the sceptre in those delightful villages, which we hope will soon inspire the pen of some Northern Boccaccio. Human opinion advances in concentric circles. Abolition swallows up the little Isms, and Socialism swallows up Abolition. Socialism long since attained the point of the circle most distant from slavery, and is now rapidly coming round to the point whence it started – that is, to slavery. Mr. Andrews, who is no humbug (except in so far as any philosopher is a humbug) Mr. Andrews, who is probably the foremost thinker in America, could, if he would, prove to the Abolitionists and Socialists, that after a furious day's drive, like that of Toby Lumpkin and his mother, they are just about to haul up at the horse pond, in a few yards of the place where they started in the morning. The Socialists, Louis Napoleon included, are trying to establish slavery, whilst abusing the word.

# XXXI

# DEFICIENCY OF FOOD IN FREE SOCIETY

The normal state of free society is a state of famine. Agricultural labor is the most arduous, least respectable, and worst paid of all labor. Nature and philosophy teach all who can to avoid and escape from it, and to pursue less laborious, more respectable, and more lucrative employments. None work in the field who can help it. Hence free society is in great measure dependent for its food and clothing on slave society. Western Europe and New England get their cotton, sugar, and much of their bread and meat from the South, from Cuba, Russia, Poland, and Turkey. After all, the mass of their population suffers continual physical want. McCulloch informs us in his edition of Adam Smith, "that the better sort of Irish laborers eat meat once a month, or once in six months; the lowest order never. The better class of English laborers eat meat twice or three times a week." Now no Southern negro would believe this if you were to swear to it. Yet it is a very favorable account of those laborers. The Irish rarely eat bread, and the English peasantry have wholly inadequate allowance of it. On the Continent, the peasantry generally live on fruits, nuts and olives, and other things, which our slaves do not seek as food at all, but as mere condiments to give a relish to their meat and bread. Agriculture is the proper pursuit of slaves, to be superintended and directed, however, by freemen. Its profits are inadequate to the support of separate families of laborers, especially of white laborers in cold climates, whose wants are greater than those of negroes at the South. The expenses of families are greatly lessened where slavery associates a large number under a common head, or master, and their labor is rendered more efficient and productive.

This is the great idea of the Socialists, and it is a truer one than the "every-man-for-himself" doctrine of the political economists. Free society is in great measure fed and clothed by slave society, which it pays for in worthless baubles, fashionable trifles, and deleterious luxuries; — without which, slave society would do much better. Everyone should study the census of the Union, in order to see how dependent the Northeast is on slave labor, and how trifling are her agricultural products.

The profits of slave farming enure chiefly to the advantage of Western Europe and our North. Practical men, therefore, at the North, so far from going to work to abolish slavery, are bringing daily a larger supply of slaves into the slave market, than ever was brought before. Add the Coolies of Asia and apprentices from Africa to the old negro slave trade, and the annual supply of new slaves exceeds by far that of any other period.

The Abolitionists will probably succeed in dissolving the Union, in involving us in civil and fratricidal war, and in cutting off the North from its necessary supply of food and clothing; but they should recollect that whilst they are engaged in this labor of love, Northern and English merchants are rapidly extending and increasing slavery, by opening daily markets for the purchase and sale of Coolies, apprentices, and Africans.

The foreign slave trade is not necessary for the supply of the slave markets. The increase of the present slaves, if humanely treated, would suffice to meet that demand. But Africans and Coolies cost less than the rearing of slaves in America, and the trade in them, whenever carried on, induces masters to work their old slaves to death and buy new ones from abroad.

The foreign slave trade, especially the Coolie trade, is

the most inhuman pursuit in which man ever engaged. Equally inhuman to the victims which it imports, and to the old slaves, whose treatment and condition it renders intolerably cruel. By directing philanthropy and public opinion in a false direction, the Abolitionists have become the most efficient propagandists of slavery and the slave trade. And slavery, such as it exists in pursuance of the foreign slave trade, shocks our sense of humanity quite as much as that of the most sensitive Abolitionists.

Since writing thus far, we met with the following in the *Charleston Mercury*:

WHEAT IN MASSACHUSETTS. — The deficiency in the production of wheat in Massachusetts alone, in 1855, for the consumption of her inhabitants, was 3,915,550 bushels; and of Indian corn, 3,420,675 bushels (*without allowing any thing for the consumption of corn by cattle*).

In 1850, the deficiency in the production of wheat in all the New England States, was equal to 1,691,502 barrels of flour; and to 3,464,-675 bushels of corn (*without allowing any thing for the consumption by cattle*).

This is 327,185 barrels more than was exported of domestic flour from all of the United States to foreign countries during the year ending 30th June, 1855, and 87,000 more barrels than was exported both of domestic and foreign flour from the United States for the same period.

We conclude, from our examination of the census, that the grain and potatoes made in New England would about feed her cattle, horses, hogs, and sheep — leaving none for her inhabitants. We lately compared carefully the census of Massachusetts and North Carolina, and found, in round numbers, that according to population, North Carolina produced annually ten times as much of human food as Massachusetts — but that Massachusetts balanced the account by producing annually ten times as many paupers and criminals as North Carolina. We also discover that the want of food in the one State and its abundance in the other, tells on the duration of human life. The morality in Massachusetts is nearly double that in North Carolina. We infer that there is ten times as much of human happiness in North Carolina as in Massachusetts. The census gives no account of the infidels and the Isms – of them there are none in North Carolina, and Massachusetts may boast that she rivals Germany, France, and Western New York in their production.

Really, it is suicidal folly in New England to talk of disunion and setting up for herself. She does not possess the elements of separate nationality. She is intelligent and wealthy; but her wealth is cosmopolitan – her poverty indigenous. Her commerce, her manufactures, and moneyed capital, constitute her wealth. Disunion would make these useless and unprofitable at home, and they would be transferred immediately to other States and Nations.

North Carolina might well set up for herself, for she can produce all the necessaries and comforts and luxuries of life within herself, and has Virginia between herself and danger on the one side, and an inaccessible sea coast on the other. But we of Virginia, being a border State, would be badly situated in case of disunion, and mean to cling to it as long as honor permits. Besides, Virginia loves her nearest sister, Pennsylvania, and cannot bear the thought of parting company with her.

Tecum vivere amem!
Tecum obeam lubens! [1]

[1] "With thee I fain would live, with thee I'd gladly die." Horace, *Odes*, III, ix, 24.

# XXXII

## MAN HAS PROPERTY IN MAN!

In the *Liberator* of the 19th December, we observe that the editor narrows down the slavery contest to the mere question whether "Man may rightfully hold property in man?"

We think we can dispose of this objection to domestic slavery in a very few words.

Man is a social and gregarious animal, and all such animals hold property in each other. Nature imposes upon them slavery as a law and necessity of their existence. They live together to aid each other, and are slaves under Mr. Garrison's higher law. Slavery arises under the higher law, and is, and ever must be, coëval and coëxtensive with human nature.

We will enumerate a few of its ten thousand modifications.

The husband has a legally recognized property in his wife's services, and may legally control, in some measure, her personal liberty. She is his property and his slave.

The wife has also a legally recognized property in the husband's services. He is her property, but not her slave.

The father has property in the services and persons of his children till they are twenty-one years of age. They are his property and his slaves.

Children have property, during infancy, in the services of each parent.

Infant negroes, sick, infirm and superannuated negroes, hold most valuable property in the services and capital of their masters. The masters hold no property in such slaves, because, for the time, they are of no value.

Owners and captains of vessels own property in the services of sailors, and may control their personal liberty. They (the sailors) are property, and slaves also.

The services and persons, lives and liberty of soldiers and of officers, belong to the Government; they are, whilst in service, both property and slaves.

Every white working man, be he clerk, carpenter, mechanic, printer, common laborer, or what else, who contracts to serve for a term of days, months, or years, is, for such term, the property of his employer. He is not a slave, like the wife, child, apprentice, sailor or soldier, because, although the employer's right to his services be equally perfect, his remedy to enforce such right is very different. In the one case, he may resort to force to compel compliance; in the other, he is driven to a suit for damages.

Again: Every capitalist holds property in his fellow men to the extent of the profits of his capital, or income. The only income possibly resulting from capital, is the result of the property which capital bestows on its owners, in the labor of other people. In our first three chapters we attempt to explain this.

All civilized society recognizes, and, in some measure, performs the obligation to support and provide for all human beings, whether natives or foreigners, who are unable to provide for themselves. Hence poor-houses, &c.

Hence all men hold valuable property, actual or contingent, in the services of each other.

If, Mr. Garrison, this be the only difficulty to be adjusted between North and South, we are sure that your little pet, Disunion, "living will linger, and lingering will die."

When Mr. Andrews and you have quite "expelled human nature," dissolved and disintegrated society, and reduced mankind to separate, independent, but conflicting monads, or human atoms – then, and not till then, will you establish the 'sovereignty of the individual,' and destroy the property of man in man.

# XXXIII

# THE COUP DE GRACE TO ABOLITION

The Abolitionists are all willing to admit that free society has utterly failed in Europe, but will assign two reasons for that failure — "Excess of population, and want of equality and liberty."

Were the population of England doubled, the labor required to support that population would be lessened, could all labor and expenses be supported alike; because the association and division of labor might be rendered more perfect, and the expenses of a single family, or single individual, might be divided among and borne by many. The Socialists and Abolitionists understand this. When one family has to support its own school, its own mill, its own mechanics, its own doctor, parson, &c., living is expensive; but where these and other expenses are divided among many, living becomes cheap; hence it is far less laborious to live in a densely settled country than in a sparsely settled one, if labor and expenses can be equally divided. The soil of England will readily support double its population, if its products be not wasted in luxury, in feeding deer, and game, and horses. England has not attained that density of population which enables men to live by the least amount of labor. Her laboring population has been thinned and labor rendered dearer and scarcer, by emigration, of late years, to America, California, and Australia — yet, in the winter of 1854, there was a general outbreak and riot of her operatives, because a fall in prices occasioned a large number of her factories to stop work, and turn their hands out of employment. This happens every day in free society, from the bankruptcy of employers, or from the glut of markets and fall of prices. We will add, that a meeting of the working men of New York, in the Park, asserted that there were 50,000 working men and women, in that city, out of employment last winter.

The competitive system (so injurious to the laboring class) is carried out with less exception or restriction in America than in Europe. Hence, considering the sparseness of our population, the laboring class are worse off in New York, Philadelphia, and Boston, than in London, Manchester, or Paris. And this begets more Socialists in the higher classes, and more mobs, riots, and trade-unions, with the laborers, than in Europe.

Finally, if it be excess of numbers, or want of liberty, that occasions the failure of free society, why are our Abolitionists and Socialists so hot and so active in upsetting and reorganizing society? They have pronounced, with entire unanimity, that free society is intolerable, whether a country be densely or sparsely settled.

The Abolitionists boast, that lands are dearer and labor cheaper in free than in slave society. Either proposition contains the admission that free laborers work more for others and less for themselves than slaves – in effect, that they are less free than slaves. The profits of land are what the landowner appropriates of the results of work of the laborer. Where he appropriates most, and leaves the laborer least, there lands are dearest, labor cheapest, and laborers least free. In Europe, lands sell much higher than at the North; hence laborers are less free in fact than at the North. In the North they sell higher than in the South, because the slaves consume more of the results of their own labor than laborers at the North, and leave less profit to the landowner. The high price of land is, in the general, an unerring indication of the poverty and actual slavery of the laboring class. Its low price, equally proves that the laborers, whether called slaves or freemen, work more for themselves, and less for the landowners, than where lands are dear. In settled countries, where all the lands are appropriated, this theory is undeniable and irrefutable.

As this is a short chapter, we take the opportunity to apologize for our discursive, immethodical and unartistic manner.

In the first place, the character of the enemy we have to contend with prevents anything like regular warfare. They are divided into hundreds of little guerrilla bands of Isms, each having its peculiar partisan tactics, and we are compelled to vary our mode of attack from regular cannonade to bushfighting, to suit the occasion.

Again, we practiced as a jury lawyer for twenty-five years, and thereby acquired an inveterate habit of cumulation and iteration, and of various argument and illustration. But, at the same time, we learned how "to make out our case," and to know when it is "made out." The lawyer who observed the Unities in an argument before a jury would be sure to lose his cause; and now the world is our jury, who are going to bring in a verdict against free society of "guilty."

We admire not the pellucid rivulet, that murmurs and meanders, in cramped and artificial current, through the park and gardens of the nobleman; but we do admire the flooded and swollen Mississippi, whose turbid waters, in their majestic course, sweep along upon their bosom, with equal composure, the occupants of the hen-roost and the poultry yard, the flocks, the herds, the crops, the uprooted forest, and the residences of man. The Exhaustive, not the Artistic, is what we would aspire to. And yet, the Exhaustive may be the highest art of argument. The best mode, we think, of writing, is that in which facts, and argument, and rhetoric, and wit, and sarcasm, succeed each other with rapid iteration.

Intonuere poli, et crebris micat ignibus æther! [1]

Again, Artistic execution is un-English. It neither suits their minds nor their tastes. Discursiveness and prurient exuber-

[1] "From pole to pole it thunders, the skies lighten with frequent flashes," Virgil, *Aeneid*, I, 90.

ancy of thought and suggestion, they often possess, but always fail when they attempt a literary or other work of Art. Indeed, we have a strong suspicion that Art went out of the world about the time the Baconian Philosophy came in.

A continuous argument, without pause or break, on a subject profoundly metaphysical, equally fatigues the writer and the reader. Nobody likes it, and very few read it. *Desipere in loco* [2] is not only a very agreeable maxim to the author, but a very wise and prudent one.

Lastly. Like Porthos, when "we have an idea," we are at once seized with a feverish anxiety to communicate it, and we think it better to break in on the regular thread of our discourse, and do so at once, than to spoil our whole discourse by having our minds occupied with two subjects at a time.

Another idea strikes us. As yet we hardly aspire to the dignity of authorship. We indulge in abandon, because, as a writer, we have no reputation to jeopard or to lose. But, should this book take, we will mount the antithetical stilts of auctorial dignity – write a book as stale and dry as "the remainder biscuit after a long voyage," and as free from originality, wit, thought or suggestiveness, as the Queen's Speech, the President's Message, or a debate in the United States Senate. We do not as yet bore the world with "respectable stupidity," because our position does not authorize it.

[2] "To jest at the proper time."

# XXXIV

## NATIONAL WEALTH, INDIVIDUAL WEALTH, LUXURY, AND ECONOMY

It is a common theory with political economists that national wealth is but the sum of individual wealth, and that as individual wealth increases, national wealth increases, *pari passu.*

We think this theory false and pernicious, and the more so because it is plausible.

All profit-bearing possessions or capital tend to exonerate their owners from labor, and to throw the labor that supports society on a part only of its members. Now, as almost all wealth is the product of labor, this diminution of labor, diminishes wealth, or, at least, increases poverty, by placing heavier burdens on the laboring class.

This, however, is a very small part of the evil effects of individual wealth. Society requires it of the rich to live according to their incomes, to fare sumptuously, to have costly dress, furniture, equipage, houses, &c., and to keep many servants.

Their incomes are spent in luxuries, and thousands of laborers are taken off from the production of necessaries to produce those luxuries, or to wait on their owners. Thus, the burden of the support of society, so far as the ordinary comforts and necessaries of life are concerned, are thrown on fewer and fewer, as private wealth and luxury increase. It requires a thousand pauper laborers to sustain one millionaire, and without them his capital will produce no profit. This accounts for the great numbers and excessive poverty of the mass in England. Half the boasted capital of England, probably two-thirds of it, is but a mortgage of the bones and sinews of the laborers, now and forever, to the capitalists. The national debt, stocks of all kinds, money at interest, and indeed all debts, represent this sort of private wealth, which is national poverty.

Sumptuous houses, parks, and all establishments that are costly to sustain and keep up, and do not facilitate, but check the production of necessaries, are also part of private wealth, and of national poverty. Four-fifths of the private wealth of England, and half of that of our Northeast, is a severe tax on labor, and a constant preventive of the accumulation of national wealth.

Private wealth at the South consists chiefly in negro laborers, and improvements of land that increase its productive capacities. Fine enclosures, improved stock, good granaries, and machines and implements for farming, comfortable negro cabins, good orchards, &c., are as strictly a part of national, as of individual wealth. Not so with the costly private dwellings in our Northern cities. The expense of building, of repairing, of furnishing, and of keeping servants for their owners or tenants is a constant drawback from productive industry, increases the burdens of the laboring poor, and diminishes national wealth. The poverty-stricken fields of New England are the necessary consequence of the luxurious expenditure in her cities. Yet that luxury is no part of national wealth, but a constant tax on it, whilst improved farms constitute almost three-fourths of all her real wealth for they feed and clothe mankind.

This is a most interesting subject; one which we have not mastered, or, if we had, this work on which we are engaged is not the proper one for its full discussion and exposition. We merely throw out a few suggestions for the consideration of the thinking and ingenuous. If we are right, luxury is the greatest sin against society; economy and industry, the chiefest of social virtues.

# XXXV

# GOVERNMENT A THING OF FORCE, NOT OF CONSENT

We do not agree with the authors of the Declaration of Independence, that governments "derive their just powers from the consent of the governed." The women, the children, the negroes, and but few of the non-property holders were consulted, or consented to the Revolution, or the governments that ensued from its success. As to these, the new governments were self-elected despotisms, and the governing class self-elected despots. Those governments originated in force, and have been continued by force. All governments must originate in force, and be continued by force. The very term, government, implies that it is carried on against the consent of the governed. Fathers do not derive their authority, as heads of families, from the consent of wife and children, nor do they govern their families by their consent. They never take the vote of the family as to the labors to be performed, the moneys to be expended, or as to anything else. Masters dare not take the vote of slaves as to their government. If they did, constant holiday, dissipation, and extravagance would be the result. Captains of ships are not appointed by the consent of the crew, and never take their vote, even in "doubling Cape Horn." If they did, the crew would generally vote to get drunk, and the ship would never weather the cape. Not even in the most democratic countries are soldiers governed by their consent, nor is their vote taken on the eve of battle. They have some how lost (or never had) the "inalienable rights of life, liberty, and the pursuit of happiness", and, whether Americans or Russians, are forced into battle without and often against their consent. The ancient republics were governed by a small class of adult male citizens who assumed and exercised the government without the consent of the governed. The South is governed just as those ancient republics were. In the county in which we live, there are eighteen thousand souls, and only twelve hundred voters. But we twelve hundred, the governors, never asked and never intend to ask the consent of the sixteen thousand eight hundred whom we govern. Were we to do so, we should soon have an "organized anarchy." The governments of Europe could not exist a week without the positive force of standing armies.

They are all governments of force, not of consent. Even in our North, the women, children, and free negroes, constitute four-fifths of the population; and they are all governed without their consent. But they mean to correct this gross and glaring iniquity at the North. They hold that all men, women, and negroes, and smart children are equals, and entitled to equal rights. The widows and free negroes begin to vote in some of those States, and they will have to let all colors and sexes and ages vote soon, or give up the glorious principles of human equality and universal emancipation.

The experiment which they will make, we fear, is absurd in theory, and the symptoms of approaching anarchy and agrarianism among them leave no doubt that its practical operation will be no better than its theory. Anti-rentism, "vote-myself-a-farm-ism," and all the other Isms, are but the spattering drops that precede a social deluge.

Abolition ultimates in "Consent Government"; Consent Government in Anarchy, Free Love, Agrarianism, &c., &c., and "Self-elected Despotism" winds up the play.

If the interests of the governors, or governing class, be not conservative, they certainly will not conserve institutions injurious to their interests. There never was and never can be an old society, in which the immediate interests of a majority of human souls do not conflict with all established order, all right of property, and all existing institutions. Immediate interest is all the mass look to; and they would be sure to revolutionize government, as often as the situation of the majority was worse than that of the minority. Divide all property to-day, and a year hence the inequalities of property would provoke a re-division.

In the South, the interest of the governing class is eminently conservative, and the South is fast becoming the most conservative of nations.

Already, at the North, government vibrates and oscillates between Radicalism and Conservatism; at present, Radicalism or Black Republicanism is in the ascendant.

The number of paupers is rapidly increasing; radical and agrarian doctrines are spreading; the women and the children, and the negroes, will soon be let in to vote; and then they will try the experiment of "Consent Government and Constituted Anarchy."

It is falsely said, that revolutions never go backwards. They always go backwards, and generally farther back than where they started. The Social Revolution now going on at the North, must some day go backwards. Shall it do so now, ere it has perpetrated an infinitude of mischief, shed oceans of blood, and occasioned endless human misery; or will the Conservatives of the North let it run the length of its leather, inflict all these evils, and then rectify itself by issuing into military despotism? We think that by a kind of alliance, offensive and defensive, with the South, Northern Conservatism may now arrest and turn back the tide of Radicalism and Agrarianism. We will not presume to point out the whole means and *modus operandi*. They on the field of action will best see what is necessary to be done.

Whilst we hold that all government is a matter of force, we yet think the governing class should be numerous enough to understand, and so situated as to represent fairly, all interests. The Greek and Roman masters were thus situated; so were the old Barons of England, and so are the white citizens of the South. If not all masters, like Greek and Roman citizens, they all belong to the master race, have exclusive rights and privileges of citizenship, and an interest not to see this right of citizenship extended, disturbed, and rendered worthless and contemptible.

Whilst the governments of Europe are more obviously kept alive and conducted by force than at any other period, yet are they all, from necessity, watchful and regardful of Public Opinion. Opinion now rules the world, but not as expressed through the ballot-box. Governments become more popular as they become more forcible. A large governing class is not apt to mistake or disregard opinion; and, therefore, Republican institutions are best adapted to the times. Under Monarchical forms, the governments of Europe are daily becoming more Republican. The fatal error committed in Western Europe is the wielding of government by a class who govern, but do not represent, the masses. Their interests and those of the masses are antagonistic, whilst those of masters and slaves are identical.

Looking to theory, to the examples of the Ancient Republics, and to England under the Plantagenets, we shall find that Southern institutions are far the best now existing in the world.

We think speculations as to constructing governments are little worth; for all government is the gradual accretion of Nature, time and circumstances. Yet these theories have occurred to us, and, as they are conservative, we will suggest them. In slaveholding countries all freemen should vote and govern, because their interests are conservative. In free states, the government should be in the hands of the land-owners, who are also conservative. A system of primogeniture, and entails of small parcels of land, might, in a great measure, identify the interests of all; or, at least, those who held no lands would generally be the children and kinsmen of those who did, and be taken care of by them. The frequent accumulation of large fortunes, and consequent pauperism of the masses, is the greatest evil of modern society. Would not small entails prevent this? All cannot own lands, but as many should own them as is consistent with good farming and advanced civilization. The social institutions of the Jews, as established by Moses and Joshua, most nearly fulfill our ideas of perfect government.

A word, at parting, to Northern Conservatives. A like danger threatens North and South, proceeding from the same source. Abolitionism is maturing what Political Economy began. With inexorable sequence Let Alone is made to usher in No-Government. North and South our danger is the same, and our remedies, though differing in degree, must in character be the same. Let Alone must be repudiated, if we would have any Government. We must, in all sections, act upon the principle that the world is "too little governed." You of the North need not institute negro slavery, far less reduce white men to the state of engro slavery. But the masses require more of protection, and the masses and philosophers equally require more of control. Leave it to time and circumstances to suggest the necessary legislation; but rely upon it, "Anarchy, plus the street constable" won't answer any longer. The Vigilance Committee of California is but a mob, rendered necessary by the inadequacy of the regular government. It is the *vis medicatrix naturæ*, vainly attempting to discharge the office of physician. That country is "too little governed" where the best and most conservative citizens have to resolve themselves into mobs and vigilance committees to protect rights which government should, but does not, protect.

The element of force exists probably in too small a degree in our Federal Government. It has neither territory not subjects. Kansas is better off; for she has a few citizens and a large and fertile territory. She is backing the Government out, if not whipping her. Massachusetts, too, has nullified her laws. Utah contemns her authority, and the Vigilance Committee of California sets her at successful defiance. She is an attempt at a *paper consent* government, without territory or citizens. Considered and treated as a league or treaty between *separate States* or *Nations*, she may yet have a long and useful existence; for then those *Nations* or *States*, seeing that she has no means of self-enforcement, self-support, or self-conservation, may, for their mutual interests, combine to sustain and defend her. Heretofore, domestic weakness and danger from foreign foes has combined the States in sustaining the Union. Hereafter, the great advantages of friendly and mutual intercourse, trade and exchanges may continue to produce a like result. But the prospects are alarming, and it is well that all patriots should know that the Union has little power to sustain and perpetuate itself.

There are three kinds of force that occur to us will sustain a government. First, "inside necessity," such as slavery, that occasions a few to usurp power, and to hold it forcibly, without consulting the many; secondly, the force of foreign pressure or aggression, which combines men and States together for common defence; and thirdly, the inherent force of a prescriptive or usurpative government, which sustains itself by standing armies. Such are all the governments of Western Europe. Not one of them could exist forty-eight hours, but for the standing armies. These standing armies became necessary and grew up as slavery disappeared. The old Barons kept the Canaille, the Proletariat, the Sans Culottes, the Nomadic Beggars in order by lashing their backs and supplying their wants. They must be fed and kept at work. Modern society tries to effect this (but in vain) by moral suasion and standing armies. Riots, mobs, strikes, and revolutions are daily occurring. The mass of mankind cannot be governed by Law. More of despotic discretion, and less of Law, is what the world wants. We take our leave by saying "THERE IS TOO MUCH OF LAW AND TOO LITTLE OF GOVERNMENT IN THIS WORLD."

Physical force, not moral suasion, governs the world. The negro sees the driver's lash, becomes accustomed to obedient cheerful industry, and is not aware that the lash is the force that impels him. The free citizen fulfills *con amore*, his round of social, political, and domestic duties, and never dreams that the Law, with its fines and jails, penitentiaries and halters, or Public Opinion, with its ostracism, its mobs, and its tar and feathers, help to keep him revolving in his orbit. Yet, remove these physical forces, and how many good citizens would shoot, like firey comets, from their spheres, and disturb society with their eccentricities and their crimes.

Government is the life of a nation, and as no one can forsee the various future circumstances of social, any more than of individual life, it is absurd to define on paper, at the birth of either the nation or individual, what they shall do and what not do. Broad construction of constitutions is as good as no constitution, for it leaves the nation to adapt itself to circumstances; but strict construction will destroy any nation, for action is necessary to national conservation, and constitution-makers cannot foresee what action will be necessary. If individual or social life were passed in mere passivity, constitutions might answer. Not in a changing and active world. Louisiana, Florida, and Texas would have been denied to the South under strict construction, and she would have been ruined. A constitution, strictly construed, is absolutely inconsistent with permanent national existence.

# XXXVI

## WARNING TO THE NORTH

BANQUO — But 'tis strange:
And oftentimes, to win us to our harm,
The instruments of darkness tell us truths;
Win us with honest trifles, to betray us
In deepest consequences. *Macbeth*

The reader must have remarked our propensity of putting scraps of poetry at the head of our chapters, or of interweaving them with the text. It answers as a sort of chorus or refrain, and, when skillfully handled, has as fine an effect as the fiddle at a feast, or the brass band on the eve of an engagement. It nerves the author for greater effort, and inspires the reader with resolution to follow him in his most profound ratiocinations and airiest speculations. We learnt it from "our Masters in the art of war" when we carried their camp and their whole park of artillery (which we are now using with such murderous effect against their own ranks). We also captured their camp equipage, books of military strategy, &c. In them we found rules laid down for the famous songs which are so harmoniously blended with the speeches at all Infidel and Abolition conventions, and Women's Rights and Free Love assemblages. They are intended to inspire enthusiasm, confirm conviction, and to "screw the courage to the sticking point." Besides, sometimes they answer admirably the opposite purpose of a sedative. Often, when Sister This One has, by her imprudent speech, outraged decency, propriety, religion, and morality, and drawn down upon her head hisses and cries of "Turn her out! Turn her out!" Brother That One bursts forth in "strains of sweetest melody," and like another Orpheus quells and quiets another hell. Not that we intend by any means to intimate that this musical brother would play Orpheus throughout, and take as long and perilous a trip to rescue his sister as Orpheus did for Eurydice. On the contrary, we suspect in such contingency he would pray to Pluto to double bar the gates, and bribe Cerberus to keep closer watch. We derive this impression from the triangular correspondence of Greeley, Andrews, and James, entitled "Love, Marriage and Divorce"; and from the actings and doings of the courts and legislature of Massachusetts—who, from the number of the divorces they grant, we should think could hardly find time to send Hiss on a visit of purification to the Convents.

Now it may be, that sometimes, when we "have gone it rather strong" (as we are very apt to do) and offended the reader, our scraps of poetry may answer the purpose of the Abolition songs, and soothe and propitiate him. Besides, they afford a sort of interlude or by-play, like that of Sancho where he slipped off from the flying horse, Clavileno, just as he and the Don had reached the constellation of the Goat, and went to playing with the little goats to relieve the giddiness of his head. I am sure, when we have, as we often do, mounted with our reader into the highest regions of metaphysics, that his head becomes a little giddy (at least ours does) and that he is thankful for a little poetry or a turn at play with our Abolition Goats. "Goats, indeed!" quoth Mr. G——, "Lions, you had better say." Well, be it lions! We are no more afraid of you than if you were lambs; and you will no sooner dare to attack us than you did the Knight of La Mancha when he vainly challenged you to mortal combat.

Let not the reader suppose that we either emulate the chivalry of the Don or the wisdom of his Squire. A Northern clime has congealed the courage of our lions and they are afraid of the "paper bullets of the brain"; yet they are vastly fond of shooting them at others, provided they are sure the shot will not be returned.

As for Sancho, we think him the wisest man we ever read after, except Solomon. Indeed, in the world of Fiction, all the wisdom issues from the mouths of fools – as witness Shakspeare's Falstaff and his fools. There is at least vraisemblance in all this; for, as in the Real world, the philosophers (e.g. our Masters in the art of war) have monopolized all the folly – where so likely to find the wisdom as among the fools?

We fear our "Little Cannibals" are growing impatient, and may be, a little jealous of our seeming preference for our goats. They are young yet and require nursing. But they are young Herculeses, born with teeth, and if any Abolition serpents attempt to strangle them in the cradle, they'll be apt to get the worst of it. The danger is, however, that the Abolitionists will steal and adopt them – for they are vastly fond of young cannibals, and employ much of their time in sewing and knitting and getting up subscriptions, to send shirts and trousers to the little fellows away over in Africa, who as indignantly repel them as King Lear did when he stripped in the storm and resolved to be his "unsophisticated self."

Now, seeing that the Abolitionists are so devoted to the uncouth, dirty, naked little cannibals of Africa, haven't we good reason to fear that they will run away with and adopt ours, when they come forth neatly dressed in black muslin and all shining with gold from the master hands of Morris and Wynne? [1] They will be sure at least to captivate the hearts of the strong-minded ladies, and if they will treat them well in infancy, we don't know but what, if they will wait till they grow up, we may spare them a husband or two from the number.

Mr. Morris has promised they shall be black as Erebus without, and white as "driven snow" within.

[1] Publishers of Fitzhugh's books.

If they can get over the trying time of infancy – if the critics don't smother them in the cradle, the boys will make their own way in the world, and get a name famous as Toussaint or Dessalines.

To be candid with the reader, we have learned lately that the physique of a book is quite as important as its metaphysique – the outside as the inside. Figure, size, proportion are all to be consulted; for books are now used quite as much for center table ornaments as for reading. We have a marble one on our center table that answers the former purpose admirably, because nobody can put puzzling questions about its contents. Now, we must write the exact amount, and no more, to enable Mr. Morris and Mr. Wynne to make our book appear externally *comme il faut.* We write this chapter in part for that purpose. The reader would not object to a page, or so, more or less of it, and Mr. Morris and Mr. Wynne will know how to curtail or omit, for they are not only masters of their own trades, but can render us valuable assistance in ours.

We return to our Cannibals, with this single remark to that morose and demure reader who is snarling at our occasional levity – "You, sir, never throw off your dignity; because you would be sure to uncover your folly."

We warn the North, that everyone of the leading Abolitionists is agitating the negro slavery question merely as a means to attain ulterior ends, and those ends nearer home. They would not spend so much time and money for the mere sake of the negro or his master, about whom they care little. But they know that men once fairly committed to negro slavery agitation – once committed to the sweeping principle "that man being a moral agent, accountable to God for his actions, should not have those actions controlled and directed by the will of another," are, in effect, committed to Socialism and Communism, to the most ultra doctrines of Garrison, Goodell, Smith and Andrews – to no private property, no church, no law, no government, – to free love, free lands, free women and free churches.

There is no middle ground – not an inch of ground of any sort, between the doctrines which we hold and those which Mr. Garrison holds. If slavery, either white or black, be wrong in principle or practice, then is Mr. Garrison right – then is all human government wrong.

Socialism, not Abolition, is the real object of Black Republicanism. The North, not the South, the true battle-ground. Like Fanny Wright, the author of American Socialism, the agitators of the North look upon free society as a mere transition state to be a better, but untried, form of society. The reader will not fully comprehend the ideas we would convey, without reading *England the Civilizer*, by Miss Fanny Wright. It is worth reading, not only as far the best history of the British constitution, but as the most correct and perfect analysis and delineation of free society – of that form of society which all Socialists and all thinking men agree cannot stand as it is. The Abolition School of Socialists like it because it is intolerable – because they consider it a transition state to a form of society without law or government. Miss Wright has the honesty to admit, that a *transition* has never taken place. No; and never will take place: because the expulsion of human nature is a pre-requisite to its occurrence.

But we solemnly warn the North that what she calls a *transition* is what every leading Abolitionist is moving heaven and earth to attain. This is their real object – negro emancipation a mere gull-trap.

In the attempt to attain "transition" seas of gore may be shed, until military despotism comes in to restore peace and security.

We (for we are a Socialist) agree with Mr. Carlyle, that the action of free society must be reversed. That, instead of relaxing more and more the bonds that bind man to man, you must screw them up more closely. That, instead of no government, you must have more government. And this is eminently true in America, where from the nature of things, as society becomes older and population more dense, more of government will be required. To prevent the attempt at transition, which would only usher in revolution, you must begin to govern more vigorously.

But we will be asked, How is this to be effected? The answer is easy. The means are at hand, and the work is begun.

The Democratic party, purged of its radicalism and largely recruited from the ranks of the old line Whigs, has become eminently and actively conservative. It is the antipodes of the Democratic party of the days of Jefferson, in the grounds which it occupies and the opinions which it holds, (what it professes to hold is another thing). Yet it has been a consistent party throughout. Consistent, in wisely and boldly adapting its action to the emergencies of the occaion. It is pathological, and practices according to prevailing symptoms. 'Tis true, it has a mighty Nosology in its Declaration of Independence, Bills of Rights, Constitutions, Platforms, and Preambles and Resolutions; but, like a goo' physician, it watches the state of the patient, and casts Nosology to the dogs when the symptoms require it. When we entered the party we were radicals, and half Abolitionists, and found inscribed on its banner, *"The world is too much governed!"* Now, we are sure the conviction has fastened itself on the heart of every good citizen, that "the world is too little governed."

The true and honorable distinction of the Democratic party is, that it has but one unbending principle — "The safety of the people is the supreme law." To this party we think the Nation and the North may confidently look for a happy exodus from our difficulties. It is pure, honest, active, and patriotic now, and will continue so as long as the dark cloud of Abolition and Socialism lowers and threatens at the North. Long and quiet possession of power will be sur to corrupt it. It will be then time to cast it aside. It is now able, and it alone is able, to grapple with and strangle the treasons of the North.

Times change, and men change with them.

Good and brave men are proud, not ashamed, of such changes. Let no false pride of seeming consistency deter us from an avowal, which omitted, may trammel and impede our action.

Our old Nosology is an effective arsenal and armory for the most ultra Abolitionists, and the more effective, because we have not *formally* repudiated it. Let "*The world is too little governed*" be adopted as our motto, inscribed upon our flag and run up to the masthead.

NOTE. – We learn that many of the old Federalists of the North, and some of the South, are joining our ranks. We welcome them. Their principles were wrong when they adopted them, but (barring their consolidation doctrines) will answer pretty well now. It was ever the misfortune of the old Federal party and the lately deceased Whig party, to be right at the wrong time. They were, as the doctors say, nosological and not pathological in practice. The Whig party of England, like the Democratic party of America, is eminently pathological, active, observant, and impressible.

# XXXVII

## ADDENDUM

*Virginia, Nov.* 18, 1856.

WM. LLOYD GARRISON, Esq.:

DEAR SIR — I have observed so much fairness in the manner in which slavery and other sociological questions are treated in the *Liberator*, that it has occurred to me you would not consider suggestions from an ultra pro-slavery man obtrusive, and might deem them worth a place in your columns. I shall not promise that the example of your liberality will be followed at the South. It is a theory of mine that "recurrence to fundamental principles" is only treason clothed in periphrastic phrase; and that the right of private judgment, liberty of the press, freedom of speech, and freedom of religion are subordinate to these "principles," and must not be allowed to assail them — else there can be no stability in government, or security of private rights. The South thinks me heretical, but feels that I am right, and takes care to trammel these sacred rights quite as efficiently by an austere public opinion, as Louis Napoleon does by law or by mere volition.

I entirely concur in a theory I heard Mr. Wendell Phillips * propound in a lecture at New Haven. I shall not attempt to give his eloquent words, for I am incapable of doing justice to his language; but the amount of his theory was, that governments are not formed by man, but are the

* Mr. Phillips is, in private life, aside from his abolition and sectional prejudices, a worthy, accomplished gentleman. He is the most eloquent and graceful speaker to whom we ever listened. He seems to distill manna and ambrosia from his lips, but is all the while firing whole broadsides of hot shot. "He is his own antithesis" — an infernal machine set to music.

gradual accretions of time, circumstance, and human exigencies; that they grow up like trees; and that man may cultivate, train and aid their growth and development, but cannot make them out and out. Now, I accept the theory, and propose, in the first place, to deter men from applying the axe to the root of our Southern institutions (that is, discussing or recurring to "fundamental principles") by moral suasion or monition, next, by tar and feathers, and, that failing, by the halter. The worst institutions that ever *grew up* in any country are better than the best that philosophers or philanthropists ever devised. As for ours, we deem them, since the days of Rome, Athens and Judea, the crack institutions of the world.

With these preliminary remarks, I will make the following suggestions or interrogations: —

Is not slavery to capital less tolerable than slavery to human masters?

Where a few, as in England, Ireland and Scotland, own all the lands, are not the mass, the common laborers, who own no capital, and possess neither mechanical nor professional skill, of necessity, the slaves to capital?

Was it not this slavery to capital that occasioned the great Irish famine, and is it not this same slavery that keeps the large majority of the laboring class in Western Europe in a state of hereditary starvation?

In old societies, where the laborers are domestic slaves, and exceed in number the demand for labor, would not emancipating them subject them at once to a mastery, or exacting despotism of capital, far more oppressive than domestic slavery?

Did not the emancipation of European serfs, or villeins, in all instances, injure their condition as a class?

In the event of the occurrence of such excess of domestic slaves, would it not be more merciful to follow the Spartan plan, and kill the surplus, than the abolition plan, which sets them all free, to live on half allowance, and to "make free labor cheaper than slave labor," by this fierce competition and underbidding to get employment?

Are there not fewer checks to superior wit, skill, and capital, and less of protection afforded to the weak, ignorant and landless mass in Northern society, than in any other ever devised by the wit of man?

Is not Laissez Faire, in English, "Every man for himself, and devil take the hindmost," your whole theory and practice of government?

When your society grows older, your population more dense, and property, by your trading, speculating and commercial habits, gets into a few hands, will not the slavery to capital be more complete and unmitigated than in any part of Europe, where a throne, a nobility and established church, stand between the bosses, bankers and landlords, and the oppressed masses?

Do not almost all well-informed men of a philosophical turn of mind in Western Europe and our North, concur in opinion that the whole framework of society, religious ethical, economic, legal and political, requires radical change?

Is not the absence of such opinion at the South, and its prevalence in free society, conclusive proof of the naturalness and necessity of domestic slavery?

Would not the North be willing to leave the settlement of the slavery question in Kansas to the public opinion of Christendom (for it will be settled by all Christendom, of whom not one in a hundred will be slaveholders) if it were not sensible that public opinion was about to decide in favor of *negro* slavery, and, therefore, that it must be forestalled by Federal legislation?

A SOUTHERNER.

Since our work was in the press, the above has appeared in the *Liberator*. We embrace the occasion to thank Mr. Garrison for his courtesy, and to make a few remarks that we hope will not be deemed ill-timed or impertinent.

A comparison of opinions and of institutions between North and South will lead to kinder and more pacific relations. Hitherto, such comparisons could not be made, because the South believed herself wrong, weak, and defenceless, and that Abolition was but an attempt to apply the brand to the explosive materials of her social edifice. She is now equally confident of her justice and her strength, and believes her social system more stable, as well as more benevolent, equitable and natural, than that of the North. Whilst she will never tolerate radical agitation and demagoguical propagandism, she is ready for philosophical argument and discussion, and for historical and statistical comparison.

A Southerner employs the term "discussion," as equivalent to agitation; for the South does not proscribe the discussion of any subject, by proper persons, at proper places, and on proper occasions. (Who are proper persons, and what proper times and places, must be left to a healthy, just and enlightened public opinion to determine.) But men shall not lecture our children, in the streets, on the beauties of infidelity; parsons shall not preach politics from the pulpit; women shall not crop the petticoat, mount the rostrum, and descant on the purity of Free Love; incendiaries shall not make speeches against the right of landholders, nor teach our negroes the sacred doctrines of liberty and equality.

We are satisfied with our institutions, and are not willing to submit them to the *experimentum in vile corpus*! If the North thinks her own worthless, or only valuable as subjects for anatomical dissection, or chemical and phrenological experiments, she may advance the cause of humanity by treating her people as philosophers do mice and hares and dead frogs. We think her case not so desperate as to authorize such reckless experimentation. Though her experiment has failed, she is not yet dead. There is a way still open for recovery.

As we are a Brother Socialist, we have a right to prescribe

for the patient; and our Consulting Brethren, Messrs. Garrison, Greeley, and others, should duly consider the value of our opinion. Extremes meet – and we and the leading Abolitionists differ but a hairbreadth. We, like Carlyle, prescribe more of government; they insist on No-Government. Yet their social institutions would make excellently conducted Southern sugar and cotton farms, with a head to govern them. Add a Virginia overseer to Mr. Greeley's Phalansteries, and Mr. Greeley and we would have little to quarrel about.

We have a lively expectation that when our Cannibals make their entreé, "Our Masters in the Art of War" will greet them with applause, instead of hisses; with a *feu de joie*, or gratulatory salute, instead of a murderous broadside. We want to be friends with them and with all the world; and, as the curtain is falling, we conclude with the valedictory and invocation of the Roman actor – "Vos valete! et plaudite!"

THE END

# INDEX

# THE JOHN HARVARD LIBRARY

*The intent of Waldron Phoenix Belknap, Jr., as expressed in an early will, was for Harvard College to use the income from a permanent trust fund he set up, for "editing and publishing rare, inaccessible, or hitherto unpublished source material of interest in connection with the history, literature, art (including minor and useful art), commerce, customs, and manners or way of life of the Colonial and Federal Periods of the United States . . . In all cases the emphasis shall be on the presentation of the basic material." A later testament broadened this statement, but Mr. Belknap's interests remained constant until his death.*

*In linking the name of the first benefactor of Harvard College with the purpose of this later, generous-minded believer in American culture the John Harvard Library seeks to emphasize the importance of Mr. Belknap's purpose. The John Harvard Library of the Belknap Press of Harvard University Press exists to make books and documents about the American past more readily available to scholars and the general reader.*